Revolutionary
RECIPĚS

Concord à la Carte

Emerson Hospital Auxiliary

Any inquiries about this book or additional copies should be directed to:

The Emerson Hospital Auxiliary
Emerson Hospital
133 ORNAC
Concord, MA 01742
978-287-3019

ISBN 0-9715498-0-X

First printing 2002   5000 copies

WIMMER
COOKBOOKS

ConsolidatedGraphics
1-800-548-2537

INTRODUCTION

The Minutemen were a hearty, diverse lot, from all the towns surrounding Concord, who answered the call on that April day in 1775 and ushered in a new era.

This collection of recipes has been contributed by our members and friends from these same towns. The food in this book captures the essence of our times, relying on the freshest ingredients and spirit of today's creative cuisine.

We hope this book will become one of your favorites.

Emerson Hospital Auxiliary
Cookbook Committee

Co-Chairmen
Beth Neeley Kubacki   Jeanne Rautiola

Committee
Leslie Cheney   Lorri Langin
Gloria Donadio   Laura Milton
Patsy Dietrich   Maryann Mullin
Ginny Farwell   Cynthia Pugliese
Susan Warner

Editor
Monica Scanlon

Production Coordinator
Molly Mink

Historical Notes
Paula Williams

Cover and Original Artwork
Victor Lazzaro

Design and Calligraphy
Maria Lazzaro

About the Artists
Victor A. and Maria Lazzaro

Victor and Maria Lazzaro, our artists, live in Redding, Connecticut, in a house designed by Victor, who is a registered architect, as well as an illustrator. They first met at The Cooper Union For The Advancement of Science and Art in New York City.

Victor then went on to obtain his architectural degree at Carnegie Mellon University, while Maria obtained her B.F.A. at Manhattanville College where she also was a member of the art faculty. Both taught at Pratt Institute in Brooklyn, New York; Maria, briefly, and Victor for many years in the Foundation Art and Interior Design departments.

Their lifelong collaboration continues to this day and both count their finest achievement, the raising of their children, Vincent, Paola, and Victor, the younger.

We would like to thank our cooks and recipe testers.
We would also like to thank the Acton Congregational Church
for allowing us to use their facilities.

The Cottage Building

*This cookbook is dedicated
to all members of the
Emerson Hospital Auxiliary,
past and present.*

Emerson Hospital Auxiliary Mission

The Emerson Hospital Auxiliary acts as a liaison between the Hospital and the communities it serves, and works in partnership with the Hospital to:
- Provide educational programs that promote community health and wellness
- Increase awareness of Hospital Services
- Support the Hospital through fundraising

The Emerson Hospital Auxiliary History

In 1911, the Deaconess Hospital in Concord, Massachusetts, opened with fourteen beds on land granted by Mrs. Charles Emerson of Concord.

In 1922, the Deaconess Association chose to sever ties with the hospital and deeded the property to the newly formed Corporation of Emerson Hospital in Concord.

In October, 1924, the Emerson Aid Society was formed to raise funds to continue a community hospital in Concord, and by November 29, 1924, Emerson Hospital received its first patient. Community support continued to grow and helped the hospital to survive.

In 1949, the Aid Society with its newly formed branches (Acton, Lincoln, Maynard and Stow) reorganized, and the name was changed to the Emerson Hospital Auxiliary. In later years, more "units" were added and soon the communities of Bedford, Boxborough, Carlisle, Sudbury and Westford were also supporting the Auxiliary.

In 1999, the Emerson Hospital Auxiliary with over 600 members from its surrounding towns celebrated its 75th anniversary. The generous commitment of these women, who have supported their hospital, has helped to make the Auxiliary a vital part of each community served by Emerson Hospital.

5

Concord, Massachusetts—A Meeting of Minds and Action

Concord, Massachusetts has a long history of American "firsts." The area was first home to over eighty Native American settlements; these first Americans were drawn to the area by bountiful fishing waters, abundant game, and sheltering trees. Purchased from the Algonquin tribe, Concord's "six miles square" became home to its first European settlers in 1635, and it was the first inland settlement in New England above the tidewater. On April 19, 1775, Concord was the center of revolt and discourse when the first "shot heard round the world" set off the American Revolution. In the ensuing years, Concord became America's first literary center and philosophical heart with Ralph Waldo Emerson, Henry David Thoreau, Nathaniel Hawthorne, Louisa May Alcott, and their families and friends calling the town "home."

Even today, a casual stroll around Concord is a walk through the places where much original to American history and thinking first began. The Old Hill Burying Ground, where the Liberty Pole stood in defiance, is still Concord's highest ground guarding the main entrance to the town's center, just as its high ridge provided shelter to the town's first settlers. Wright Tavern, where both the Minutemen and the British gathered at various times during the morning of April 19, 1775, still stands at the foot of the high ridge. Concord's Common, where the Minutemen trained and marched, is still a green mound in the town's center, and the Colonial Inn, where illegal munitions were hidden away, still anchors one end of the square. Walking down Monument Street, strollers pass by The Old Manse, home to the Revolution's own fiery, spiritual leader Reverend William Emerson. Turning sharply left, they enter the narrow lane and move toward the Concord River, The Old North Bridge, French's Minuteman Statue, and the meadows of Barrett's Farm.

It is a short walk from Concord's town center to Barrett's Farm, and every American who walks it must surely ask themselves, "Why this place; why Concord?" As with all history, American or otherwise, the answers lie not in the places but in the people who lived the events…the Concord people who looked out over the political landscape of their times…the Concord people whose vision was shaped by their own dreams and beliefs…the Concord people who came together with others, determined their own fate, and chose to act.

In general, history originates in the individuals who nurture what Plato called the "examined" life. Concord citizens have a long-standing history of living examined lives. Concord's own Ralph Waldo Emerson offered a transcendental philosophy that challenged and trusted the individual to fully examine and analyze all experiences as personal history. Emerson said, "There is no history. There is only Biography…The new individual must work out the whole problem of science, letters and theology for himself…" In the specific history surrounding the American Revolution, John Adams wrote a friend in 1818, "The Revolution was effected before the war commenced. The Revolution was in the minds and hearts of the people; a change in their religious sentiments of their duties and obligations…This radical change in the principles, opinions, sentiments and affections of the people was the real American Revolution."

Appetizers

The Minuteman Statue

The Minuteman Statue

After the long march from Boston commencing at ten o'clock the night before...after capturing Paul Revere on the town's outskirts...after the early morning skirmish on Lexington Green...after Revere telling the British the town knew they were coming...after viewing the not-so-distant Buttrick Farm, the British troops coming down the constricted lane to the North Bridge to the beat of drum and fife on the morning of April 19, 1775 arrived at the bridge to find no one there. The militia had retired over the bridge to a mile north at Punkatasset Hill. The militia could only be seen by the British when they returned to the hill overlooking the bridge, at about 9:00. They knew exactly where to find rebel munitions and supplies; they had detailed maps and inventories supplied by Concord's Tory loyalists. They represented the Crown in overpowering numbers and regal might; they believed this little town of rebels could ill-afford confronting such a noble force. The majority of British never left Concord center. Seven companies of soldiers were sent to the bridge. Three were posted around the bridge, on the West Bank while the four others marched to Barrett's farm. The Old Manse could be glimpsed off to the left, and across the Concord River, the confined lane emptied into the open farm fields of Minuteman Captain David Brown. The British were at the bridge for a good hour before they saw the militia. Smoke could be seen rising from the town. The British soon retreated ripping up bridge planks as they went in an effort to protect themselves. The Militia came down the hill to face their opponents. The British fired the first shot. Major John Buttrick gave the order to return fire, "The Shot Heard 'Round the World." Both sides were restricted by the narrow road and wet lands bordering it. Even today, the lane still narrows between trees and rock fence, The Old Manse stands sentry off to the side, the Concord River quietly meanders and curves, the hill still rises beyond the restored bridge. Three British soldiers were killed at the bridge fight. Two were buried where they fell at the bridge, the third in the town center where he died after the fight. The bridge itself is a replica, and rising behind it is the Minuteman Statue, commissioned by Concord and dedicated at the first centennial celebration in 1875. Created by Concordian Daniel Chester French, it was his first major work; mid point in his illustrious career would be the seated Lincoln in Washington's Lincoln Memorial. The Melville Memorial in Concord's Sleepy Hollow Cemetery is one of his last. French's Minuteman is the yeoman soldier standing at the ready with a plow at his feet and rifle in his hand...ready at a minute's notice to defend his land and liberty. His countenance bears witness to the patriot's determined resolve, and that resolve must have been the biggest surprise of all for the British facing the Minutemen on April 19, 1775.

Appetizers

Asparagus with Prosciutto

4   ounces whipped cream
    cheese
¼   teaspoon garlic, finely
    minced
Pinch of salt
Freshly ground pepper, to
taste
12 thin slices of prosciutto, cut
    crosswise into halves
24 asparagus spears, cut to 4
    inches and partially cooked

• Preheat oven to 350 degrees.

• Combine whipped cream cheese, minced
  garlic, salt and pepper

• Spread prosciutto with cheese mixture and
  roll around one asparagus spear. Repeat
  with remaining prosciutto and asparagus.
  Arrange on baking sheet.

• Heat in oven for 3 to 4 minutes until
  heated through.

• Serve immediately.

Serves 8

Hot Beef Dip

8   ounces cream cheese,
    softened
2   tablespoons green pepper,
    finely chopped
2   tablespoons onion,
    chopped
2   tablespoons milk
1   jar (2.5 ounce) chipped
    beef (dry beef), finely
    chopped
½   cup sour cream
¼   teaspoon pepper
½   cup walnuts, chopped
Corn chips

• Preheat oven to 350 degrees.

• In a 2-quart casserole, combine cream
  cheese, green pepper, onion, milk,
  chipped beef, sour cream and pepper.

• Top with chopped walnuts.

• Bake for 15 to 20 minutes.

• Serve with large corn chips.

Yield: 3 cups

Sausage Stroganoff Dip

2   pounds sausage of your
    choice
4   tablespoons flour
2   cups milk
2   large onions, chopped
6   ounces fresh mushrooms,
    sliced
¼   cup butter
2   teaspoons soy sauce
2   tablespoons
    Worcestershire sauce
Salt and freshly ground
    pepper, to taste
Paprika, to taste
2   cups sour cream

- Brown sausage, occasionally pouring off grease. Break sausage up into small pieces.

- Sprinkle sausage with flour. Add milk.

- Simmer until slightly thickened. Set aside.

- Sauté onions and mushrooms in butter until onions are tender.

- Add to sausage mixture.

- Stir in soy sauce, Worcestershire sauce, salt, pepper and paprika.

- Cook until mixture bubbles.

- Remove from heat. Add sour cream.

- Serve hot with Melba toast.

Yield: 6 cups

Festive Cranberry Brie

1   can (8 ounce) whole
    cranberry sauce, crushed
2   tablespoons packed brown
    sugar
¼   teaspoon rum or orange
    extract
⅛   teaspoon ground nutmeg
1   round Brie cheese
    (8 ounce)
2   tablespoons pecans,
    chopped

- Preheat oven to 500 degrees.

- Combine crushed cranberry sauce, brown sugar, rum and ground nutmeg.

- Peel off top rind of Brie cheese, leaving ¼-inch rim. Top Brie with cranberry mixture and sprinkle with chopped pecans.

- Bake for 4 to 5 minutes.

- Serve with crackers or bread.

Serves 6 to 8

May microwave instead of using conventional oven. Microwave for 1 minute on high.

Warm Bleu Cheese Dip

7 **slices bacon, chopped**

2 **cloves garlic, minced**

8 **ounces cream cheese, softened**

¼ **cup half-and-half**

4 **ounces bleu cheese**

2 **tablespoons chives, chopped**

Tabasco sauce, to taste

3 **tablespoons smoked almonds, finely chopped**

- Preheat oven to 350 degrees.

- Cook bacon in a large skillet over medium-high heat until nearly crisp.

- Drain the drippings from the skillet and add the garlic. Cook until the bacon is crisp.

- Beat cream cheese in a mixing bowl until light.

- Add half-and-half and beat until smooth.

- Stir in the bacon mixture, bleu cheese, chives and Tabasco sauce.

- Spoon into a baking dish and cover with foil.

- Bake for 30 minutes or until heated through.

- Sprinkle with almonds. Bake uncovered until bubbly.

- Serve with crackers or vegetables.

Yield: 1½ to 2 cups

Warm Crab and Artichoke Dip

¼ cup cream cheese, at room temperature

½ cup mayonnaise

Salt and freshly ground pepper, to taste

¾ cup (4 ounces) crabmeat, well drained

¼ cup plus 2 tablespoons Parmesan cheese, grated, divided

3 tablespoons marinated artichoke hearts, drained and chopped

2 tablespoons green onion, sliced

2 tablespoons red bell pepper, diced

2 tablespoons celery, diced

1 tablespoon flat-leaf parsley, finely chopped

1½ teaspoons sherry wine vinegar

½ teaspoon Tabasco sauce

Toasted baguette slices or crackers

- Preheat oven to 400 degrees.

- Beat cream cheese in large bowl until smooth. Add mayonnaise, beating just until blended. Season with salt and pepper.

- Using a rubber spatula, fold in crabmeat, ¼ cup Parmesan cheese, artichoke hearts, green onion, bell pepper, celery, parsley, vinegar and Tabasco sauce.

- Transfer crab mixture to 2-cup soufflé pan. Top with remaining 2 tablespoons of Parmesan cheese.

- Bake until crab mixture is warm and cheese melts, about 15 minutes.

- Transfer to platter, surround with toasts and serve.

Yield: about 1½ cups

You may substitute red wine vinegar for sherry wine vinegar.

Clams al Forno

36-40	**littleneck clams, cleaned and scrubbed**
2	**large onions, thinly sliced**
1	**jalapeño pepper, seeded and chopped**
½	**teaspoon dried red pepper flakes**
¾	**cup dry white wine**
½	**cup water**
2	**tablespoons fresh garlic, minced**
½	**cup canned tomatoes in heavy purée, chopped**
8	**tablespoons unsalted butter, cut up**
3	**scallions, cut into julienne strips**
1	**lemon cut into 6 wedges**

• Preheat oven to 500 degrees.

• Place the clams in a single layer in a baking dish.

• Scatter onions, jalapeño pepper, red pepper flakes, wine, water, garlic, tomatoes, and butter over the clams.

• Roast the clams for 9 minutes. Turn and roast for additional 9 to 10 minutes longer, until they pop open. Discard any clams that do not open.

• To serve, place 6 clams in each bowl and divide the broth among them. Serve piping hot, garnished with scallions and lemon wedges.

Serves 6 to 8

15

Clams Casino

20	littleneck clams
1	onion, chopped
2	cloves garlic, minced
½	green pepper, finely chopped
½	cup butter
1	cup parsley, chopped
1	cup dry bread crumbs
1	cup Parmesan cheese, grated

Salt and freshly ground pepper, to taste

8-10 slices uncooked bacon, cut into ½-inch squares

- Preheat oven to 350 degrees. Wash clams thoroughly under cold running water, discarding any with broken shells and those with necks that do not retract when prodded gently with finger.

- In an 8 to 10 quart steamer or casserole, place 4 cups water and bring to a boil over high heat.

- Add clams, cover tightly and steam for 5 to 8 minutes, turning them in the pot once or twice with a slotted spoon.

- With tongs or a slotted spoon, transfer the clams to a deep platter or serving bowl. All the shells should be open. Discard any clams that remain shut.

- Remove the clams from their shells and chop finely.

- Clean 20 half shells.

- Sauté onion, garlic and green pepper in the butter until soft.

- Add chopped clams, parsley, bread crumbs, cheese, salt and pepper and mix well.

- Stuff cleaned shells with clam mixture and top with bacon squares.

- Bake for 10 to 15 minutes. Place under broiler until bacon browns.

Yield: 20 appetizers

Lemon Parmesan Artichoke Bottoms

2 cans (14 ounces each) artichoke bottoms, rinsed, drained and patted dry

1½ cups Parmesan cheese, grated

½ cup mayonnaise

3 large cloves garlic, minced

2 teaspoons fresh lemon juice

1 teaspoon lemon peel, grated

Salt and freshly ground pepper to taste

¼ cup pine nuts

Fresh parsley, chopped (optional)

- Preheat oven to 375 degrees.

- Lightly grease 8-inch square baking dish. Place artichoke bottoms, rounded sides down, in prepared dish.

- Combine Parmesan, mayonnaise, garlic, lemon juice, and lemon peel in medium bowl. Season to taste with salt and pepper.

- Mound mayonnaise mixture in artichokes. Sprinkle with pine nuts.

- Bake artichokes until heated through, about 20 minutes.

- Garnish with parsley and serve.

Yield: 14 to 16 hors d'oeuvres

Lobster Bundles

2   scallions

12 ounces lobster meat, cooked

1   cup feta cheese, crumbled

2   tablespoons Dijon mustard

6   ounces cream cheese, softened

Salt and freshly ground pepper, to taste

2   tablespoons fresh tarragon, chopped

1   tablespoon white wine

Vegetable cooking spray

36 wonton wrappers (3x3-inches each)

- Preheat oven to 375 degrees.

- Trim and slice scallions, using green part only.

- In a medium bowl, toss lobster with scallion and feta cheese.

- Mix with mustard, cream cheese, salt, pepper, tarragon and wine.

- Spray mini muffin tins with vegetable spray. Place 1 wonton wrapper in each cup.

- Place a heaping teaspoon of lobster mixture in each cup. Fold sides on top to seal or twist to enclose.

- Spray each bundle with cooking spray.

- Bake for 12 to 15 minutes or until lightly brown.

Yield: 36 appetizers

Bundles can be prepared on a cookie sheet instead of mini-muffin tins. Fill each wonton as described, pull up sides and twist together to seal. Do not overfill. Place on cookie sheets sprayed with cooking spray. Spray each wonton and bake as directed.

Mushroom Croustades

1	package (16 ounce) high quality firm white bread, thinly sliced
6	tablespoons butter, divided
3	tablespoons shallots, minced
½	pound fresh mushrooms, finely chopped
2	tablespoons flour
1	cup heavy cream
1½	tablespoons fresh chives, minced
1	tablespoon fresh parsley, minced
½	teaspoon lemon juice
½	teaspoon salt
⅛	teaspoon cayenne pepper

• Preheat oven to 400 degrees.

• Melt 2 tablespoons of the butter.

• Cut a 3-inch round from each slice of bread. Brush rounds with melted butter and gently fit rounds into miniature muffin tins to form cups. Bake 10 minutes or until lightly browned. Cool.

• In a heavy skillet, sauté shallots in ¼ cup butter for 1 minute. Stir in mushrooms and simmer uncovered until all liquid has evaporated, about 10 minutes.

• Remove from heat and stir flour into mushrooms. Pour cream over mushrooms and return to heat.

• Stirring constantly, bring mushrooms to a boil and cook another minute or until mixture becomes very thick.

• Remove from heat and add chives, parsley, lemon juice, salt and cayenne pepper.

• Spoon hot mushroom mixture into the warmed toast shells and serve.

Yield: 24 appetizers

Filling may be made in advance. Cover and refrigerate. To serve, heat filling in the microwave. Warm shells in the oven to maintain crispness. Fill and serve.

The filled toast shells may also be frozen. Freeze in the muffin tins. Once frozen, remove and place into plastic bags. To serve, bring to room temperature and heat in oven until warm.

Mushroom Palmiers

1	pound fresh mushrooms
1½	medium onions, peeled and quartered
5	tablespoons butter
2	tablespoons flour
1	teaspoon fresh lemon juice
1½	teaspoons dried thyme or 2 tablespoons finely chopped fresh thyme
½	teaspoon Tabasco sauce

Salt and freshly ground black pepper, to taste

1½	packages (17.25 ounce) frozen puff pastry, thawed (3 sheets)
2	eggs
4	teaspoons water

• In a food processor, finely chop mushrooms. Transfer to plate and set aside.

• Add onion to processor and finely chop.

• In large skillet, melt butter over medium heat. Add mushrooms and onion and cook until juice evaporates, stirring occasionally, about 8 minutes.

• Add flour, lemon juice, thyme and Tabasco.

• Season with salt and pepper.

• Reduce heat to low and cook about 2 minutes. Set aside to cool.

• Preheat oven to 400 degrees.

• Place 1 unfolded pastry sheet on flat surface. Spread evenly with ⅓ mushroom mixture.

• Roll up from both long edges into center, pressing 2 rolls together.

• Repeat with remaining 2 pastry sheets.

• Wrap tightly in plastic wrap and freeze 1 hour. (May be prepared to this point and frozen. Let thaw partially before proceeding.)

(continued on next page)

Mushroom Palmiers continued

- Slice into ¼-inch thick slices, using serrated knife.

- Place, cut side down, on ungreased baking sheet, 1-inch apart.

- In small bowl, combine eggs and water and whisk to blend. Brush over tops of Palmiers and bake 18 to 20 minutes.

Yield: 4 to 5 dozen

Shrimp and Pesto Pizzettas

1 **container (6 ounce) prepared basil pesto**
1 **package (4 pieces) thin white roll-up mountain bread, such as lavash**
1 **package (7 ounce) three-cheese shredded Italian blend**
1 **pound small shrimp, shelled, rinsed, drained, and patted dry**

- Preheat oven to 350 degrees.

- Spread ¼ of prepared pesto on each piece of roll-up bread.

- Sprinkle with shredded cheese and cover with shrimp.

- Arrange on a cookie sheet and bake 10 to 12 minutes or until cheese bubbles.

- Cut each into 6 to 8 wedges. Serve hot or at room temperature.

Serves 8 to 10

Mushroom Strudel

1¼ pounds (6 cups) mushrooms, finely minced

2 tablespoons shallots, finely chopped

1 teaspoon salt

¼ teaspoon pepper

3-4 teaspoons curry powder

1 tablespoon sherry wine

¾ cup butter, divided

1 cup sour cream

¾ cup plus 2 tablespoons bread crumbs

1 pound frozen phyllo dough, thawed

• Preheat oven to 375 degrees.

• Sauté mushrooms, shallots, salt, pepper, curry powder and sherry in ¼ cup butter until liquid evaporates, about 15 minutes. Set aside to cool.

• When cool, add sour cream and 2 tablespoons bread crumbs.

• Unwrap the thawed phyllo dough and spread on a cool damp cloth. Cover unused dough with a damp towel to keep it moist while you are working.

• Melt remaining ½ cup of butter.

• Lay out one layer of dough on a damp cloth and brush with melted butter and sprinkle with bread crumbs. Repeat process to make 4 total layers, using ¼ cup melted butter and ½ of the remaining bread crumbs (about 6 tablespoons).

• Spoon half of the mushroom mixture in a 2 to 3-inch wide strip at the short end of the dough. Fold over about 1 inch of dough along the long side of the dough. Roll up dough as for a jelly roll.

• Repeat the process with the remaining phyllo dough, butter, bread crumbs and mushroom filling, making a second strudel.

• Place the two strudels on greased baking sheets. Bake for 25 to 30 minutes.

Serves 16

Scallops with Leeks and Garlic Oil

3 cups water

2 pounds leeks, white and pale green parts only, cut into ½-inch pieces

6 tablespoons unsalted butter, divided

Ground nutmeg

1 pound bay scallops, connective muscle removed

1½ teaspoons fresh thyme, chopped, or ½ teaspoon dried, crumbled thyme

Salt and freshly ground pepper to taste

3 tablespoons balsamic vinegar or red wine vinegar

2 tablespoons garlic, chopped

½ cup peanut oil

• Bring water to a boil in a heavy medium saucepan. Add leeks and cook until tender, about 10 minutes. Drain well, reserving leeks and liquid separately.

• Return liquid to saucepan. Boil until liquid is reduced to ¼ cup, about 13 minutes.

• Melt 3 tablespoons of the butter in a heavy medium skillet over medium heat. Add leeks and sauté until golden, stirring occasionally, about 12 minutes. Season to taste with salt and nutmeg. Cover to keep warm.

• Melt remaining 3 tablespoons butter in another heavy medium skillet over medium high heat. Add bay scallops and thyme. Season with salt and pepper.

• Sauté scallops until just cooked through, about 4 minutes. Using slotted spoon, transfer scallops to bowl. Cover to keep warm.

• Add reduced leek cooking liquid to same skillet and boil until reduced to sauce consistency, about 3 minutes.

• Pour reduced leek liquid into blender. Add balsamic vinegar and garlic. With blender running, gradually pour in oil. Season to taste with salt and pepper.

• Arrange leeks on platter. Spoon scallops over leeks and drizzle generously with sauce.

• Serve, passing remaining sauce separately.

Serves 4 as an appetizer

Spicy Meatballs

1   **pound lean ground beef**
¾   **cup seasoned dry bread crumbs**
2   **tablespoons onion, finely chopped**
1   **tablespoon ketchup**
4   **drops Tabasco sauce**
½   **teaspoon prepared mustard**
2   **eggs, well beaten**
½   **teaspoon salt**
¼   **teaspoon pepper**
1   **tablespoon Parmesan cheese, grated**

- In a large mixing bowl, combine ground beef, bread crumbs, onion, ketchup, Tabasco, mustard, eggs, salt, pepper and Parmesan cheese. Mix well. Shape into small 1-inch balls.

- Sauté in a large non-stick skillet until browned. Set aside.

If preferred, place meatballs on broiler pan and bake at 425 degrees for about 12 minutes.

Sauce

½   **cup ketchup**
½   **cup chili sauce**
¼   **cup cider vinegar**
½   **cup packed brown sugar**
2   **tablespoons onion, finely chopped**
1   **tablespoon Worcestershire sauce**
4   **drops Tabasco sauce**
½   **teaspoon dry mustard**
3   **drops Angostura bitters**
1   **teaspoon salt, or to taste**
¼   **teaspoon pepper**

- Combine ketchup, chili sauce, vinegar, brown sugar, onion, Worcestershire sauce, Tabasco, mustard, bitters, salt and pepper. Bring to a boil.

- Reduce heat and simmer 5 minutes.

- Add meatballs and simmer an additional 10 minutes. Transfer to chafing dish to keep warm.

Yield: about 3½ dozen meatballs

Angostura bitters may be found where drink mixers are sold.

Spicy Shrimp

½ **cup olive oil**

2 **tablespoons Cajun/Creole seasoning**

2 **tablespoons fresh lemon juice**

2 **tablespoons fresh parsley, chopped**

1 **tablespoon honey**

1 **tablespoon soy sauce**

Pinch cayenne pepper

1½ **teaspoons dry mustard**

1 **pound uncooked large shrimp, shelled and deveined**

French bread

Lemon wedges

• Preheat oven to 450 degrees.

• Combine olive oil, Cajun seasoning, lemon juice, parsley, honey, soy sauce, cayenne pepper and mustard.

• Place into a 9x13-inch baking dish. Add shrimp and refrigerate for 1 hour.

• Bake for about 10 minutes, stirring occasionally.

• Serve on French bread with lemon wedge as garnish.

Serves 6 to 8

25

Spinach Pesto Appetizer

2½ cups nonfat cottage cheese, drained

1 package (10 ounce) frozen chopped spinach, thawed and squeezed to remove excess moisture

1 package (8 ounce) reduced fat cream cheese, cut into pieces

¼ cup Romano cheese, grated

1 large whole egg plus 2 large egg whites

2 cloves garlic, minced

2 teaspoons dried basil

¼ teaspoon salt

⅛ teaspoon pepper

Cherry tomatoes for garnish

Whole fresh basil leaves for garnish

• Preheat oven to 325 degrees. Spray a 9-inch springform pan with nonstick spray and set aside.

• Place cottage cheese, spinach, cream cheese, Romano cheese, egg, egg white, garlic, basil, salt and pepper into a food processor. Process until smooth.

• Spoon mixture into prepared pan. Smooth top with a spatula. Bake for 1 hour, or until firm. Cool on wire rack.

• To serve, unmold and garnish with cherry tomatoes and/or basil leaves.

• Serve with assorted crackers or small party breads.

Serves 12

You may substitute 2 extra large whole eggs for the large eggs plus 2 egg whites.

Middle Eastern Hummus

2   cans (14. 5 ounce) chick-
    peas, rinsed and drained
Juice of 1 large lemon, or to
    taste
6-8 tablespoons plain nonfat
    yogurt
3-4 tablespoons tahini paste
1-2 cloves garlic
Salt and freshly ground
    pepper, to taste
Garnish Ingredients
Extra-virgin olive oil
Parsley, minced
Olives, green or black,
    chopped
Paprika

- Place chickpeas, lemon juice, yogurt, tahini paste, garlic, and salt and pepper in a food processor. Blend well.

- Pour into serving bowl. Drizzle with olive oil. Garnish with parsley, olives and paprika.

- Serve with small crackers, corn chips or small party breads.

Yield: 3 cups

Curry and Chutney Pâté

8   ounces cream cheese
1   cup Cheddar cheese,
    grated
3-4 scallions, minced
2   teaspoons curry powder
1   bottle (8 ounce) chutney

- Combine cream cheese, Cheddar cheese, scallions and curry powder.

- Line a small, flat-bottomed mold with plastic wrap and press cheese mixture into mold. Chill.

- Invert cheese mixture onto plate and remove mold and plastic wrap.

- Spoon chutney on top of cheese. Serve with crackers.

Yield: 3 cups

Brandied Mushroom Pâté

2   tablespoons brandy

⅓   cup pistachio nuts, skinned
     and coarsely chopped

½   pound fresh mushrooms,
     coarsely chopped

2   tablespoons unsalted
     butter

2   tablespoons shallots,
     minced

½   cup dry white wine

1   teaspoon salt

3   drops Tabasco sauce

⅛   teaspoon mace

8   ounces cream cheese,
     softened

• Pour brandy over pistachio nuts and let stand while making pâté.

• Sauté mushrooms in butter. Add shallots and cook 2 to 3 minutes, stirring constantly.

• Add wine and continue cooking over medium heat 10 to 15 minutes, or until most of the wine has evaporated. Remove from heat.

• Stir in salt, Tabasco and mace. Cool.

• Place in blender with cream cheese and process until smooth. Fold in pistachio nuts.

• Place in a mold or crock and refrigerate covered at least 5 hours before serving.

• Serve with crackers, chips or small party breads.

Yield: 1½ cups

Polynesian Ginger Dip

1   cup mayonnaise
1   cup sour cream
¼   cup onion, finely chopped
¼   cup fresh parsley, minced
¼   cup water chestnuts, finely chopped
3   tablespoons chopped candied ginger, plus additional for garnish
2   cloves garlic, minced
1   tablespoon soy sauce

• Combine mayonnaise, sour cream, onion, parsley, water chestnuts, 3 tablespoons ginger, garlic, and soy sauce.

• Refrigerate until ready to serve.

• Garnish with additional chopped candied ginger.

• Serve with potato chips or fresh vegetables.

Serves 10 to 15

Sun-Dried Tomato Artichoke Dip

⅓   cup sun-dried tomatoes, simmered 2 minutes and drained
⅓   cup toasted pine nuts
3   tablespoons Parmesan cheese, grated
2   tablespoons parsley
1   tablespoon olive oil
1   clove garlic
½   cup roasted red peppers
1   jar (6 ounce) marinated artichoke hearts

• Combine tomatoes, pine nuts, Parmesan cheese, parsley, olive oil, garlic, red peppers and artichoke hearts in a food processor. Process until smooth. Refrigerate 1 hour before serving. Serve with crackers.

Yield: 2 cups

29

Two very distinctive and delicious eggplant appetizers that will surely please you and your company!

Eggplant Caponata I

¼   **cup olive oil**

1   **onion, chopped**

4   **cloves garlic, minced**

1   **medium eggplant, peeled and chopped**

2   **green peppers, seeded and chopped**

1   **cup celery, chopped**

1   **can (8 ounce) pitted black olives, drained and chopped**

1   **cup mushrooms, chopped**

1   **can (8 ounce) tomato sauce**

2   **tablespoons red wine vinegar**

¼   **cup light brown sugar**

¼   **teaspoon dried basil**

Salt and freshly ground pepper, to taste

- Heat oil in a large skillet. Add onion and garlic and sauté until tender.

- Add eggplant, green pepper and celery.

- Cook, covered, stirring occasionally, for about 15 minutes.

- Add olives, mushrooms and tomato sauce. Mix thoroughly.

- Add vinegar, brown sugar and basil.

- Simmer uncovered until all ingredients are tender, about 15 minutes. Season with salt and pepper.

- Serve at room temperature with chips, crackers or party breads.

Serves 12 to 16

May be made in advance and refrigerated.

May be served warm as a vegetable side dish.

Eggplant Caponata II

2 **pounds eggplant, peeled and cubed in ½-inch cubes**

½ **cup olive oil, divided**

2 **cups chopped celery**

¾ **cup chopped onions**

⅓ **cup wine vinegar mixed with 4 teaspoons sugar**

3 **cups crushed tomatoes**

2 **tablespoons tomato paste**

6 **large green olives, slivered**

2 **tablespoons capers**

2 **teaspoons anchovy paste**

Salt and freshly ground pepper, to taste

½ **cup pine nuts, (optional)**

- Sprinkle eggplant with salt and place in paper towel-lined colander. Cover with more paper towels and place a heavy pot of water on top to press for 1 to 2 hours.

- Sauté celery in ¼ cup olive oil until almost tender.

- Add onions. Sauté until both are tender. Transfer to bowl.

- Sauté eggplant cubes in ¼ cup olive oil about 8 minutes.

- Return celery and onions to pan and stir in vinegar, tomatoes, tomato paste, olives, capers, anchovy paste, salt and pepper. Bring to a boil. Reduce heat and simmer uncovered for about 15 minutes.

- Add pine nuts. Correct seasoning. Cool completely and refrigerate.

Yield: 8 cups

Serve in antipasto or with pita bread.

31

Goat Cheese Log

8	ounces cream cheese
6	ounces goat cheese
3	tablespoons green onion, minced
3	tablespoons parsley, minced
¼	tablespoon lemon zest
¾	cup ground pistachios

- On a piece of waxed paper, flatten cream cheese into a 5x7-inch rectangle. Flatten goat cheese on top of cream cheese.

- Sprinkle with green onion, parsley and lemon zest. Roll into a log.

- Roll log in pistachios before serving.

- Accompany with assorted crackers.

Serves 10 to 12

Gorgonzola Pistachio Mold

1	pound cream cheese, softened
½	pound Gorgonzola cheese
1	cup unsalted butter, softened
1	cup fresh parsley, chopped
1	cup pistachios, shelled and chopped

- Line an 8x4-inch loaf pan or mold with plastic wrap, draping excess wrap over sides of pan.

- Combine cream cheese, Gorgonzola cheese and butter. Blend well.

- Spread one third of the mixture into the pan. Sprinkle with parsley. Cover with another ⅓ of mixture. Sprinkle with pistachios. Top with remaining cheese mixture. Chill until firm.

- Invert mold onto serving plate. Remove plastic wrap.

- Serve at room temperature with chips, crackers or party breads.

Serves 12 to 16

Herbed Garlic Cheese Spread

16　ounces cream cheese, softened

¼　cup mayonnaise

2　teaspoons Dijon mustard

2　tablespoons chives, finely chopped

2　tablespoons fresh dill, finely chopped, or 1 tablespoon dried dill

1　large clove garlic, minced

• Beat together cream cheese, mayonnaise, mustard, chives, dill and garlic.

• Chill and serve with assorted crackers, chips or party breads.

Serves 10 to 12

Marinated Goat Cheese

8　firm goat cheese rounds, 2 to 3 ounces each, sliced

1½　cups extra-virgin olive oil

4　bay leaves

1　tablespoon mixed black and green peppercorns

1½　tablespoons dried thyme

3　large cloves garlic cut into slivers

3　tablespoons fresh basil, slivered

1　tablespoon dried pink peppercorns

• Place the goat cheese slices on an oven-proof platter or flat dish large enough to hold them without touching.

• Heat the oil, bay leaves, mixed peppercorns and dried thyme in a small saucepan over medium-high heat until you hear the mixture begin to sizzle and pop.

• Immediately remove from the heat and pour over the cheeses.

• Scatter the slivered garlic in the marinade and sprinkle with the basil and pink peppercorns. Marinate in the refrigerator overnight to firm up cheeses.

• Bring to room temperature before serving.

• Serve with crackers or baguette slices.

Yield: 8 appetizer servings or
24 hors d'oeuvre

33

Mushroom, Walnut and Olive Spread

1   **medium onion, minced**

3   **tablespoons vegetable oil**

1   **pound mushrooms, finely chopped**

¼   **cup dry white wine**

1   **teaspoon Worcestershire sauce**

½   **teaspoon dried hot red pepper flakes**

1¼ **cups walnuts, toasted and chopped**

½   **cup kalamata olives, pitted and chopped**

¼   **cup parsley, minced**

¼   **cup scallions, minced**

1   **tablespoon fresh thyme, minced**

4   **ounces cream cheese, softened**

Salt and freshly ground pepper to taste

Toast points and crackers for serving

- In a large skillet cook the onion in the oil over moderately low heat, stirring until translucent, about 5 minutes.

- Add mushrooms and cook for 5 minutes. Add wine and simmer mixture until all the liquid has evaporated. Stir in the Worcestershire sauce and hot pepper flakes.

- Combine the walnuts, olives, parsley, scallions and thyme in a bowl. Add the mushroom mixture and the cream cheese and stir until combined. Season with salt and pepper to taste.

- Transfer the spread to a crock and serve with toast points and crackers.

Yield: 3 cups

Pesto Torte

1 **pound unsalted butter, at room temperature**

1 **pound cream cheese, at room temperature**

2½ **cups packed fresh basil**

1 **cup Parmesan cheese, grated**

⅓ **cup olive oil**

1 **clove garlic**

¼ **cup pine nuts (optional)**

- Beat butter and cream cheese in a mixer.

- In a blender or food processor, to make pesto, pulse the basil, Parmesan cheese, olive oil, garlic and pine nuts until smooth.

- Line a medium-size mold (5 to 6 cups) with plastic wrap, making sure wrap hangs over sides of mold.

- Place 4 fresh basil leaves on bottom of mold. Make several layers of the cheese and pesto, beginning and ending with a cheese layer.

- Cover with plastic wrap and refrigerate overnight.

- Unmold by pulling on the plastic wrap.

- Serve with sliced baguettes or crackers.

Serves 16 to 20

Citrus and Clove Shrimp

5   cups water

1½ cups dry white wine

Juice of ½ lemon

Juice of ½ lime

¼   teaspoon ground cloves

1   tablespoon whole black
    peppercorns

1   tablespoon salt

1   bay leaf (optional)

2   2½-inch long dried hot
    chilies

1   large onion

3   pounds uncooked large
    shelled shrimp

Marinade

1½ tablespoons white wine
    vinegar

1   tablespoon fresh lemon
    juice

1   tablespoon fresh lime juice

¼   teaspoon ground cloves

Salt and freshly ground
    pepper, to taste

½   cup extra-virgin olive oil

1   clove garlic, thinly sliced

Lemon and lime wedges for
    garnish

• In an 8-quart stockpot or saucepan, combine water, wine, lemon juice, lime juice,
  ground cloves, peppercorns, salt, bay leaf,
  chilies and onion. Bring to a boil and boil
  for 5 minutes.

• Add shelled shrimp and cook, stirring
  occasionally, until just cooked, about
  3 minutes.

• Drain shrimp in a colander. Cool 5 minutes.

• For marinade, whisk together white wine
  vinegar, lemon juice, lime juice, ground
  cloves, salt and pepper to taste.

• Whisk in olive oil in a stream until
  marinade is emulsified. Stir in garlic.

• In a large bowl, combine shrimp and
  marinade. Marinate shrimp, covered and
  chilled, for 8 hours or overnight.

• Serve shrimp with lemon and lime
  wedges.

Serves 12

Marinated Shrimp Wrapped in Pea Pods

1   pound uncooked large
     shrimp (28 to 30), peeled
     and deveined
½   cup olive oil
3   tablespoons fresh lemon
     juice
3   tablespoons Dijon mustard
2   cloves garlic, finely minced
Dash sugar
Salt and freshly ground
     pepper, to taste
15   snow pea pods

• Cook shrimp in a large pot of boiling
  water for 2 to 3 minutes. Immerse shrimp
  in ice water to cool and drain well.

• Combine olive oil, lemon juice, mustard,
  garlic, sugar, and salt and pepper in a
  covered jar. Shake well.

• Pour over shrimp and marinate for 24 hours.

• Remove string from pea pods and blanch
  in boiling water for 30 seconds. Immerse
  immediately in ice water and drain well.

• With a sharp knife, split the pea pods in half
  lengthwise to make 30 separate halves. Chill.

• Just before serving, drain shrimp and wrap
  each one with a pea pod half. Fasten with
  a toothpick.

Yield: 30 pieces.

Tortilla Pinwheels

8   ounces cream cheese,
     softened
2   tablespoons sour cream
½   teaspoon garlic powder
1   tablespoon dried Italian
     dressing mix
4   tablespoons scallions,
     finely chopped
1   roasted red pepper, finely
     sliced
5   large flour tortillas

• Combine cream cheese, sour cream,
  garlic powder and Italian seasoning.

• Spread lightly on tortillas, making certain
  it spreads to the edge.

• Sprinkle scallions and red peppers on
  tortillas. Roll tightly. Refrigerate to chill.

• Cut into ½-inch pieces and serve.

Yield: 24 hors d'oeuvre

37

Vodka Spiked Cherry Tomatoes with Pepper Salt

3 pints firm small red and
   yellow cherry tomatoes
½ cup vodka
3 tablespoons white-wine
   vinegar
1 tablespoon superfine
   granulated sugar
1 teaspoon fresh lemon zest,
   finely grated
3 tablespoons kosher salt
1½ tablespoons black pepper,
   coarsely ground

- Cut a small "x" in skin of blossom end of each tomato.

- Blanch tomatoes, 5 at a time, in a saucepan of boiling water 3 seconds. Immediately transfer with a slotted spoon to a bowl of ice and cold water to stop cooking.

- Drain and peel, transferring to a large shallow dish.

- Stir together vodka, vinegar, sugar, and zest until sugar is dissolved.

- Pour over tomatoes, gently tossing to coat.

- Marinate, covered and chilled, at least 30 minutes and up to 1 hour.

- Stir together salt and pepper and serve with tomatoes for dipping.

Yield: 60 hors d'oeuvres

Tomatoes can be peeled and vodka marinade prepared 1 day ahead and kept separately, covered and chilled.

Brunch & Breads

Monument Square and the Colonial Inn

Monument Square and the Colonial Inn

In October 1774, the Town Common, later known as Monument Square, was the center of more than just the town's comings and goings. With the growing concerns about British heavy-handedness and absolute control of Boston, the town of Concord became a center of colonial government and patriotic resistance. In the Concord Meetinghouse, the First Provincial Congress was called "...to maintain the rights of the people." Delegates representing the towns of Massachusetts met, elected John Hancock president, authorized the formation of armed companies for protection and defense, and determined the best course of action. One decision was to move supplies, munitions, and valuables from Boston and other more susceptible outposts to secret places within Concord. It is rumored the church communion silver was "stored" at the Common's Wright Tavern in a barrel of soft soap. Barrels of flour were stationed in varied houses; some harbored cannon balls and shot and powder. In February 1775, the Town Common provided the training ground for the Second Minuteman Company of Concord; being one of three such Concord companies, places and times for training were judiciously set aside. Above the Town Common, the Liberty Pole stood sentry on Hill Burying Ground, and the original ridge and dwellings angled off the Common. The Colonial Inn of today anchors Monument Square, but when Concord's Minutemen marched and drilled on the Common, the inn was actually three buildings. The center one was used as a Provincial storehouse during the Revolution. Concord's Town Common offered a harbor for patriots and self-government and a hiding place for the supplies and munitions needed to carry out the will of the people.

Brunch & Bread

Apple - Pear Coffee Cake

10 tablespoons butter, divided

1 cup sugar

2 eggs

2 cups flour

1 teaspoon baking powder

1 teaspoon baking soda

½ teaspoon salt

8 ounces sour cream

1¼ cups cooking apples (about 2 apples), peeled and finely chopped

¾ cup pear (about 1 pear), peeled and finely chopped

1 teaspoon vanilla extract

1 cup firmly packed brown sugar

½ cup pecans, chopped

1 teaspoon ground cinnamon

• Preheat oven to 350 degrees.

• With an electric mixer at medium speed, cream 8 tablespoons butter, gradually adding sugar and beating well.

• Add eggs, one at a time, beating well after each addition.

• Combine flour, baking powder, baking soda and salt.

• Add to creamed mixture alternately with sour cream, beginning and ending with flour mixture, mixing after each addition.

• Fold in apples and pears. Stir in vanilla.

• Spread batter in a greased 13x9x2-inch baking pan.

• Combine brown sugar, pecans, 2 tablespoons butter and cinnamon. Sprinkle evenly over batter.

• Bake for 45 to 50 minutes or until a wooden pick inserted in center comes out clean.

Serves 12 to 15

Fresh Blueberry Coffee Cake

1¼ cups fresh blueberries
1⅓ cups sugar, divided
2   cups plus 2 tablespoons flour, divided
½   cup butter, softened
2   eggs
1   teaspoon baking powder
½   teaspoon salt
8   ounces sour cream
1   teaspoon vanilla or almond extract
½   cup pecans or walnuts, chopped

Glaze
¾   cup sifted confectioners' sugar
1   tablespoon warm water
1   teaspoon vanilla or almond extract

- Preheat oven to 350 degrees.

- Combine blueberries, ⅓ cup sugar and 2 tablespoons flour in a small saucepan. Cook over medium heat 5 minutes or until thickened, stirring constantly. Set aside.

- Cream butter. Gradually add remaining 1 cup sugar, beating well at medium speed of an electric mixer. Add eggs, one at a time, beating well after each addition.

- Combine remaining 2 cups flour, baking powder and salt. Add to creamed mixture alternately with sour cream, beginning and ending with flour mixture. Stir in vanilla.

- Spoon half of batter into a heavily greased 10-inch tube pan. Spoon half of reserved blueberry mixture over batter. Repeat procedure with remaining batter and blueberry mixture. Swirl knife through batter.

- Sprinkle with pecans. Bake for 50 minutes. Let cool in pan 5 minutes.

- Transfer to a serving plate.

- To make glaze, combine sugar, water and extract in a small bowl. Stir with a wire whisk until smooth. Drizzle glaze over warm coffee cake.

Serves 12 to 16

42

Light Raspberry Coffee Cake

1   cup fresh raspberries
3   tablespoons brown sugar
1   cup flour
⅓   cup sugar
½   teaspoon baking powder
¼   teaspoon baking soda
⅛   teaspoon salt
½   cup plain lowfat yogurt
2   tablespoons butter, melted
1   teaspoon vanilla
1   large egg
1   tablespoon sliced almonds

Glaze
¼   cup confectioners' sugar
¼   teaspoon vanilla
Milk

- Preheat oven to 350 degrees.

- Combine raspberries and brown sugar. Set aside.

- In a large bowl, combine flour, sugar, baking powder, baking soda and salt.

- In a separate bowl combine yogurt, butter, vanilla and egg, stirring well.

- Add yogurt mixture to the flour mixture, stirring until just moist.

- Spoon ⅔ of the batter into an 8-inch round cake pan coated with cooking spray.

- Top with the raspberry mixture, then the remaining batter.

- Sprinkle with sliced almonds.

- Bake for 40 minutes until wooden tooth-pick comes out clean when inserted into the middle of the cake.

- Let cool 10 minutes.

- To make glaze, combine confectioners' sugar, ¼ teaspoon vanilla and enough milk to create the consistency for drizzling over the top of the cake.

Serves 8 to 10

Raspberry Cream Cheese Coffee Cake

2¼ **cups flour**
1 **cup sugar, divided**
¾ **cup butter**
½ **teaspoon baking powder**
½ **teaspoon baking soda**
¼ **teaspoon salt**
¾ **cup sour cream**
1 **teaspoon almond extract**
2 **eggs**
8 **ounces cream cheese, softened**
½ **cup raspberry preserves**
½ **cup sliced almonds**

• Preheat oven to 350 degrees.

• Grease and flour the bottom and sides of a 10-inch springform pan.

• In a large bowl, combine flour and ¾ cup sugar. Using a pastry blender or fork, cut in the butter until mixture resembles coarse crumbs.

• Set aside 1 cup of this crumb mixture and combine remaining mixture with baking powder, baking soda, salt, sour cream, almond extract and one egg, blending well.

• Spread batter over bottom and 2 inches up sides of the pan. (Batter should be about ¼ inch thick on the sides.)

• In a small bowl, combine cream cheese, ¼ cup sugar and 1 egg, blending well. Pour into batter-lined pan.

• Carefully spoon preserves evenly over the cream cheese mixture.

• In a small bowl, combine reserved 1 cup of crumb mixture and almonds. Sprinkle over preserves.

• Bake for 45 to 55 minutes or until cream cheese filling is set and crust is deep golden brown. Cool in pan for 15 minutes.

• Remove sides of pan and serve warm or cool. Store in refrigerator.

Serves 16

44

Sleep-Over Coffee Cake

2   **cups flour**
1   **cup sugar**
1   **cup buttermilk**
⅔   **cup butter, softened**
½   **cup brown sugar**
2   **large eggs**
2   **tablespoons dry milk powder**
1   **tablespoon cinnamon**
1   **teaspoon baking soda**
1   **teaspoon baking powder**
½   **teaspoon salt**

Topping

½   **cup brown sugar**
½   **cup walnuts or pecans, chopped**
½   **teaspoon ground nutmeg**
¼   **cup butter, melted**

- Grease and flour a 9x13x2-inch baking pan.

- In a large bowl, using an electric mixer, combine flour, sugar, buttermilk, ⅔ cup butter, ½ cup brown sugar, eggs, dry milk powder, cinnamon, baking soda, baking powder and salt. Mix at low speed until well-blended, about 4 minutes.

- Pour into prepared pan.

- For topping, mix ½ cup brown sugar, nuts and nutmeg. Sprinkle evenly over batter.

- Refrigerate overnight.

- Preheat oven to 350 degrees.

- Drizzle melted butter over cake. Bake for 30 minutes until top is a rich golden brown.

- Cool for 15 minutes. Serve warm.

Serves 8 to 10

45

Sour Cream Coffee Cake

1   **cup butter, softened**
2   **cups sugar**
½   **teaspoon salt**
1   **teaspoon vanilla**
2   **eggs**
2   **cups flour**
1½ **teaspoons baking powder**
1   **cup sour cream**

Topping
4   **tablespoons brown sugar**
1   **tablespoon cinnamon**
½   **cup pecans, chopped**

- Preheat oven to 350 degrees. Grease and flour Bundt pan.

- Cream butter, sugar, salt and vanilla. Add eggs and mix thoroughly.

- Sift together flour and baking powder. Add to creamed mixture a small amount at a time, mixing well after each addition.

- Fold in the sour cream and mix well. Set aside.

- For topping, mix brown sugar, cinnamon and pecans in a small bowl.

- Place half the batter in Bundt pan. Sprinkle with half of the topping mix. Cover with remaining batter, then sprinkle with remaining topping mix.

- Bake for 60 to 70 minutes.

Serves 10 to 12

Serve with fresh fruit, raspberry coulis or fruited whipped cream.

Irish Soda Bread

¼ **cup plus 1 tablespoon unsalted butter, divided**
4 **cups flour**
¼ **cup sugar**
3 **teaspoons baking powder**
1 **teaspoon salt**
2 **tablespoons caraway seeds**
2 **cups raisins**
1⅓ **cups buttermilk or sour milk**
1 **whole egg plus 1 egg yolk, divided**
1 **teaspoon baking soda**
1 **tablespoon water**

- Preheat oven to 375 degrees.

- Grease a deep 2½-quart casserole with 1 tablespoon butter.

- In a large bowl sift together flour, sugar, baking powder and salt. Stir in caraway seeds.

- Add ¼ cup butter and cut in with a pastry blender until mixture is like coarse corn meal.

- Stir in raisins.

- In a small bowl beat buttermilk, 1 whole egg and baking soda until blended.

- Turn dough out on to a floured board and knead about 3 minutes until smooth. Shape into a ball and place in casserole dish.

- With a sharp knife cut an "x" ½ inch deep over top surface.

- Mix egg yolk and water and brush over top.

- Bake for 60 to 65 minutes. Cool 10 minutes and remove from pan.

Yield: 1 loaf

Orange Bread

1   **cup sugar**
2   **cups flour**
½   **teaspoon salt**
1   **teaspoon baking powder**
½   **teaspoon baking soda**
Juice of 2 large oranges (remove zest before juicing)
¼   **cup butter, melted**
1   **teaspoon vanilla**
1   **egg, beaten**
½   **cup coconut**

Topping

2   **tablespoons sugar**
2   **teaspoons orange zest**

- Preheat oven to 350 degrees. Grease an 8x4-inch loaf pan and line it with waxed paper.

- In a large bowl, combine sugar, flour, salt, baking powder and baking soda.

- Add enough boiling water to orange juice to make 1 cup. Add melted butter, vanilla and beaten egg.

- Make a hole in the center of the flour mixture and add the liquids, mixing well.

- Fold in coconut.

- Place dough mixture into the loaf pan.

- For topping, combine 2 tablespoons sugar with orange zest. Sprinkle over loaf.

- Bake for 1 hour.

Yield: 1 loaf

Wonderful toasted, served warm with butter.

Blueberry Loaf

8 tablespoons unsalted
butter, melted and cooled

1¼ cups sugar, plus additional
to sprinkle top of loaf

2 eggs

2 cups flour

2 teaspoons baking powder

½ teaspoon salt

½ cup milk

2 teaspoons lemon zest,
grated (optional)

1½ cups blueberries

- Preheat oven to 350 degrees. Grease a 9x5-inch loaf pan.

- Beat butter and sugar until fluffy. Add eggs, beating in one at a time.

- Combine flour, baking powder and salt.

- Add half of the flour mixture to the butter. Beat just to mix.

- Beat in milk, followed by remaining flour mixture. Do not overbeat.

- Mix in lemon zest if desired.

- Fold in blueberries with a rubber spatula.

- Spoon into prepared loaf pan and sprinkle with sugar.

- Bake for 45 to 50 minutes.

Serves 8 to 10

Spiced Pumpkin Loaf

1¾ cups flour
1   teaspoon baking powder
1   teaspoon baking soda
½   teaspoon salt
1   cup canned pumpkin
⅔   cup sugar
⅓   cup sour cream
⅓   cup vegetable oil
3   tablespoons orange
    marmalade
1   egg, beaten
1   teaspoon cinnamon
½   teaspoon ground ginger
¼   teaspoon nutmeg, freshly
    grated
⅛   teaspoon ground cloves
⅔   cup walnuts, chopped

Cream Cheese Spread

8   ounces cream cheese,
    softened
½   cup orange marmalade

• Preheat oven to 350 degrees.

• Grease and flour a 9x5-inch loaf pan, line with wax paper, then grease and flour wax paper. Set aside.

• Combine flour, baking powder, baking soda and salt, stirring well.

• Combine pumpkin, sugar, sour cream, oil, 3 tablespoons marmalade, egg, cinnamon, ginger, nutmeg and cloves in a medium mixing bowl. Beat well at medium speed of an electric mixer.

• Add flour mixture to pumpkin mixture, beating well.

• Stir in walnuts.

• Pour batter into prepared pan. Bake for 40 to 50 minutes or until a wooden pick inserted into center comes out clean. Cool in pan for 10 minutes.

• Remove from pan. Remove wax paper and let cool completely on a wire rack.

• Make a cream cheese spread, beating together the cream cheese and ½ cup orange marmalade. Serve alongside cooled loaf.

Serves 8 to 10

Cranberry Muffins

1 tablespoon butter, softened, plus 4 tablespoons butter, melted and cooled
1 cup firm fresh cranberries
2¾ cups flour
¾ cup sugar
4 teaspoons baking powder
½ teaspoon salt
1 cup milk
1 egg, lightly beaten

- Preheat oven to 400 degrees.

- With a pastry brush, spread 1 tablespoon softened butter over the inside surfaces of a medium-sized 12 cup muffin tin (each cup should be about 2½ inches across).

- Wash the cranberries under cold running water and pat dry on paper towels.

- Coarsely chop cranberries in a food processor. Set aside.

- Combine flour, sugar, baking powder and salt and sift into a deep mixing bowl.

- Stirring constantly with a large spoon, pour in milk in a thin stream.

- When the milk is absorbed, stir in the egg and 4 tablespoons of cooled, melted butter.

- Add chopped cranberries and continue to stir until well combined.

- Ladle batter into each muffin cup, filling about ⅔ full.

- Bake in middle of oven for 30 minutes, or until muffins are puffed and brown on top and a toothpick inserted in the center comes out clean.

- Run a knife around the edge of each cup to loosen muffins. Turn out and serve warm.

Yield: 12 muffins

51

Boston's Best Blueberry Muffins

½	**cup butter**
1	**cup sugar**
2	**eggs**
2	**cups flour, unsifted**
2	**teaspoons baking powder**
½	**teaspoon salt**
½	**cup milk**
1	**teaspoon vanilla**
2-2½	**cups fresh whole blueberries**
2	**teaspoons sugar for topping**

- Preheat oven to 375 degrees.

- On low speed of hand mixer in a large bowl, cream butter and sugar until fluffy.

- Add eggs, one at a time and mix until blended.

- Sift together the flour, baking powder and salt. Add to creamed mixture alternately with milk and vanilla, mixing well.

- Add whole blueberries and mix with spoon, being careful not to break up berries.

- Pour into a greased 12 muffin tin. Sprinkle with sugar. Bake for 30 minutes. Cool and serve.

Yield: 12 muffins

Lemon Cornmeal Blueberry Muffins

Zest of 2 large lemons, grated (about 2 tablespoons)
1   **cup sugar**
½   **cup vegetable oil**
1   **large egg**
1   **cup buttermilk**
1½ **cups flour**
⅓   **cup cornmeal**
1   **teaspoon baking soda**
Scant ¼ teaspoon salt
1   **cup blueberries**

Glaze
3   **tablespoons fresh lemon juice**
1½ **tablespoons sugar**

- Preheat oven to 375 degrees.

- Line a 12 muffin tin with paper liners or grease them.

- In a large mixing bowl with a wooden spoon, stir together zest, sugar, oil and egg.

- Stir in the buttermilk, then the flour, cornmeal, baking soda and salt.

- Fold in blueberries. Let the batter rest for 15 minutes.

- Fill muffin cups 7/8ths full.

- Bake for 20 to 22 minutes until they are lightly browned and a toothpick inserted into the center comes out clean.

- Cool in the pan for 5 minutes before dipping them in the glaze.

- To make the glaze, stir lemon juice and sugar together in a small bowl until sugar is completely dissolved.

- Quickly dip the tops of the warm muffins into the glaze. Allow to cool for 15 minutes before serving.

Yield: 12 muffins

Muffins can be frozen. After they have cooled, place on a cookie sheet in the freezer. Once frozen, they can be stored in a heavy plastic bag. To reheat, place frozen muffins in a preheated 300 degree oven for 10 minutes or microwave on medium power in increments of 20 seconds until warm.

Nantucket Morning Glory Muffins

1¼ cups sugar

2¼ cups flour

1 tablespoon cinnamon

2 teaspoons baking soda

½ teaspoon salt

½ cup shredded coconut

½ cup raisins

2 cups carrots, grated
   (4 large carrots)

1 apple, shredded

1 can (8 ounce) crushed
   pineapple, drained

½ cup pecans or walnuts

3 eggs

1 cup vegetable oil

1 teaspoon vanilla

- Preheat oven to 350 degrees.

- Sift together the sugar, flour, cinnamon, baking soda and salt into a large bowl.

- Add coconut, raisins, carrots, apple, pineapple and nuts and stir to combine.

- In a separate bowl whisk eggs with oil and vanilla.

- Pour egg mixture into the bowl with flour mixture and blend well.

- Spoon batter into muffin tins lined with papers, filling each cup to the brim.

- Bake for 35 minutes or until a toothpick inserted into the center comes out clean.

- Let cool in the pan for 10 minutes, then turn out on a rack to cool.

Yield: 16 muffins

These muffins need 24 hours for "ripening" to develop their full flavor.

Triple Chocolate Muffins

3	ounces unsweetened chocolate
3	ounces semisweet chocolate plus 3 ounces (½ cup) semisweet chocolate chips, divided
¼	cup unsalted butter
½	cup flour
½	teaspoon baking powder
¼	teaspoon salt
2	eggs
½	cup sugar
1	teaspoon vanilla extract
1	teaspoon instant coffee granules or powder
½	cup walnuts, chopped

- Preheat oven to 350 degrees.

- Butter a 12-muffin tin.

- Combine unsweetened chocolate, 3 ounces semisweet chocolate and butter in top of a double boiler over simmering water. Stir often until melted and smooth. Set aside and cool slightly.

- In a small bowl combine flour, baking powder and salt. Set aside.

- In a separate bowl combine eggs, sugar, vanilla and coffee. Using a hand mixer, beat until light and about double in volume.

- Beat in the chocolate mixture and then the flour mixture, just until blended.

- Stir in the chocolate chips and walnuts. The mixture will be stiff, almost like a dough.

- Spoon into prepared muffin cups, filling each about ⅔ full. Smooth top of each muffin.

- Bake until muffins look dry on top, about 15 minutes. Do not overbake. The centers should remain moist.

- Cool in the tins for 10 minutes. Remove.

Yield: 12 muffins

Cranberry Scones

1¾ cups flour
⅓ cup sugar
1 teaspoon baking powder
½ teaspoon baking soda
⅔ cup buttermilk
⅓ cup sweetened, dried cranberries
⅓ cup butter, melted and cooled

- Preheat oven to 400 degrees.

- Combine flour, sugar, baking powder and baking soda.

- Stir in buttermilk, cranberries and melted butter just until evenly moistened.

- On a greased 12x15-inch baking sheet, spoon dough into 6 to 8 portions, keeping slightly apart.

- Bake for 18 to 20 minutes until well browned. Serve hot or cold.

Yield: 6 to 8 scones

For plain scones, omit the fruit and, if desired, add cinnamon to taste.

Orange French Toast

Oil and butter for griddle
3 tablespoons maple syrup, plus additional for serving
3 tablespoons whipping cream
3 tablespoons orange-flavored liqueur
½ teaspoon salt
6 eggs
¼ teaspoon nutmeg, freshly grated
Grated orange rind from 1 large orange
1 loaf Italian bread, sliced very thin

- Grease a griddle with oil and butter. Preheat griddle to 375 degrees.

- Lightly beat syrup, cream, liqueur, salt, eggs, nutmeg and orange rind.

- Dip slices of bread in egg mixture and cook on griddle until lightly browned.

- Serve with warm maple syrup.

Serves 6

56

Oven Baked Apple Pancake

¾ **cup pancake mix**

½ **cup milk**

3 **eggs**

⅓ **cup sugar, divided**

2 **large apples (3 cups sliced)**

¼ **cup butter**

¼ **cup walnuts or pecans, chopped**

1 **teaspoon cinnamon**

- Preheat oven to 450 degrees.

- Combine pancake mix, milk, eggs and 1 teaspoon sugar. Mix well.

- In a 9 or 10-inch ovenproof skillet over medium heat, melt butter and sauté apples until tender.

- Remove skillet from heat and sprinkle apples with nuts.

- Pour batter evenly over apples and nuts.

- Mix cinnamon with remaining sugar and sprinkle over batter.

- Cover skillet with lid or foil and bake for 10 to 12 minutes or until pancake is puffed and sugar is melted.

- Loosen side of pancake from skillet. Cool slightly. Cut into wedges.

Serves 4

Oven Pancake

8   **eggs**
2   **cups milk**
2   **cups flour**
2   **teaspoons sugar**
1½ **teaspoons salt**
½   **cup butter**
Lemon wedges
Confectioners' sugar
Fresh berries (or other fruits)
Whipped cream

- Use a 15-inch round, 3-inch deep paella pan to make one large pancake or four 9 to 10 -inch round pie pans to make four smaller pancakes.

- In a large bowl whisk together eggs, milk, flour, sugar and salt until well blended. Let stand at room temperature for 30 minutes before baking.

- Preheat oven to 500 degrees.

- Place butter in pan(s) and place pan(s) in oven just until butter melts.

- Remove from oven and swirl the butter around to coat pans.

- Pour pancake batter into pan(s) and bake for 15 to 20 minutes or until pancake has risen above the edges of the pan(s), is golden on top and has set in the center.

- Transfer to the table immediately. Cut into wedges, squeeze lemon over each serving, and top with a sprinkling of confectioners' sugar, a spoonful of berries (or other fruit), and a dollop of whipped cream, if desired.

Serves 8

Baked Eggs and Spinach Casserole

5   **packages (10 ounces each) frozen chopped spinach, thawed and drained**

1¼   **teaspoons salt, divided**

8   **tablespoons butter**

8   **tablespoons flour**

2½   **cups milk**

2½   **cups Cheddar cheese, shredded**

10   **eggs**

Freshly ground pepper, to taste

- Preheat oven to 325 degrees.

- In a 13x9-inch baking dish, arrange spinach in an even layer and sprinkle evenly with 1 teaspoon salt.

- With a spoon, make 10 indentations in the spinach.

- In a medium saucepan over low heat, melt butter. Add flour and stir until smooth.

- Gradually stir in milk and cook, stirring constantly until sauce is thickened.

- Stir in cheese and heat just until cheese is melted.

- Break one egg into each indentation. Sprinkle eggs with ¼ teaspoon salt and pepper to taste.

- Pour cheese sauce over eggs.

- Bake for 30 to 35 minutes until the eggs are set.

Serves 10

Brunch Eggs with Spanish Sauce

Eggs

½ cup butter
1 loaf toasting white bread
6 eggs
3 cups milk
¾ teaspoon dry mustard
¾ teaspoon white pepper
1 pound Cheddar cheese, grated

Sauce

3 tablespoons vegetable oil
⅓ cup onion, chopped
¼ cup green pepper, chopped (optional)
¾ cup fresh mushrooms, sliced
1 tablespoon cornstarch
1 can (16 ounce) tomatoes with all liquid
1 teaspoon salt
Freshly ground pepper, to taste
2 teaspoons sugar
Dash cayenne pepper

Eggs

- Butter both sides of bread and cut in cubes.
- Combine eggs, milk, mustard and pepper.
- Layer bread cubes and cheese in a buttered 13x9-inch casserole.
- Pour egg mixture over top.
- Cover and refrigerate overnight.
- Preheat oven to 350 degrees.
- Bake uncovered for 40 to 45 minutes or until set.

Sauce

- Brown onions, peppers and mushrooms in the oil.
- Combine cornstarch with 2 tablespoons liquid from the tomatoes and add to browned vegetables.
- Add tomatoes with the rest of their liquid, salt, pepper, sugar and cayenne pepper.
- Cook over low heat, stirring often for 15 to 20 minutes.
- Serve with the cooked brunch eggs.

Serves 8

Goat Cheese and Artichoke Strata

2 cups whole milk

¼ cup olive oil

8 cups sourdough bread, diced

1½ cups whipping cream

5 large eggs

1 tablespoon garlic, chopped

½ teaspoon salt

¼ teaspoon pepper

¼ teaspoon nutmeg

12 ounces goat cheese, crumbled

2 tablespoons fresh sage, chopped

1 tablespoon fresh thyme, chopped

½ teaspoon Herbs de Provence

12 ounces smoked ham, chopped (optional)

3 jars (6.5 ounces each) marinated artichoke hearts, halved

1 cup packed grated Fontina cheese

1½ cups Parmesan cheese, grated

- In a large bowl mix milk, oil and bread and let stand 10 minutes until liquid is absorbed.

- Whisk together whipping cream, eggs, garlic, salt and pepper and nutmeg in a separate bowl until well blended.

- Add crumbled goat cheese to cream mixture.

- Mix sage, thyme and Herbs de Provence in a third bowl.

- Toss chopped ham and artichokes together in a bowl.

- In a 13x9x2-inch baking dish, layer ½ of the bread mixture, then ½ of the artichoke and ham mixture, then ½ of the herb mix, then ½ of each of the Fontina and Parmesan cheeses. Cover with ½ of the cream mixture.

- Repeat, using the remaining ingredients and ending with the cream mixture.

- Cover and chill for 24 hours.

- When ready to serve, preheat oven to 350 degrees.

- Bake uncovered for 1 hour until firm in the center.

Serves 8 to 12

Ham and Artichoke Strata

2   cans (8 ounces each)
    artichoke hearts, drained
12 thin slices baked ham
4   tablespoons butter
¼   cup flour
2   cups milk, warmed
⅛   teaspoon seasoned salt
⅛   teaspoon cayenne pepper
¼   teaspoon nutmeg
⅛   teaspoon paprika
⅛   teaspoon white pepper
⅔   cup Swiss cheese,
    shredded, divided
⅔   cup Parmesan cheese,
    grated, divided
¼   cup dry sherry
⅔   cup buttered bread crumbs

• Preheat oven to 350 degrees.

• If artichokes are large, cut in half. Wrap 2 halves in one slice of ham and arrange closely in a lightly buttered 9x13x2-inch glass baking dish. (Dish may be prepared to this point ahead. Cover and refrigerate).

• In a saucepan melt butter over medium heat and blend in flour, stirring until smooth.

• Remove from heat and gradually add milk, stirring until smooth.

• Return to heat and cook until thickened, stirring constantly.

• Add salt, pepper, nutmeg, paprika and white pepper and ⅓ cup each of Swiss and Parmesan cheeses. Stir over low heat until melted.

• Remove from heat and blend in sherry.

• Pour sauce over ham rolls.

• Combine bread crumbs and remaining ⅓ cup of cheeses. Sprinkle over sauce.

• Bake for 25 to 30 minutes or until brown and bubbly.

Serves 6 to 8

Seafood and Artichoke Casserole

1 can (14 ounce) artichoke hearts, drained
1 pound fresh medium-sized shrimp, cooked, peeled and deveined
1 pound fresh crabmeat, cleaned
½ pound fresh mushrooms, sliced
6½ tablespoons butter, divided
4½ tablespoons flour
1½ cups half-and-half
1 tablespoon Worcestershire sauce
¼ cup dry sherry
Salt and white pepper, to taste
¼ cup Parmesan cheese, freshly grated
Paprika, to taste
Parsley, chopped, for garnish

- Preheat oven to 375 degrees.

- Arrange artichokes in a buttered 3-quart baking dish.

- Spread shrimp and crabmeat over them.

- Sauté mushrooms in 2 tablespoons butter for about 5 minutes. Arrange over seafood.

- In a large heavy saucepan, melt remaining 4½ tablespoons butter and blend in flour.

- Cook and stir 5 minutes over medium heat.

- Slowly add cream, cooking and stirring constantly until thickened and smooth.

- Stir in Worcestershire sauce, sherry, salt and white pepper.

- Pour over seafood in casserole and sprinkle with cheese and paprika.

- Bake for 20 minutes. Sprinkle with chopped parsley before serving.

Serves 6 to 8

‑

Leek Tart

2 tablespoons butter

2 pounds leeks (white and tender green parts only), split lengthwise, cleaned thoroughly and cut into ¼-inch strips

½ teaspoon salt

Freshly ground black pepper, to taste

2 large eggs

½ cup cream (heavy, half-and-half, or light)

¼ teaspoon nutmeg

1 9-inch prepared crust in a buttered quiche, tart or pie pan

• Melt butter in skillet over medium heat. Add leeks, salt and pepper. Cover and cook until leeks are very soft with little color. Reduce heat as they cook, about 30 minutes.

• Preheat oven to 400 degrees.

• Beat together eggs, cream and nutmeg until well combined.

• Add leeks and pour into uncooked pastry shell.

• Bake until golden and custard is set: 20 to 30 minutes. Let rest in pan 10 minutes. Cut and serve.

Serves 6

Soups & Salads

Wright Tavern

Wright Tavern

Seeking refreshment after the early morning march from Boston and the brief unpleasantness on Lexington Green, British Major Pitcairn entered Wright Tavern, which operated as British Headquarters from seven o'clock until noon on April 19, 1775. He had paraded into Concord at the head of seven hundred red-coated troops, stretched out in impressive columns and marching along to fife and drum. It had been a noisy parade into town, in that marching to their own fife and drum and barely two-hundred yards in front of Pitcairn's troops were the Concord Minutemen, numbering one-hundred and fifty. Considering the way the day would end, it was peculiar that Concord's Minutemen functioned as an escort of sorts for the British at the day's beginning, but the Minutemen were simply being practical and displaying the good American common sense that would govern the day's outcome. Having seen Pitcairn's seven hundred well-arrayed men approach outside Concord at Meriam's Corner, the one hundred and fifty Minutemen determined their fight that day would be better waged elsewhere. They had promptly done an about-face, marched back to Concord in front of Pitcairn and his columned troops, warned residents of the British imminent approach, and hurried on to Barrett's Farm. Upon his Concord arrival, Pitcairn climbed up Old Burying Ground Hill with his commander Colonel Smith. He saw the growing number of Minutemen forming on the other side of Concord River. Detachments were sent to the North and South Bridges, along with a contingent assigned to take Colonel Barrett's farm where the British had been told the main munitions were quartered. A few troops stayed in the town and started searching for rebel stores. When hidden supplies were found, the soldiers dumped them in the town's millpond outside the Wright Tavern. Thinking matters well in hand and retreating to the tavern, Major Pitcairn ordered a brandy and was served. It is rumored he swirled his drink with his finger and said he would so stir Yankee blood before the day was out. Up the road at the North Bridge, things had really begun to stir, and Pitcairn's sojourn at Wright Tavern had to sustain his disastrous flight back to Boston with his demoralized troops.

Soup & Salad

Hot

Cold

Chili/Stew

Salads and Dressings

Antique Show Minestrone

4   ounces bacon, diced

2   tablespoons butter

4   cloves garlic, minced

2   carrots, peeled and diced
    into ¼-inch pieces

1   onion, peeled and diced
    into ¼-inch pieces

1   leek (white part and 1-inch
    green) well-rinsed,
    quartered and cut into
    ¼-inch slices

3   cups green cabbage, finely
    shredded

2   zucchini, quartered
    lengthwise and cut into
    ¼-inch thick slices

1   Idaho potato, peeled and
    cut into ¼-inch dice

4   cups chicken broth

2   cups beef broth

2   tablespoons tomato paste

2   tablespoons dried oregano

1½ teaspoons dried basil

1   teaspoon black pepper,
    coarsely ground

Salt, to taste

5   tablespoons fresh flat-leaf
    parsley, chopped, divided

¾   cup dried red kidney
    beans, cooked and drained,
    or 1 can (15.5 ounce)
    kidney beans

4   ripe plum tomatoes, cut
    into ¼-inch dice

½   cup tiny bow-shaped pasta

- Cook bacon in large soup pot over low heat to render fat. Do not let it brown.

- Add butter, garlic, carrots, onion and leek and raise heat slightly.

- Cover and wilt vegetables for 10 minutes, stirring occasionally.

- Add cabbage, zucchini, potato, chicken and beef broths and tomato paste. Bring to a boil.

- Reduce heat and add oregano, basil, pepper, salt, and 2 tablespoons parsley.

- Simmer over medium heat for 15 minutes.

- Add kidney beans, plum tomatoes and pasta. Simmer until pasta is tender, about 10 minutes.

- Adjust seasoning. Stir in remaining 3 tablespoons parsley.

Serves 6 to 8

Asparagus Soup

4   large onions, chopped

8   tablespoons unsalted
     butter

8   cups chicken stock

2   pounds fresh asparagus,
     divided

½   cup heavy cream

Salt and freshly ground
     pepper, to taste

• Melt butter in large soup pot.

• Add chopped onions and cook until soft
  and light brown in color, about 30 minutes.

• Add chicken stock to pot and bring to
  a boil.

• Cut asparagus into 1-inch pieces, saving
  a few tips to use as a garnish. Set saved
  tips aside.

• Add asparagus pieces to stock and
  simmer, covered, 45 to 50 minutes or
  until asparagus is very soft. Cool slightly.

• Using blender or food processor, purée
  soup in batches, 2 cups at a time, until
  smooth.

• Return puréed soup to the pot. Add
  reserved asparagus tips and heavy cream.
  Simmer 5 minutes.

• Season with salt and pepper.

Serves 10

Black Bean "Cassoulet" Soup

1	pound dried black (turtle) beans
½	cup olive oil
1½	cups yellow onions, diced
6	cloves garlic, crushed
1	very meaty ham bone or 1 smoked ham hock
3	quarts water
1¾	tablespoons ground cumin
1	tablespoon dried oregano
1-2	bay leaves
½	tablespoon coarse (kosher) salt
½	tablespoon ground black pepper

Pinch cayenne pepper

4	tablespoons fresh flat-leaf parsley, chopped, divided
1	pound fresh garlic sausage
3	sweet Italian sausage links
3	hot Italian sausage links
½	pound bratwurst
1½	medium-sized sweet red peppers, cored, seeded and diced
2	tablespoons dry sherry
1½	tablespoons dark brown sugar
1	tablespoon fresh lemon juice

Sour cream

- Soak black beans in water to cover overnight.

- In a large heavy stockpot heat oil over low heat. Add onions and garlic. Sauté until limp, about 10 minutes.

- Drain and rinse beans and add to stockpot. Add ham bone and 3 quarts of water. Stir in cumin, oregano, bay leaves, salt, pepper, cayenne, and 2 tablespoons parsley. Heat to boiling. Reduce heat to medium and cook uncovered at a slow rolling boil for 2 hours, skimming foam from top and stirring occasionally.

- Meanwhile, grill sweet, hot and garlic sausage and bratwurst. Cut hot and sweet sausage and bratwurst into 1-inch pieces. Remove casings from garlic sausage and cut into ½-inch pieces.

- In a food processor fitted with a steel blade, process 2 cups of beans until smooth. Return beans to pot, cooking for an additional 30 minutes.

- Add all the sausages and red peppers and cook for another 30 minutes.

- Remove ham bone, shred meat and return meat to pot. Stir in sherry, sugar and lemon juice.

(continued on next page)

Black Bean "Cassoulet" Soup continued

• Cook over medium heat until beans are very soft and soup is thick, 30 to 45 minutes. Stir in remaining 2 tablespoons parsley. Adjust seasoning.

• Ladle soup into bowls and dollop each serving with sour cream.

Serves 8

Emerson Auxiliary Christmas Shop Soup

3   **slices bacon**
1   **cup onion, chopped**
½   **cup celery, chopped**
1   **teaspoon dried basil**
1   **can (14.5 ounce) beef broth**
1   **can (10.5 ounce) bean with bacon soup**
2   **cups water**
1   **can (28 ounce) whole tomatoes, crushed**
½   **cup bowtie pasta**
1   **cup cabbage, shredded**
1   **cup zucchini, sliced**

• In a large saucepan, fry bacon. Remove and crumble. Cook onion and celery in bacon fat. Add basil. Season to taste.

• Add broth, soup, water, tomatoes and pasta. Bring to a boil, cover and reduce heat to simmer 15 minutes.

• Add cabbage and zucchini. Cook 15 minutes longer, stirring often.

Serves 8 to 10

Hearty Lentil Soup

1	**pound ground beef**
1	**cup celery, chopped**
1	**cup carrot, chopped**
1	**cup onion, chopped**
1	**cup cabbage, chopped**
16	**ounces dried lentils, rinsed**
1	**teaspoon green pepper, chopped**
1	**teaspoon salt**
½	**teaspoon ground pepper**
1	**bay leaf**
2	**beef bouillon cubes**
1	**can (46 ounce) tomato juice**
4	**cups water**

- Brown beef over medium heat, about 5 minutes.

- Stir in all remaining ingredients.

- Cover and bring to a boil. Reduce heat and simmer 90 minutes, uncovered. Stir occasionally.

Serves 8 to 10

A great soup to serve after outside winter activities.

Italian Style Lentil Soup

1 package (16 ounce) dried lentils
¼-½ pound salt pork
1 onion, chopped
3-4 stalks celery, chopped
2-3 cloves garlic, minced
2 cans (28 ounce) crushed tomatoes
4 cups chicken broth
Salt and freshly ground pepper, to taste
Parsley flakes, to taste
1 can (6 ounce) tomato paste (optional)
4-6 carrots, peeled and cut into bite-sized pieces
½ pound small, shaped pasta (e.g., Ditalini), cooked
Parmesan cheese, freshly grated, for garnish

• Wash lentils thoroughly and rinse several times.

• Render salt pork over low heat. Add onions and celery and cook until soft. Add garlic and brown.

• Add lentils and cook for 5 minutes, stirring constantly.

• Add crushed tomatoes and chicken broth. Season to taste with salt, pepper and parsley.

• Simmer 1 hour. If desired, add tomato paste to thicken.

• Add carrots. Cook until tender.

• Add pasta. Correct seasoning.

• Serve with grated cheese.

Serves 8 to 10

Minestrone with Sweet Sausage and Tortellini

⅓   cup olive oil
1   large yellow onion, cut into thin rings
4   large carrots, peeled and thickly sliced
1   fennel bulb, chopped
2   large potatoes, peeled and diced
1   green bell pepper, cored, seeded and cut into ½-inch squares
3   medium-sized zucchini, diced
1½ cups green beans, diagonally sliced
1   medium-sized green cabbage, shredded
5   cups beef stock
5   cups water
1   can (35 ounce) Italian plum tomatoes
2   tablespoons dried oregano
1   tablespoon dried basil
Salt and freshly ground pepper, to taste
Outer rind of a 2-inch chunk of Parmesan or Romano cheese
1½ cups canned cannellini (white kidney) beans, drained
1   pound cheese-stuffed tortellini
1½ pounds sweet Italian sausage, pan fried, drained and sliced
Fontina cheese, freshly grated

• Heat oil in a large stockpot over medium heat. Add onion and sauté for 10 to 15 minutes. Stir in carrots and sauté 2 to 3 minutes, tossing occasionally.

• Add, one at a time, fennel, potatoes, green pepper, zucchini and green beans, sautéing each vegetable 2 to 3 minutes before adding the next. Stir in cabbage and cook 5 minutes more.

• Add stock, water, tomatoes (with their juices), oregano, basil, and salt and pepper to taste. Bury cheese rind in middle of soup. Heat to boiling. Reduce heat and simmer, covered, over low heat for 2½ to 3 hours. Soup will be very thick.

• Fifteen minutes before serving stir in cannellini beans and tortellini. Raise heat to cook tortellini, stirring occasionally to keep them from sticking to bottom of pot. Just before serving, stir in sausage. Remove cheese rind and discard.

• Ladle minestrone into shallow pasta bowls and garnish generously with Fontina cheese.

Serves 10 to 12

74

Quick Spinach and Tortellini Soup

2 tablespoons olive oil

2 ounces pancetta or bacon, finely diced

1-3 cloves garlic, minced

1 medium onion, finely chopped

9 cups chicken broth

2 teaspoons dried Italian herb blend or a mixture of oregano, basil or parsley

9 ounces cheese tortellini

1 can (28 ounce) crushed tomatoes packed in purée

8 ounces fresh spinach, rinsed well, stemmed and coarsely chopped

Salt and freshly ground pepper, to taste

1 cup Parmesan cheese, freshly grated

• Heat olive oil in a stockpot over medium-high heat. Add pancetta, garlic and onion. Cook, stirring frequently, until lightly browned, 10 to 15 minutes.

• Add chicken broth and Italian herbs. Bring to a boil and stir in tortellini. Simmer uncovered until tortellini is cooked, 10 to 12 minutes.

• Stir in crushed tomatoes and simmer another 5 minutes.

• Add spinach and cook just until wilted, about 3 minutes.

• Season to taste with salt and pepper.

• Ladle hot soup into bowls and top with a liberal sprinkling of grated cheese.

Serves 6 to 8

Shrimp, Tofu and Spinach Soup

<table>
<tr><td>1</td><td>package (2 ounce) cellophane noodles (bean threads)</td></tr>
<tr><td>1</td><td>tablespoon oil</td></tr>
<tr><td>1</td><td>tablespoon fresh ginger, grated</td></tr>
<tr><td>3</td><td>cloves garlic, minced</td></tr>
<tr><td>½</td><td>teaspoon curry powder</td></tr>
<tr><td>1½</td><td>quarts chicken stock or broth</td></tr>
<tr><td>3</td><td>tablespoons Asian fish sauce</td></tr>
<tr><td>2</td><td>teaspoons soy sauce</td></tr>
<tr><td>1½</td><td>teaspoons sugar</td></tr>
<tr><td>¾</td><td>teaspoon Asian sesame oil</td></tr>
<tr><td>⅛</td><td>teaspoon salt</td></tr>
<tr><td>⅛</td><td>teaspoon dried red pepper flakes</td></tr>
<tr><td>¼</td><td>pound shiitake mushrooms, stems removed and caps cut into thin slices</td></tr>
<tr><td>½</td><td>pound spinach, stems removed, leaves washed and cut into 1½-inch pieces (about 5 cups)</td></tr>
<tr><td>4</td><td>scallions including green tops, cut into 1-inch pieces</td></tr>
<tr><td>½</td><td>pound firm tofu, cut into 1-inch cubes</td></tr>
<tr><td>½</td><td>pound fresh medium shrimp, shelled and deveined</td></tr>
<tr><td>1½</td><td>tablespoons lemon juice</td></tr>
</table>

- Place noodles in medium bowl, cover with hot water, and leave to soften about 15 minutes. Drain and cut into 4-inch pieces.

- In a large pot, heat oil over moderate heat.

- Add ginger and garlic and cook, stirring, 2 minutes. Add the curry and cook 1 minute longer.

- Add stock, fish sauce, soy sauce, sugar, sesame oil, salt and red pepper flakes. Bring to a boil.

- Add sliced mushrooms. Reduce heat and simmer for 4 minutes.

- Add spinach, scallions and tofu. Simmer just until spinach wilts, about 1 minute.

- Add shrimp and noodles and cook until just done, about 2 minutes.

- Stir in lemon juice.

Serves 4

Buttermilk Bay Clam Chowder

1   **dozen medium-sized
    chowder clams in the shell,
    scrubbed and rinsed**
½   **cup butter**
3   **onions, peeled and chopped**
2   **white boiling potatoes,
    peeled and diced**
2   **ripe medium-sized
    tomatoes, peeled, seeded
    and chopped**
**Salt and freshly ground white
    pepper, to taste**
1   **bay leaf**
½   **teaspoon dried thyme**
2   **cups light cream or
    half-and-half**

- Steam clams in a large covered pot in a small amount of boiling water until they open. Remove clams as they open and continue to steam unopened ones a few minutes more. Discard any clams that do not open.

- Reserve 2 cups clam broth from top of pan after any sand has settled to bottom. Add water if necessary to make 2 cups liquid.

- Shuck clams. Chop and set aside.

- Wash and dry pot.

- Melt butter in pot. Sauté onions gently until translucent but not brown.

- Add potatoes. Toss to coat with butter. Sauté 1 to 2 minutes.

- Add tomatoes, salt and pepper, bay leaf and thyme.

- Return chopped clams to pot along with reserved clam broth. (Chowder can be made ahead to this point and refrigerated.)

- Just before serving, heat to boiling, then reduce heat to simmer and stir in cream.

- Continue to cook over low heat until soup is hot. Do not boil.

Serves 4 to 6

If you do not have fresh clams, substitute 1 can (approximately 12 ounces) whole baby clams and 2 bottles clam juice. Add water if necessary to make 2 cups liquid.

Cream of Potato and Artichoke with Lobster

2	**lobsters, 1 pound each**
2	**tablespoons extra-virgin olive oil**
1	**shallot, minced**
2	**cups vegetable broth**
2	**potatoes, peeled and cubed**
½	**pound canned artichoke bottoms, trimmed and cubed**

Salt, to taste

Saffron, to taste

2	**tablespoons heavy cream**
8	**thin slices Tuscan bread, toasted**
4	**sprigs chervil**

- Boil lobsters in a pot of salted water until shells are red, about 10 minutes. Drain and remove meat from shells, taking care to keep claw meat intact.

- Heat oil in a pot and sauté shallot until golden. Pour in broth. Add potatoes and artichokes. Bring mixture to a boil and cook for 10 minutes. Season with salt to taste.

- Purée in a food processor or blender and return to pot. Warm over medium heat. Dilute a pinch of saffron in cream and whisk into soup.

- Divide lobster meat into 4 soup bowls and ladle soup over it. Garnish each bowl with 2 slices of bread, a lobster claw, and a sprig of chervil.

Serves 4

Fish Chowder

½ **cup butter**

3 **cups onion, diced**

¼ **cup carrot, finely grated**

2 **teaspoons garlic, minced**

½ **cup flour**

12 **cups concentrated fish stock**

4 **pounds chowder fish fillets, cut into chunks (2 pounds cod, 1 pound monkfish, 1 pound cusk or other variety)**

2 **cups light cream**

1 **cup Monterey Jack cheese, finely grated**

Salt and freshly ground black pepper, to taste

• Heat butter in saucepan until softened and sauté onions, carrots and garlic, stirring frequently, about 5 minutes. Remove from heat and gradually stir in flour. Return to heat and stir for about 4 minutes.

• Meanwhile, begin heating stock in a large pot. Whisk stock into flour mixture. Bring stock mixture to a boil, whisking constantly. Reduce heat and simmer for 10 minutes.

• Add fish and simmer 10 minutes. Stir in cream and cheese and simmer until cheese melts, about 5 to 8 minutes.

• Add salt and pepper to taste.

Serves 10 to 12

When reheating, warm chowder slowly to avoid boiling the cream.

Frozen fish stock, bottled clam juice and fish bouillon cubes are available at most fish markets and grocery stores.

Scallop-Corn Chowder

1	tablespoon butter
1	cup onion, chopped
½	cup celery, diced
⅓	cup red bell pepper, seeded and diced
1	clove garlic, minced
¼	cup flour
1½	cups red potatoes, diced
1	cup frozen whole kernel corn
¼	teaspoon salt
¼	teaspoon dried thyme
⅛	teaspoon ground pepper
3	bottles (8 ounce) clam juice
½	cup water
1	pound bay scallops
¼	cup fresh parsley, chopped

- Melt butter in a Dutch oven over medium heat.

- Add onion, celery, red bell pepper and garlic.

- Sauté 8 minutes or until tender.

- Sprinkle onion mixture with flour. Stir well.

- Cook 1 minute, stirring constantly.

- Add potatoes, corn, salt, thyme, pepper, clam juice and water. Stir well.

- Bring to a boil. Cover, reduce heat and simmer 15 minutes.

- Add scallops. Cover and cook 3 minutes.

- Sprinkle with parsley.

Serves 7

Cream of Broccoli, Mushroom and Leek Soup

6 tablespoons butter, divided
2 cups beef stock, divided
2 cups chicken stock, divided
2 pounds broccoli, coarsely chopped
¾ pound mushrooms, sliced
½ pound leeks, split and coarsely chopped
⅓ cup white wine
½ small shallot, minced
⅛ teaspoon dried basil
1 cup half-and-half
1¼ cups whipping cream
Salt and freshly ground pepper, to taste

• Combine 2 tablespoons each of butter, beef and chicken stock in a large skillet over medium-high heat. Add broccoli and cook until soft. Purée in a blender or food processor in 3 batches, adding at least 1/2 cup stock with each batch. Transfer to large saucepan or Dutch oven and add remaining stock. Heat through, stirring occasionally. Cover and keep warm over low heat.

• Heat remaining 4 tablespoons butter in skillet. Sauté mushrooms and leeks lightly. Add to soup.

• In a heavy-bottomed medium saucepan over medium heat, combine wine, shallot and basil. Cook until all liquid evaporates, watching carefully to avoid scorching.

• Meanwhile, heat half-and-half and whipping cream in small saucepan just until hot. Whisking constantly, add cream mixture in slow steady stream to shallot-basil mixture and cook over medium heat until reduced by ⅓. Whisk cream mixture into warm soup. Season with salt and pepper.

Serves 6 to 8

Soup may be frozen.

Butternut Squash, Apple and Ginger Soup

3-4 pounds butternut squash, peeled, cored, and cut into large chunks

3 tablespoons unsalted butter

3 small Granny Smith apples (about 1¼ pounds), cored, peeled and chopped

1½ cups yellow onion, finely chopped

3 tablespoons fresh ginger, minced and peeled

2 cloves garlic, peeled and chopped

6-7 cups vegetable broth

1 teaspoon salt

½ teaspoon ground black pepper

½ cup whipping cream (optional)

8 ounces crème fraîche or sour cream

4 ounces bleu cheese, crumbled

Toasted pumpkin seeds (optional)

- Preheat oven to 450 degrees. Spray a large roasting or jelly-roll pan with cooking spray. Roast squash until tender.

- In a large pot over moderate heat, melt butter. Add apple, onion, ginger and garlic. Cook uncovered, stirring occasionally, until lightly browned (15 to 20 minutes). Add broth, baked squash, salt and pepper. Simmer partially covered for 30 to 35 minutes, stirring occasionally. Remove from heat and cool.

- Purée soup in batches in a food processor. (Soup may be prepared to this point up to 3 days in advance. Cool, cover and refrigerate.)

- Return soup to pan. Add optional cream and heat, stirring often, until steaming, about 5 minutes. Adjust seasoning.

- In a small metal bowl, combine crème fraîche and bleu cheese and blend until smooth. Ladle hot soup into bowls and garnish with crème fraîche mixture and pumpkin seeds.

Serves 8

Corn and Carrot Soup

3-4 large ears of corn (to make 2 cups kernels)

1½ tablespoons unsalted butter

2½ cups carrot, thinly sliced

1   medium onion, diced

3   cups potatoes, unpeeled and diced

5   cups chicken stock or low-sodium broth

Salt and freshly ground pepper, to taste

½   tablespoon fresh thyme leaves (or ½ teaspoon dried thyme)

½   cup heavy cream

• Remove kernels from cob with a sharp knife. Scrape off pulp and add it to kernels.

• Heat butter in a Dutch oven or large pot over medium-high heat. Add carrots and onion and cook until onion is soft, about 4 minutes. Add potato, corn, stock, salt and pepper. Cover and bring to a boil.

• Reduce heat and simmer until vegetables are tender, about 20 minutes. Stir in thyme.

• Using a slotted spoon, place about 1½ cups of vegetables in a food processor and process to a coarse purée. Pour purée back into pot and bring to a simmer. Stir in cream and let soup bubble gently for 15 minutes or until slightly creamy. Soup will thicken as it stands.

Serves 6

Cream of "Anything" Soup

2   cups of "anything" (carrots, turnips, parsnips, celery, or a mix of any vegetables)

1   onion, chopped

1   stalk celery, chopped

3   cups chicken broth

3   tablespoons butter

3   tablespoons flour

½   cup cream

Salt and freshly ground pepper, to taste

• In a large pot, cook "anything", onion and celery in chicken broth. When vegetables are tender, transfer to blender or food processor and purée.

• Add butter to pot, melt and stir in flour.

• Slowly add cream while stirring. Do not boil.

• Return puréed mixture to pot. Whisk constantly while bringing to serving temperature.

• Adjust seasoning.

Serves 5 to 6

83

Cream of Wild Rice Soup

½ cup wild rice (3 ounces)
2½ cups water
4 cups chicken broth
(or 6 chicken bouillon
cubes and 4 cups water)
2 tablespoons butter
1 tablespoon onion, minced
¼ cup flour
½ tablespoon salt (or to taste)
1¼ cup carrot, coarsely grated
3 tablespoons slivered
almonds
1 pint half-and-half
2 tablespoons dry sherry
Parsley or chives, minced, for
garnish

- Combine rice and water. Cook as directed on rice package or until water is absorbed and rice is tender.

- Heat chicken broth and set aside.

- In a medium saucepan, melt butter and sauté onion until tender. Blend in flour.

- Gradually add broth, stirring constantly with wire whisk until mixture thickens slightly.

- Stir in cooked rice. Add salt, carrots and almonds. Simmer 5 minutes.

- Blend in half-and-half and sherry. Heat to serving temperature.

- Garnish with parsley or chives

Serves 6 to 7

* cook carrots longer

Creamy Cauliflower Cashew Soup

6 cups vegetable stock or water
1 large onion, coarsely chopped
1 medium carrot, coarsely chopped
1 head cauliflower (about 1 pound), divided into florets
4 cloves garlic, coarsely chopped
Freshly ground pepper, to taste
½ teaspoon dried tarragon, crushed
¾ cup cashews, lightly toasted
2-3 teaspoons lemon juice
Salt, to taste
1 tablespoon fresh parsley, minced

• Combine stock, onion, carrots, cauliflower and garlic in a stockpot. Bring to a boil and cook until tender, about 20 minutes. Add pepper and tarragon. Remove from heat. Cool.

• Place cashews and enough soup to cover in a blender or food processor. Purée, adding more soup as necessary, until smooth. Pour into bowl.

• Purée ⅔ of remaining soup, leaving about ⅓ chunky.

• Transfer cashew purée and all of soup back to stockpot. Heat gently. Season with lemon juice and salt. Serve hot, garnished with parsley.

Serves 4 to 6

Mushroom Barley Soup

1	**cup raw pearl barley**
8-9	**cups chicken or beef stock, divided**
5	**tablespoons tamari**
5	**tablespoons dry sherry**
1	**heaping cup onion, chopped**
2-3	**cloves garlic, minced**
3	**tablespoons butter**
1½	**pounds fresh mushrooms, sliced**
1	**teaspoon salt**

Freshly ground black pepper, to taste

- In an 8-quart saucepan, cook barley in 1 cup of stock, 20 minutes or until tender. Add remaining stock, tamari and sherry.

- Sauté onions and garlic in butter until soft. Add mushrooms and salt. Continue cooking until mushrooms are tender. Add mushroom mixture to soup, including any liquid.

- Add a generous grind of pepper and simmer, covered, for 20 minutes over low heat. Correct seasoning.

Serves 6 to 8

Tamari may be found in the Oriental food section of most supermarkets and food shops

Mushroom Chive Bisque

1½	**pounds mushrooms**
½	**cup butter**
¼	**teaspoon dry mustard**
¼	**cup flour**
2	**cups chicken broth**
2	**cups light cream**
⅓	**cup chives, minced**
¼	**cup dry sherry**

Salt, to taste

- In a food processor, chop mushrooms, including stems.

- In a heavy saucepan, sauté mushrooms in butter until soft.

- Add dry mustard and flour. Cook 1 to 2 minutes. Add chicken broth and cook until thickened.

- Add cream, chives, and sherry. Season with salt to taste.

Serves 4

Tomato Soup Provençal

⅓   cup olive oil

4   leeks, rinsed, dried and
    minced

3   carrots, minced

1   medium red onion,
    chopped

3   cloves garlic, minced

Zest of 1 orange, grated

1   tablespoon dried thyme

1   teaspoon fennel seeds

1   teaspoon saffron threads

12 ripe tomatoes, seeded and
    diced

3   cans (35 ounce) plum
    tomatoes, undrained

2   quarts chicken stock

1   cup orange juice

Salt and freshly ground
    pepper, to taste

1   cup fresh basil, chopped

Goat cheese log, sliced for
    garnish

- Heat oil in large stockpot over high heat. Add leeks, carrots, onion and garlic. Cook and stir for 15 minutes. Add orange zest, thyme, fennel and saffron, cooking and stirring for 3 minutes.

- Add fresh and canned tomatoes, stock and orange juice. Simmer over medium heat for 30 minutes. Remove from heat and purée in batches. Add salt and pepper to taste. Return soup to pot and bring to simmer. Just before serving, stir in basil. Garnish bowl with a slice of goat cheese.

Serves 8 to 10

Roasted Yellow Pepper Soup and
Roasted Tomato Soup with Serrano Cream

Pepper Soup
10 yellow peppers
4 tablespoons shallots, chopped
⅔ teaspoon dried thyme
Salt and freshly ground pepper, to taste
1⅓ tablespoons butter
2 cups chicken broth plus additional for thinning soup
⅓ cup heavy cream
Juice of 1 lemon

Tomato Soup
4 plum tomatoes, quartered lengthwise
5-7 large cloves garlic, unpeeled
4 tablespoons shallots, chopped
⅔ teaspoon dried oregano
Salt and freshly ground pepper, to taste
1⅓ tablespoons butter
2 cups chicken broth, plus additional for thinning soup
⅓ cup heavy cream
2 tablespoons lemon juice

Serrano Cream
2 large cloves garlic, minced
⅔ teaspoon salt
4 fresh serrano or jalapeño peppers, seeded, and chopped fine (wear rubber gloves)
⅔ cup sour cream or crème fraîche

To roast peppers

• Preheat oven on broil. Cut peppers in half. Remove seeds. Place peppers, skin side up, on foil-lined cookie sheet. Broil 2 to 3 inches from heat until skins are charred and black. Remove from oven and place in closed ziplock bag for 15 minutes. Peel charred skin from peppers and discard. Chop peppers coarsely.

Pepper Soup

• In a heavy saucepan over moderately low heat, cook shallots, thyme, salt and pepper in butter until shallots are soft. Do not brown.

• Add peppers and chicken broth and simmer, covered for 15 minutes.

• In a blender or food processor, purée soup in batches until very smooth. Pour through a sieve back into clean saucepan.

• Whisk in cream and lemon juice. Add additional chicken broth until soup is desired consistency.

Tomato Soup

• Preheat oven to 350 degrees.

• Spread tomatoes, skin side down, on 2 foil-lined jelly-roll pans. Add garlic to one of the pans.

• Bake for 1 hour or until tomatoes are very soft and their skins are dark brown. Cool.

(continued on next page)

Roasted Yellow Pepper Soup and Roasted Tomato Soup with Serrano Cream continued

- Meanwhile, in a heavy saucepan over moderately low heat, cook shallots, oregano, salt and pepper in butter until shallots are soft.

- Remove skin from garlic cloves. Add garlic, tomatoes and broth. Simmer, covered for 15 minutes.

- In a blender or food processor, purée soup until very smooth. Pour through a sieve back into clean saucepan. Whisk in cream and lemon juice.

If necessary, add chicken broth until tomato and pepper soups are the same consistency.

Serrano Cream

- Mash garlic with salt into a paste.

- In a blender, blend together chili peppers, garlic paste and sour cream until just mixed. Do not overprocess or cream will curdle. Press through a fine sieve set over a small bowl.

To serve soup

- Heat each soup separately until hot but not boiling. Ladle ½ cup of each soup into separate measuring cups. Slowly pour soups simultaneously into a shallow soup bowl from opposite sides of bowl. Drizzle with serrano cream.

Both soups and cream can be made up to 2 days in advance and refrigerated in tightly sealed containers.

Cold Cucumber Soup

2	**tablespoons butter**
¼	**cup onion, chopped, or 1 leek, sliced and cubed**
2	**cups cucumber, diced and unpeeled**
2	**cups chicken stock**
1	**cup watercress leaves**
½	**cup uncooked potato, finely diced and peeled**
2	**sprigs parsley**
½	**teaspoon salt**
¼	**teaspoon ground pepper**
¼	**teaspoon dry mustard**
1	**cup light cream or half-and-half**

Chives, cucumber and radishes, chopped, for garnish

- Melt butter in a saucepan and cook onions until transparent. Add cucumber, stock, watercress, potato, parsley, salt, pepper and mustard and bring to a boil. Simmer 15 minutes or until potatoes are tender. Cool slightly. Purée in a food processor. Correct seasoning. Chill.

- Before serving, stir in cream. Garnish with chopped chives, cucumber and radishes.

Serves 4

Gazpacho

3   **cloves garlic, minced**

1   **cucumber, peeled, seeded and diced**

2   **sweet red peppers, cored, seeded and diced**

1   **jalapeño pepper, cored, seeded and diced (more to taste)**

1   **medium red onion, chopped**

5   **ripe tomatoes, seeded and chopped**

5   **cups tomato-vegetable juice cocktail**

½   **cup lime juice**

1   **tablespoon ground cumin**

Salt and freshly ground pepper, to taste

Lump crabmeat for garnish (optional)

Avocado, peeled and sliced, for garnish (optional)

• Combine garlic, cucumber, red and jalapeño peppers, onion, tomatoes, tomato-vegetable juice and lime juice in a large bowl. Purée half this mixture in a processor. Add purée to remaining mixture and stir thoroughly. Season to taste with cumin, salt and pepper. Refrigerate.

• Before serving, garnish with crabmeat and avocado.

Serves 6

Chilled Blueberry Soup

2	**pints fresh Maine blueberries**
¾-1	**cup maple syrup**
2	**tablespoons lemon juice**
1	**tablespoon lime juice**
6-8	**sprigs lavender**
1	**cup buttermilk**
1	**cup half-and-half or light cream**

• Pick over and wash blueberries. In a large saucepan, simmer berries, syrup, lemon and lime juices for 30 minutes. Cool. Purée in a blender until smooth. Chill.

• In a medium bowl, soak lavender in buttermilk and half-and-half for 1 hour. Strain, removing lavender.

• Combine chilled soup base with cream mixture. Chill 4 hours.

• Serve in chilled bowls. Garnish with lavender ice cubes (lavender blossoms frozen in blueberry juice).

Serves 6 to 8

Lavender is available in gourmet section of most grocery stores.

Iced Strawberry Soup

2	**pints strawberries**
½	**cup cold water**
½	**cup orange juice**
½	**cup sugar, or to taste**
⅛	**teaspoon ground cardamom**
2	**cups plain yogurt**
	Strawberries for garnish, sliced
	Sprigs of mint for garnish (optional)

• Wash and hull strawberries. Reserve a few strawberries for garnish. Purée strawberries with water in blender or food processor. Pour mixture into a large bowl.

• Add orange juice, sugar and cardamom, stirring until sugar is dissolved. Blend in yogurt. Chill.

• Serve in chilled bowls garnished with additional sliced strawberries and a sprig of mint.

Serves 4 to 6

Two Melon Soup

1   **ripe cantaloupe, seeded and flesh diced**
2   **tablespoons fresh lemon juice**
1   **small honeydew, seeded and flesh diced**
2   **tablespoons fresh lime juice**
1½ **teaspoons minced fresh mint, or to taste**
Mint sprigs for garnish (optional)
Plain yogurt for garnish (optional)

• In a blender, purée cantaloupe with lemon juice until mixture is smooth. Refrigerate, covered, for at least 3 hours.

• In a clean blender, purée honeydew with lime juice and mint until mixture is smooth. Refrigerate, covered for at least 3 hours.

• At serving time, transfer purées to separate measuring cups or other containers with spouts. With one cup in each hand, simultaneously pour equal amounts of purées into individual serving bowls, keeping purées separate. Garnish with sprig of mint and a dollop of yogurt.

Serves 6

Purées may be prepared up to 2 days in advance. Stir well before pouring.

Serve for breakfast with a generous dollop of plain lowfat yogurt.

Black Bean Chili

1	**pound dried black beans**
4	**cups water**
1	**bay leaf**
2	**medium onions, peeled and chopped**
4	**large cloves garlic, peeled and chopped**
1	**red bell pepper, cored, seeded and finely chopped**
1	**tablespoon vegetable oil**
1	**can (28 ounce) tomatoes, coarsely chopped, including juice**
2	**tablespoons tomato paste**
1	**tablespoon ground cumin**
2	**teaspoons paprika**
½	**teaspoon cayenne**
4	**teaspoons chili powder**
1	**teaspoon dried oregano**
1	**tablespoon dark brown sugar**
1½	**teaspoons salt**

Freshly ground black pepper, to taste

2 **cups frozen corn kernels**

Monterey Jack cheese, grated, for garnish (optional)

- Soak beans in water to cover overnight.

- Drain beans and place in a large stockpot with 4 cups water. Add bay leaf and simmer for 25 to 30 minutes, until beans are tender but still slightly chewy.

- While beans are simmering, slowly cook onions, garlic and red pepper in oil for 12 to 15 minutes. Stir into bean pot.

- Add tomatoes, tomato paste, cumin, paprika, cayenne, chili powder, oregano, brown sugar, salt and pepper. Simmer for 1 hour.

- Add corn 20 minutes before serving and simmer to heat through.

- Serve hot, sprinkled with cheese.

Serves 6 to 8

94

Green Chili Stew

1½ pounds pork, cut in small pieces

1 pound mild green chili, chopped, or 4 cans (4 ounce)

2 cans (28 ounce) tomatoes, crushed or whole

2 cloves garlic, crushed

½ cup parsley, chopped

½ teaspoon sugar

¼ teaspoon ground clove

2 teaspoons ground cumin

1 cup red wine

Salt to taste

Flour to thicken

- Brown meat. Add chopped chili, tomatoes, garlic, parsley, sugar, clove, cumin, wine and salt. Simmer 2 hours. Add flour to thicken if needed.

- Serve with flour tortillas or over burritos.

Serves 4 to 6

Smoky Pork Chili

3	strips bacon, cut into ¼-inch pieces
1½	pounds pork tenderloin, cut into ¾-inch pieces
1	tablespoon cooking oil
2	onions, chopped
4	cloves garlic, minced
2	teaspoons paprika
2	teaspoons ground cumin
1	teaspoon ground coriander
¼	teaspoon cayenne pepper
1¼	teaspoons salt
2	cups canned tomatoes with their juice, chopped
1½	cups low-sodium chicken broth or chicken stock
1	tablespoon tomato paste
1	can (19 ounce) kidney beans, drained and rinsed
¾	cup Cheddar cheese, grated (about 3 ounces)

- In a large pot, cook bacon until crisp. Remove with slotted spoon. Drain on paper towel and set aside.

- Add half of pork to pot and cook over moderate heat until pork begins to brown, about 3 minutes. Remove.

- Repeat with remaining pork. Remove.

- Add cooking oil to pot. Reduce heat to low and stir in onions and garlic.

- Cover and cook, stirring occasionally until onions are soft, about 10 minutes.

- Stir in paprika, cumin, coriander, cayenne and salt. Cook, stirring, for 1 minute.

- Add tomatoes and their juice, chicken broth and tomato paste.

- Bring to a boil. Reduce heat and simmer, partially covered, for 15 minutes.

- Add beans and cook 5 minutes longer.

- Stir in pork tenderloin with any accumulated juices and bacon. Cook until meat is just done, about 5 minutes longer.

- Serve topped with grated Cheddar cheese.

Serves 4

Arugula, Oranges and Grilled White Onion Salad

Citrus Dressing

3 tablespoons fresh lime juice
2 tablespoons apple cider
1 tablespoon honey
1 tablespoon red wine vinegar
1 tablespoon water
1 tablespoon shallots, minced
½ teaspoon dry mustard
½ teaspoon salt
½ teaspoon pepper
½ teaspoon vegetable oil

Salad

1 tablespoon vegetable oil
12 small white onions, quartered
1 tablespoon water
6 ounces mixed baby lettuces
5 ounces arugula leaves
4 oranges, peeled and cut into segments
3 teaspoons caraway seeds, divided

- Make the dressing by combining in a small bowl the lime juice, apple cider, honey, vinegar, water, shallots, mustard, salt and pepper. Slowly whisk in ½ teaspoon oil. Set aside.

- For the salad, in a skillet, heat 1 tablespoon oil over medium heat. Add the onions and toss to coat.

- Carefully add water and continue to cook, stirring frequently, until the onions begin to turn brown on the edges. Set aside to cool slightly.

- In a large mixing bowl, toss lettuces and arugula with the dressing.

- Add the orange segments, the onions and a few of the caraway seeds and toss again to combine.

- Arrange on individual plates. Sprinkle with remaining caraway seeds before serving.

Serves 6

Asparagus and Yellow Bell Pepper Salad with Balsamic Vinaigrette

1½ **pounds asparagus, trimmed**

½ **cup olive oil**

4 **cloves garlic, flattened**

¼ **cup balsamic vinegar or 3 tablespoons red wine vinegar**

1 **tablespoon dark brown sugar**

Salt and freshly ground pepper, to taste

1 **head radicchio, thinly sliced**

1 **large yellow bell pepper, finely diced**

• Cook asparagus in large pot of boiling salted water until just tender but still firm to bite, about 3 minutes. Drain. Transfer asparagus to bowl of ice water and cool. Drain well.

• Heat olive oil in heavy small skillet over low heat. Add garlic cloves and sauté until light brown, about 10 minutes.

• Add balsamic vinegar and cook 2 minutes.

• Add sugar and stir until dissolved.

• Season to taste with salt and pepper.

• Discard garlic.

• Arrange radicchio on large platter. Top with asparagus. Sprinkle bell pepper over radicchio and asparagus.

• Spoon enough dressing to coat. Serve, passing remaining dressing separately.

Serves 6

Balsamic Roasted Pears with Pepper and Honey

2 **tablespoons unsalted butter**

2 **firm-ripe Bosc pears, halved lengthwise and cored**

3 **tablespoons balsamic vinegar**

4 **ounces mild fresh goat cheese, cut into 4 pieces, at room temperature**

¼ **cup honey**

Freshly ground pepper, to taste

- Preheat oven to 400 degrees.

- Melt butter in an 8-inch square glass baking dish in middle of oven, about 3 minutes.

- Arrange pears in the butter, cut sides down, in a single layer and roast in middle of oven until tender, about 20 minutes.

- Pour vinegar over pears and roast 5 minutes more.

- Transfer pears, cut sides down, to serving plates with cheese. Spoon juices from baking dish over pears.

- Drizzle pears and cheese with honey and sprinkle with pepper.

Serves 4

Caesar Salad

1-2	cloves garlic, crushed
2	teaspoons salt
½	teaspoon celery salt
2	teaspoons dry mustard
2	teaspoons Worcestershire sauce
½	teaspoon pepper
½	cup freshly squeezed lemon juice
½	cup extra-virgin olive oil
2	heads romaine lettuce

Croutons, to taste
Grated Parmesan cheese for garnish

- Whisk together garlic, salt, celery salt, dry mustard, Worcestershire sauce, ground pepper and lemon juice.

- Slowly add olive oil and whisk for 1 minute more.

- Tear romaine into bite-sized pieces and place in a bowl.

- Toss with dressing.

- Sprinkle with Parmesan cheese and croutons.

Serves 8

Chinese Salad

1	cup vegetable oil
½	cup plus 2 tablespoons sugar, divided
¼	cup red wine vinegar
2	tablespoons soy sauce
½	cup sesame seeds
2	packages (3 ounce) Ramen soup noodles
½	cup butter
1	head bok choy or Napa cabbage, chopped
3	green onions, sliced
4	ounces sliced almonds

- For dressing, mix oil, ½ cup sugar, red wine vinegar and soy sauce. Chill.

- Brown sesame seeds, noodles and 2 tablespoons sugar in butter. Cool.

- Mix with bok choy and onions.

- Just before serving, pour dressing over salad and garnish with almonds.

Serves 6 to 8

100

Crisp Fried Prosciutto and Blueberry Salad

2   tablespoons olive oil

6   slices prosciutto

4   ounces mixed salad greens

2   red or white (or one of each) chicory, separated

4   tablespoons pine nuts, toasted

Dressing

4   tablespoons extra-virgin olive oil

2   tablespoons balsamic vinegar

Salt and freshly ground pepper, to taste

4   ounces blueberries

Parmesan cheese, shaved, for garnish

• Heat 2 tablespoons oil in a frying pan. Add the prosciutto and fry over medium heat until crisp and golden. Drain on paper towel. Scrape the oil and bits from the pan and transfer to a small saucepan. Set aside.

• Crumble the cooled prosciutto into bite-sized pieces.

• Place salad greens in a large bowl. Add the chicory, prosciutto and pine nuts. Toss well.

• To make dressing, add the olive oil and vinegar to the saucepan containing the reserved oil and bits. Season with salt and pepper. Add the blueberries. Heat gently until the liquid just reaches the boiling point.

• Immediately pour the dressing over the salad. Toss again and transfer to serving plates. Scatter Parmesan cheese over salads and serve.

Serves 6 to 8

Mixed Greens with Pears and Raspberries

3   **tablespoons raspberry-flavored vinegar**
2   **tablespoons apple juice**
1   **tablespoon extra-virgin olive oil**
1   **tablespoon honey**
⅛   **teaspoon salt**
⅛   **teaspoon pepper**
2   **cups spinach, torn**
2   **cups Boston lettuce, torn**
2   **cups curly endive, torn**
2   **cups fresh pears, cubed (about 2 medium)**
1   **cup raspberries**

- Combine vinegar, apple juice, oil, honey, salt and pepper in a small bowl. Stir well with a wire whisk.

- Combine spinach, lettuce, endive, pears and raspberries in a large bowl. Toss gently.

- Divide salad among 6 individual plates and drizzle with dressing.

Serves 6

Mixed Greens with Pears, Fennel and Shaved Parmesan

2 **bunches watercress, tough stems removed**

3 **cups salad lettuce, coarsely torn**

1 **small head radicchio, leaves separated**

1½ **cups fresh fennel stalks, sliced**

3 **tablespoons pine nuts, toasted**

2 **ripe Bosc pears, peeled, cored and thinly sliced**

1 **cup Parmesan cheese, shaved**

⅔ **cup Garlicky Dressing (see Index)**

- Toss the watercress, lettuce, radicchio and fennel together in a large salad bowl.

- Scatter pine nuts, pears and Parmesan cheese over the greens.

- Toss the salad with enough dressing to coat.

- Serve immediately.

Serves 6

Use a vegetable peeler to shave the Parmesan cheese.

Pecan and Apple Salad

1	**head red leaf lettuce**
1	**head Bibb lettuce**
1	**cup watercress leaves**
2	**Red Delicious apples**
¾	**cup Crunchy Glazed Pecans, chopped (recipe follows)**
¾	**cup Feta or blue cheese, crumbled**

Dressing

½	**cup walnut or vegetable oil**
¼	**cup cider vinegar**
2	**tablespoons shallots, minced**
2	**tablespoons lemon juice, freshly squeezed**
1	**tablespoon maple syrup**
¼	**teaspoon salt**
¼	**teaspoon pepper**

- Tear red leaf and Bibb lettuce into bite-sized pieces and place in a large salad bowl. Add watercress leaves.

- Cut apples into very thin wedges and place on top of greens.

- Sprinkle pecans and cheese over salad.

- To make dressing, place oil, vinegar, shallots, lemon juice, maple syrup, salt and pepper in a small jar. Shake until well combined.

- Drizzle dressing over salad. Toss gently and serve immediately.

Serves 8 to 10

Crunchy Glazed Pecans

¼	**cup butter**
¼	**cup light corn syrup**
2	**tablespoons water**
1	**teaspoon salt**
6	**ounces pecan halves**

- Preheat oven to 250 degrees. Line a baking sheet with parchment.

- Combine butter, corn syrup, water and salt in a medium saucepan and bring to a boil. Add pecans and stir to coat.

- Spread nuts evenly on baking sheet. Bake 1 hour, stirring every 10 minutes. Cool.

Salad with Oranges and Caramelized Almonds

½   **head Romaine lettuce**

1   **cup celery, sliced into bite-sized pieces**

1   **tablespoon parsley, chopped**

2   **green onions, sliced**

1   **can (10 ounce) Mandarin oranges**

2   **tablespoons sugar**

¼   **cup slivered almonds**

Dressing

½   **teaspoon salt**

2   **tablespoons sugar**

Dash pepper

Dash Tabasco sauce

2   **tablespoons white vinegar**

¼   **cup vegetable oil**

- Tear lettuce into bite-sized pieces and top with celery, parsley, onions and oranges.

- Melt 2 tablespoons sugar in skillet until melted and caramelized. Add almonds. Set aside to cool.

- For dressing, mix together salt, sugar, pepper, Tabasco sauce, vinegar and oil.

- Toss salad with dressing. Top with caramelized almonds.

Serves 4

Classic Spinach Salad

1   bag (10 ounce) fresh spinach, washed and trimmed
1   package (4 ounce) fresh bean sprouts
1   can (8 ounce) sliced water chestnuts
2   hard-boiled eggs, chopped
8   slices bacon, cooked crispy
1   small red onion, sliced into rings

Dressing

1   cup oil
½   cup red wine vinegar
½   cup sugar
⅓   cup ketchup
Dash salt

• In a large salad bowl, mix spinach, sprouts, water chestnuts, eggs, bacon and red onion.

• In a covered jar, shake the oil, vinegar, sugar, ketchup and salt.

• When ready to serve, pour enough dressing over salad to moisten.

Serves 4 to 6

Strawberry Spinach Salad

⅓   cup white vinegar
¼   cup sugar
2   teaspoons Dijon mustard
¼-½ cup scallions, minced
Juice of ½ lemon
1   cup oil
1½ teaspoons poppy seeds
Salt, to taste
6-8 cups fresh spinach
1   pint strawberries
½   cup pecans, toasted in 1 tablespoon butter

• Whisk vinegar, sugar, mustard, scallions, lemon juice, oil, poppy seeds and salt.

• Wash spinach. Remove coarse stems. Break spinach into bite-sized pieces.

• Wash and hull strawberries.

• To assemble salad, toss spinach with dressing. Arrange strawberries and pecans on top of spinach. If you try to toss everything together, the berries and nuts will end up on the bottom of the bowl.

Serves 6 to 8

Spinach, Strawberry and Orange Salad

1 **bag (10 ounce) fresh spinach, washed and trimmed**
1 **pint strawberries, washed, hulled and sliced**
1 **can (10 ounce) Mandarin oranges, drained**
2 **stalks celery, sliced**
1 **can (20 ounce) pineapple chunks (optional)**

Dressing
½ **cup sugar**
2 **tablespoons sesame seeds**
2 **tablespoons poppy seeds**
1 **tablespoon Worcestershire sauce**
½ **cup oil**
¼ **cup cider vinegar**
1 **medium onion, diced**
Sunflower seeds for garnish

Goes well with fish or chicken.

- Tear spinach. Wash. Roll in towel and refrigerate.

- Toss together spinach, strawberries, oranges, celery and pineapple. Set aside.

- To make dressing, blend sugar, sesame seeds, poppy seeds, Worcestershire sauce, oil, vinegar and onion in a blender.

- Pour dressing over spinach. Sprinkle with sunflower seeds.

Serves 6 to 8

Black Bean Corn Salad

1 can (15 ounce) black beans, drained	• Combine beans, corn, tomatoes, scallions, bell pepper and jalapeño pepper.
1-2 cups frozen corn, thawed	
2 plum tomatoes	• In a bowl, whisk vinegar, cumin, mustard and oil. Pour over salad and add cilantro. Chill.
1 red bell pepper, diced	
½ cup scallions, diced	
1 bell pepper, chopped	*Serves 6*
1 jalapeño pepper, chopped	
2 tablespoons red wine vinegar	
2 teaspoons ground cumin	
1 teaspoon Dijon mustard	
3 tablespoons olive oil	
2-3 teaspoons fresh cilantro, chopped	

Broccoli Coleslaw

1 bag (16 ounce) broccoli coleslaw	• Mix together coleslaw, Ramen noodles, sunflower seeds and almonds. Set aside.
2 packages (3 ounce) Chicken Ramen noodle soup, broken up, seasoning packets reserved	• Mix oil, vinegar, sugar and reserved soup seasoning packets.
½ cup sunflower seeds	• Pour mixture over coleslaw. Chill at least 30 minutes before serving.
½ cup almonds, sliced	
½ cup oil	• Serve chilled.
½ cup white vinegar	
½ cup sugar	*Serves 6 to 8*

New Potato and Asparagus Salad

2 **pounds new potatoes, about 5 medium-sized**
1 **pound asparagus, trimmed**
1 **tablespoon Dijon mustard**
1 **tablespoon lemon juice**
¼ **cup olive oil**
2 **tablespoons chives, snipped**
½ **teaspoon salt**
½ **teaspoon black pepper**

- Add potatoes to a large pot of water and bring to a boil. Cook until potatoes are tender, about 20 minutes. Drain. Cool slightly and cut into wedges.

- Add asparagus to a large pot of boiling water and cook until tender-crisp. Drain and rinse in cold water. Cut asparagus into 1½-inch pieces.

- Toss potatoes and asparagus in a large bowl.

- Combine mustard and lemon juice in a small bowl. Gradually whisk in oil.

- Pour over salad. Add chives, salt and pepper and toss.

- Serve at room temperature.

Serves 4

Potato and Romaine Salad with Creamy Dijon Dressing

Dressing

3   **tablespoons Dijon mustard**
2   **tablespoons water**
1   **tablespoon white wine vinegar**
1   **teaspoon salt**
1   **teaspoon ground pepper**
1¼ **cups olive oil**
2   **tablespoons chilled whipping cream**
2   **tablespoons fresh basil, chopped, or 2 teaspoons dried basil**
1   **tablespoon fresh parsley, chopped**

Salad

2   **pounds red-skinned potatoes**
5   **tablespoons cider vinegar**
¼ **cup olive oil**
2   **tablespoons white wine vinegar**
1   **large head romaine lettuce, coarsely chopped**
2   **tablespoons capers, drained**

- For dressing, blend mustard, water, vinegar, salt and pepper in a food processor.

- With machine running, add oil in slow, steady stream.

- Add cream. Blend mixture until thick and creamy.

- Mix in basil and parsley.

- Dressing may be prepared 1 day in advance. Cover and refrigerate. Bring to room temperature before using. Thin dressing with water if it becomes too thick.

- For salad, cook potatoes in large pot of boiling water until tender, about 30 minutes. Drain and cool. Peel potatoes. Cut into ⅓-inch thick slices.

- Transfer potatoes to large bowl. Sprinkle with cider vinegar.

- Potatoes can be made to this point up to 4 hours in advance. Store at room temperature.

- Whisk oil and wine vinegar in another large bowl. Add lettuce and toss to coat.

- Add capers to potatoes.

- Pour enough dressing over potatoes to coat. Spoon potato mixture over lettuce and serve.

Serves 6

Soup & Salad

Red Potato Salad with Fresh Peas

2 **pounds small red potatoes, with skin, washed and cut into halves or quarters**
1 **medium Vidalia or sweet onion, chopped**
¼ **cup cider vinegar, divided**
½ **teaspoon salt**
2 **tablespoons mayonnaise**
1 **tablespoon Dijon mustard**
¼ **cup plain yogurt**
Freshly ground black pepper
4 **leaves fresh mint, chopped, or 1 tablespoon fresh dill, minced**
1 **pound fresh peas, shelled**

• Bring a large pot of salted water to a boil. Add potatoes and cook 15 minutes or until potatoes are tender when pierced with a sharp knife.

• Drain potatoes and place in a large bowl with onions, 2 tablespoons of the vinegar, and the salt.

• Gently stir potatoes to combine all ingredients.

• Cover bowl with plastic wrap and let sit at room temperature for 30 minutes to blend flavors.

• In a small bowl, whisk together remaining 2 tablespoons vinegar, mayonnaise, mustard, yogurt and pepper just until smooth.

• Pour dressing over marinated potatoes and stir to blend.

• Sprinkle mint or dill over salad and scatter peas over all.

• Store salad in a covered container and chill until ready to serve.

Serves 8

111

Winter Salad of Black-Eyed Peas, Kidney Beans and Barley

¾   **cup dried red kidney beans, picked over and rinsed well, or 1 (16 ounce) can of red kidney beans, drained and rinsed well**

½   **cup dried or 1 cup frozen black-eyed peas, thawed**

½   **cup pearl barley**

1   **teaspoon salt, divided**

½   **cup fresh or frozen corn kernels**

⅓   **cup fresh flat-leaf parsley, finely chopped**

2   **tablespoons fresh cilantro, finely chopped**

2   **tablespoons red onion, finely diced**

¼-½   **teaspoon crushed red pepper**

3   **tablespoons olive oil**

Zest and juice of 2 large limes

½   **teaspoon ground cumin**

- If using dried kidney beans and black-eyed peas, place in two separate large bowls, cover with water and let soak for at least 6 hours or overnight. (Quick soaking method: In 2 medium saucepans, cover the beans with water and boil over moderately high heat for 2 minutes. Remove from the heat, cover and let soak for 1 hour.) Drain off the soaking liquid and rinse the beans.

- In 2 medium saucepans, cover soaked and drained beans and peas with 2 to 3 inches of water. Cover the pans and simmer over moderate heat until tender but not mushy, 50 to 60 minutes for the kidney beans and 20 to 25 minutes for the black-eyed peas. Skim foam. Test often for doneness. Let cool slightly in their liquid, then drain well.

- In a serving bowl, combine cooked or canned kidney beans with cooked or thawed black-eyed peas.

- Meanwhile, in a saucepan, simmer the barley in 2 cups of water and ½ teaspoon salt until tender but chewy, about 40 minutes. Drain well and add to the beans.

- In the same saucepan, cook the corn in a small amount of water until crisp-tender, about 5 minutes for fresh corn and 2 minutes for frozen. Drain well and add to beans and barley. The recipe can be made to this point up to two days in advance. Cover and refrigerate.

(continued on next page)

Winter Salad of Black-Eyed Peas, Kidney Beans and Barley continued

- Stir in the parsley, fresh cilantro, onion and crushed red pepper.

- In a small bowl, whisk together the oil, remaining salt, lime zest, lime juice and cumin. Pour over salad, toss gently and serve.

Serves 6

Rice and Artichoke Salad

2   boxes (6 ounce) chicken flavored rice pilaf
2   jars (6 ounce) marinated artichoke hearts
¾   cup mayonnaise
1   tablespoon curry
1   green pepper, diced
20 green olives, chopped
1   onion or 12 scallions, diced

- Prepare rice according to directions on package.

- Strain artichoke hearts, saving marinade. Cut hearts into 2 to 3 pieces each.

- Mix mayonnaise, marinade from artichokes and curry.

- Stir artichokes, pepper, olives and onion into rice mixture.

- Add mayonnaise mixture and combine well.

- Refrigerate overnight and serve cold.

Serves 6

113

Orzo Rice Salad

1   **cup wild rice, uncooked**
1   **cup orzo pasta, uncooked**
1   **tablespoon parsley, chopped**
¾   **cup green onion, chopped**
¾   **cup pecans, chopped**
1   **cup celery, sliced**
¼   **cup white wine (fruity)**
¾   **cup dried cranberries**

Dressing

2   **tablespoons orange juice concentrate**
2   **tablespoons rice wine vinegar**
1   **teaspoon fresh ginger, grated**
¼   **cup olive oil**
Salt and white pepper, to taste
Red leaf or chard lettuce

• Cook wild rice and orzo according to package directions. Cool.

• Combine parsley, green onions, pecans and celery.

• Add wine to cranberries in a saucepan and simmer for 5 minutes. Toss into salad.

• For dressing, in blender, place orange juice, rice vinegar and ginger. Turn blender on low speed and slowly add oil. Toss into salad. Salt and pepper to taste.

• Serve on bed of red leaf or chard lettuce.

Serves 8

Sweet and Sour Orzo Salad

1½ cups uncooked orzo
1   cup cucumber, peeled, seeded and chopped
½   cup green onions, chopped
1   cup carrots, chopped and parboiled 1 to 2 minutes, then cooled
½   cup white vinegar
2   tablespoons oil
3   tablespoons sugar
1   teaspoon salt
1   tablespoon fresh dill or 1 teaspoon dried dill
⅛   teaspoon ground red pepper
Toasted sesame seeds for garnish

- Cook orzo according to package directions. Rinse in cool water and drain.

- In a large bowl, combine orzo, cucumber, green onions and carrots. Set aside.

- Combine vinegar, oil, sugar, salt, dill and red pepper.

- Stir dressing into pasta and vegetables.

- Cover and refrigerate at least 1 hour.

- Sprinkle with toasted sesame seeds before serving.

Serves 10

Wild Rice Salad

2   cups cooked wild rice, cooled
1   cup pecans, coarsely chopped
1   cup golden raisins
4   scallions, sliced
Grated rind of 1 orange
¼   cup olive oil
⅓   cup orange juice
1¼   teaspoons salt, or to taste
Freshly ground black pepper

- Gently combine rice, pecans, raisins, scallions, orange rind, olive oil, orange juice, salt and pepper.

- Let stand at least 2 hours, or overnight in the refrigerator.

- Serve at room temperature.

Serves 6 to 8

Tortellini Salad

9   ounces frozen cheese-
    stuffed tortellini
½   cup olive oil
¼   cup wine vinegar
¼   cup scallions, sliced
½   teaspoon salt
3   cloves garlic, minced
2   tablespoons fresh basil,
    chopped
1   tablespoon fresh dill weed,
    chopped
¼   cup flat-leaf parsley,
    chopped
1   can (13.75 ounce) artichoke
    hearts, drained and
    quartered
1   large tomato, peeled and
    sliced
½   cup feta cheese, crumbled
½   cup black olives, sliced

• Cook frozen tortellini according to package directions. Drain and set aside.

• Make dressing by mixing olive oil, vinegar, scallions, salt, garlic, basil, dill and parsley.

• In a large bowl, combine cooked tortellini, artichoke hearts, tomato, feta cheese and olives.

• Pour dressing over tortellini and toss gently.

• Refrigerate several hours before serving.

Serves 10

Couscous and Chicken Salad
with Orange Balsamic Dressing

4½ **cups water**

3 **cups couscous
(two 10 ounce boxes)**

1 **cup dried currants**

1 **(3 pound) roasted chicken,
skinned, boned and cut
into bite-size pieces**

1½ **cups roasted red bell
peppers (from a jar),
drained and diced**

1 **can (15.5 ounce) chick-peas
(garbanzo beans), rinsed
and drained**

1 **cup Kalamata olives, pitted
and chopped**

1 **bunch green onions,
chopped**

½ **cup fresh cilantro, chopped**

Dressing

¾ **cup orange juice**

3 **tablespoons balsamic
vinegar or red wine
vinegar**

3 **tablespoons orange peel,
grated**

1 **tablespoon ground cumin**

½ **cup olive oil**

**Salt and freshly ground
pepper, to taste**

Romaine lettuce leaves

- To prepare salad, bring the water to a boil in a large saucepan. Add couscous and currants. Cover, remove from heat and let stand 5 minutes. Fluff with a fork. Transfer to large bowl and cool.

- Mix chicken, bell peppers, chick-peas, olives, onions, and cilantro into cooled couscous.

- For dressing, mix orange juice, vinegar, orange peel and cumin in a bowl.

- Gradually mix in oil.

- Pour dressing over salad and toss. Season with salt and pepper.

- Line a large bowl with romaine leaves. Top with couscous salad.

Serves 8

Dressing may be prepared the day before and refrigerated.

117

Curried Chicken Pasta Salad

8   **ounces large pasta shells, cooked and drained (3 cups)**

8   **ounces boneless skinless chicken breasts (about 2), cooked and cubed**

¾   **cup apple curry chutney (about an 8 ounce jar)**

¾   **cup celery, chopped**

¼   **cup sour cream or plain yogurt**

¼   **cup mayonnaise**

2   **tablespoons chives, chopped**

2   **tablespoons raisins**

½   **teaspoon salt**

¼   **teaspoon ground black pepper**

⅛   **teaspoon cayenne pepper**

2   **tablespoons slivered almonds, toasted**

• In a large bowl, combine pasta, chicken, chutney, celery, sour cream, mayonnaise, chives, raisins, salt, black pepper and cayenne pepper.

• Refrigerate 1 hour.

• Sprinkle with almonds before serving.

Serves 4 to 6

You may substitute the chutney of your choice for the apple curry chutney by adding to your chutney diced apples and curry.

Curried Seafood Salad

2 tablespoons peach chutney
1 cup mayonnaise
2 tablespoons tarragon vinegar
2 tablespoons vegetable oil
2 teaspoons curry powder
3-4 tablespoons half-and-half
1 head lettuce
4 stalks celery, chopped
4 green onions, chopped
½ pound cooked medium shrimp
½ pound cooked crabmeat
Selection of condiments, such as toasted coconut, toasted slivered almonds, chopped green onions, raisins, and peach chutney

- For the dressing, in a blender or food processor fitted with a metal blade, mix the chutney, mayonnaise, tarragon vinegar, oil, curry powder and half-and-half. Adjust seasoning. The curry flavor should just bite. Dressing may be made up to 2 days in advance and refrigerated.

- Tear lettuce into bite-sized pieces and place in a salad bowl.

- Add celery and green onions.

- Stir in shrimp and crabmeat, reserving some pieces as garnish.

- Toss with dressing.

- Garnish with reserved pieces of seafood.

- Serve condiments in separate bowls.

Serves 6 to 8

To toast nuts, place on a baking sheet in a 350 degree oven for 10 to 15 minutes, stirring occasionally.

Peach Chutney is sometimes called Yankee Chutney and contains peaches, raisins, red pepper, apples, lemon and spices.

119

Grilled Steak Salad

1-1½	**pounds boneless sirloin steak**
¼	**cup vegetable oil**
2	**tablespoons soy sauce**
2	**tablespoons dry sherry**
2	**cloves garlic, minced**
1	**tablespoon fresh ginger, grated**
2-3	**tomatoes, cut into wedges**
¼	**cup green onions, cut into ½-inch pieces**
½	**pound mushrooms, sliced**
	Oriental dressing
	Lettuce leaves, chopped
1	**cup onion and garlic croutons**

Oriental Dressing

¼	**cup soy sauce**
2	**tablespoons lime juice**
2	**cloves garlic, minced**
1	**teaspoon fresh ginger, minced**
1	**teaspoon orange rind, grated**
1	**teaspoon Dijon mustard**
½	**teaspoon Tabasco sauce**
½	**teaspoon sugar**

- Place steak in plastic bag with oil, soy sauce, sherry, garlic and ginger. Marinate at least 30 minutes.

- Grill 5 minutes per side. Cool and cut into thin slices.

- Combine steak, tomatoes, green onions and mushrooms. Set aside

- For dressing, mix soy sauce, lime juice, garlic, ginger, orange rind, mustard, Tabasco sauce and sugar.

- Toss steak salad with dressing. Serve over chopped lettuce and garnish with croutons.

Serves 8

Lime, Avocado and Shrimp Salad

Dressing

⅓ cup fresh lime juice

1 tablespoon Dijon mustard

Salt and freshly ground pepper, to taste

½ cup olive oil

½ cup vegetable oil

1 tablespoon shallots, minced

Zest of 1 lime, grated

3 tablespoons fresh chives, chopped

Salad

2 ripe avocados, pitted, peeled and sliced in large pieces

2 tablespoons fresh lime juice

1 pound large cooked shrimp, peeled and deveined

1 red bell pepper, stemmed, seeded and diced into ⅛-inch pieces

1 cup plum tomatoes, seeded and diced into ⅛-inch pieces

4 scallions with 3 inches green left on, thinly sliced on diagonal

3 tablespoons fresh mint leaves, coarsely chopped

- Prepare the dressing by whisking together the lime juice, mustard, salt and pepper in a small bowl.

- Slowly drizzle in the olive and vegetable oils, whisking continuously until thickened.

- Stir in shallots and lime zest.

- About 15 minutes before serving, add the chives.

- For the salad, place avocado slices in a large bowl and toss with 2 tablespoons lime juice.

- Add cooked shrimp, bell pepper, tomatoes and scallions. Fold together.

- Toss gently with ½ cup of the dressing.

- Just before serving, toss with fresh mint leaves. Serve with extra dressing on the side.

Serves 6

Oriental Turkey Salad

6	**cups cooked turkey (breast meat preferred), cubed**
2	**cups seedless white grapes, halved**
1	**can (8 ounce) water chestnuts, thinly sliced**
1	**cup celery, chopped**
½	**cup green onion, chopped**

Dressing

2	**cups mayonnaise**
2	**tablespoons soy sauce**
2	**tablespoons lemon juice**
1-1½	**tablespoons curry powder**
3	**tablespoons mango chutney, minced (optional)**
6-8	**ounces dry-roasted cashews**
1	**pound fresh bean sprouts**
8-10	**small bunches white grapes for garnish**

- In a large bowl, gently toss the turkey, grapes, water chestnuts, celery and onion. Refrigerate until 1 hour before serving.

- Mix mayonnaise, soy sauce, lemon juice, curry powder and chutney until well blended.

- Fold in cashews.

- To serve, combine dressing with turkey mixture. Arrange bean sprouts on individual plates or a large platter. Mound turkey salad in center. Garnish with grapes.

Serves 8 to 10

Spicy Shrimp Salad

1½ **pounds medium shrimp, shelled and deveined**
1 **tablespoon fresh lemon juice**
1½ **tablespoons balsamic vinegar**
¼ **teaspoon Tabasco sauce**
¼ **teaspoon salt (optional)**
⅓ **cup olive oil**
½ **medium red onion, chopped**
1 **green pepper, cut in strips**
1 **avocado, diced**
1 **cup cherry tomatoes, cut in half**
¼ **pound snow peas**
Romaine lettuce

- Cook shrimp in pot of boiling salted water until pink and loosely curled, 1 to 2 minutes. Cool.

- In a small bowl, whisk together lemon juice, vinegar, Tabasco sauce and salt. Gradually whisk in olive oil. In refrigerator, marinate shrimp in mixture for several hours or overnight.

- When ready to serve, gently toss together the shrimp, onion, green pepper, avocado, tomatoes and snow peas.

- Line a large platter or 4 individual plates with lettuce. Mound salad in center.

Serves 4

Bleu Cheese Dressing

2	**cups mayonnaise**
1	**cup sour cream**
½-¾	**pound bleu cheese, crumbled**
½-1	**teaspoon garlic, minced**
1-1½	**teaspoons fresh lemon juice**

Salt and freshly ground pepper, to taste

• Thoroughly mix mayonnaise, sour cream, bleu cheese, garlic, lemon juice and salt and pepper.

• Refrigerate at least 24 hours before serving.

Yield: 4 cups

Chatterbox French Dressing

6	**tablespoons sugar**
1	**teaspoon salt (optional)**
1	**teaspoon celery salt**
1	**teaspoon dry mustard**
1	**tablespoon ketchup**
1	**tablespoon onion juice or 1 teaspoon onion powder**
3	**tablespoons vinegar**
1	**cup olive oil**

Juice of ½ lemon

• Combine sugar, salt, celery salt, mustard, ketchup, onion juice, vinegar, oil and lemon juice in a bowl and beat with an eggbeater until well blended.

• Pour into a jar, cover and refrigerate.

Yield: 1½ cups

Garlicky Salad Dressing

2   cloves garlic, finely
    chopped
½   cup fresh lemon juice
1   cup extra-virgin olive oil
½   teaspoon anchovy paste or
    1 anchovy fillet, chopped
½   teaspoon salt
¼   teaspoon black pepper

• Place the garlic, lemon juice, olive oil, anchovy paste, salt and pepper in a food processor or blender and process until smooth.

Yield: 1½ cups

Dressing keeps for 2 to 3 days. Great all-around dressing for greens, marinating vegetables and drizzling on grilled fish or chicken.

Honey Salad Dressing for Fruit

⅔   cup sugar
1   teaspoon dry mustard
1   teaspoon paprika
¼   teaspoon salt
1   teaspoon celery salt
⅓   cup honey
5   tablespoons vinegar
1   tablespoon lemon juice
1   teaspoon onion, grated
1   cup salad oil

• Mix together sugar, mustard, paprika, salt and celery salt.

• Add honey, vinegar, lemon juice and grated onion.

• Place in a blender and add oil slowly while mixing.

Yield: 2 cups

125

Creamy Parmesan, Basil and Pine-Nut Dressing

2 tablespoons grated
  Parmesan cheese
2 tablespoons basil leaves
1 tablespoon toasted pine
  nuts
½ teaspoon minced garlic
⅓ cup olive oil
2½ tablespoons balsamic
  vinegar

- In a food processor or blender, puree the Parmesan cheese, basil, pine nuts and garlic.

- Slowly add the oil, processing continuously.

- Add the vinegar and pulse to combine.

Yield about 1/2 cup

This creamy dressing is especially good with spicy greens such as arugula and radicchio.

No-Fat Ginger Soy Dressing

¼ cup fresh lime juice
2 tablespoons soy sauce
2 tablespoons Asian fish
  sauce
1 tablespoon minced mint
1 tablespoon minced cilantro
2 teaspoons minced fresh
  ginger
1½ teaspoons sugar
¼ teaspoon crushed red
  pepper
Salt and freshly ground black
  pepper to taste

- In a glass or stainless-steel bowl, combine the lime juice, soy sauce, fish sauce, mint, cilantro, ginger, sugar and red pepper. Season with salt and black pepper and whisk to blend.

Yield about 2/3 cup

This is best served with spicy greens or Asian cabbage or greens.

Poultry & Meat

The Old Manse

The Old Manse

With the approach road to Barrett's Farm at the front and to the side and the North Bridge and Concord River in the backyard of The Old Manse, the Reverend William Emerson and his family had front row seats during the morning hours of April 19, 1775. The minister had brought his family to The Manse in 1770, and the long history between the property and the Emerson-Ripley family began then, with family ownership lasting one hundred and sixty nine years. The house lays claim to fame beyond its revolutionary geography; among others, it sheltered two particularly revered men of letters who defined American thought and beliefs, not with guns but with words. With the family tree firmly rooted all the way back to Concord's Puritan founder Reverend Peter Bulkeley, the Reverend William Emerson was Ralph Waldo Emerson's grandfather. Ralph Waldo Emerson visited and lived at The Old Manse at various points in his life; he drafted his first published essay, *Nature,* at The Old Manse in 1835. His essay was the beginning definition of Transcendental thinking and offered a uniquely American voice and belief in the "common man" to see, think and comprehend all that surrounds him; Emerson's essay was a revolution of thinking and words. Nathaniel Hawthorne rented The Manse in 1842 when he came out of his self-imposed Salem exile to marry Sophia Peabody. The newlyweds moved into The Old Manse for an extended three year honeymoon; there Hawthorne was freed of his gloomy loneliness and discovered a soul-mate in his wife. Their etched messages to one another are still on The Old Manse back windows looking across the meadow to the North Bridge. From the windows of The Old Manse, the defining beginnings of the "American Experiment" were glimpsed, and inside its walls, some of the words that helped explain and define America to itself were set to paper. In The Old Manse in August 1776, the fiery, revolutionary Reverend William Emerson prepared his last message to his congregation. With the first anniversary of the battle passed, he wrote, "...Britain's tyrannic power, however hard to bear, has taught us lessons we should ne'er have learned without her, has taught us our own strength and how to live without her. She'll sway her iron sceptre over this world no more; a glory this, too bright for all but those who hold the golden sceptre of peace and righteousness..."

Poultry

Chicken

Cornish Hen

Turkey

Meat

Beef

Veal

Lamb

Pork

Roast Chicken with Maple Pepper Glaze and Sweet Potatoes

2 pounds sweet potatoes, peeled and cut into 1½-inch pieces

2 tablespoons cooking oil, divided

1 teaspoon salt, divided

1¼ teaspoons ground black pepper, divided

1 chicken (3 to 3½ pounds)

1 tablespoon butter, cut into small pieces

6 tablespoons pure maple syrup

1½ tablespoons bourbon

- Preheat oven to 425 degrees.

- In a large roasting pan, toss sweet potatoes with 1 tablespoon of the oil, ½ teaspoon of the salt and ¼ teaspoon of the pepper. Push potatoes to edge of the pan, leaving space in the center for chicken.

- Rub the cavity of the chicken with ¼ teaspoon salt and ⅛ teaspoon pepper. Twist the wings behind the back and tie the legs together. Place the chicken, breast side up, in the center of the roasting pan. Coat the chicken with the remaining ¼ teaspoon salt and ⅛ teaspoon pepper. Dot with butter. Roast chicken for 30 minutes.

- Meanwhile, in a small bowl, combine the maple syrup, bourbon and remaining ¾ teaspoon pepper. Remove the roasting pan from the oven and stir the potatoes. Brush the chicken with 2 tablespoons of the glaze and drizzle ½ tablespoon of glaze over potatoes. Return the pan to the oven and cook for about 30 minutes, stirring the potatoes and brushing the chicken with remaining glaze 2 more times. Transfer chicken and potatoes to a plate and let rest in a warm spot for about 10 minutes.

- Meanwhile, pour off the fat from the roasting pan. Add any accumulated juices from the chicken to the liquid in the pan. Serve the chicken with the pan juices and sweet potatoes.

Serves 4

Rustic Garlic Chicken

2   **tablespoons cooking oil**

1   **chicken (about 3 to 3½ pounds), cut into 8 pieces**

1   **teaspoon salt, divided**

¼   **teaspoon ground black pepper**

3   **heads garlic, cloves separated**

2   **tablespoons flour**

1   **cup dry white wine**

1   **cup low-sodium chicken broth or stock**

2   **tablespoons butter**

2   **tablespoons fresh parsley, chopped**

- Preheat oven to 400 degrees.

- In a Dutch oven, heat the oil over moderately high heat. Sprinkle the chicken with ½ teaspoon of the salt and the pepper. Cook the chicken until well browned, turning, about 8 minutes in all, and remove from the pot.

- Reduce the heat to moderate. Add the garlic and sauté until it starts to brown, about 3 minutes. Sprinkle the flour over the garlic and stir until combined. Return the chicken to the pot, cover and bake for 15 minutes.

- Remove the pot from the oven and place it on a burner. Remove the chicken pieces from the pot and place on a warm serving platter.

- Over moderately high heat, whisk in the wine and simmer for 1 minute. Whisk in the broth and the remaining ½ teaspoon salt and simmer until starting to thicken, about 3 minutes. Turn the heat off, whisk in the butter and pour the sauce over the chicken. Sprinkle with the parsley.

Serves 4

Serve cooked garlic cloves unpeeled. Each guest squeezes the garlic out of the skin onto the plate to eat with the chicken.

Chicken Breasts with Gruyère and Mushrooms

3   **chicken breasts, boned and skinned**

2   **eggs, well beaten**

½   **teaspoon salt**

1   **cup fine bread crumbs**

1   **tablespoon dried herb mixture of your choice**

8   **tablespoons butter**

½   **pound fresh mushrooms, sliced**

4   **ounces Gruyère cheese, shredded**

1   **cup chicken broth**

Juice of 1 lemon

- Preheat oven to 350 degrees.

- Cut chicken breasts into strips. Combine egg and salt. Marinate chicken in egg for 1 hour in refrigerator.

- Mix bread crumbs with the dried herbs. Roll chicken in bread crumbs and herbs to coat. Melt butter in a large skillet and brown the chicken lightly.

- Transfer to a 1½-quart casserole and top with sliced mushrooms. Sprinkle with cheese and pour broth over all. Bake for 30 minutes, or until heated through. Squeeze fresh lemon juice over casserole just before serving.

Serves 6

Chicken Artichoke Piccata

1	pound chicken breasts, skinned and boned
¼	cup flour
2	tablespoons butter
2	tablespoons olive oil
½	cup white wine
½	cup chicken stock
Juice of 1 lemon	
6	tablespoons parsley, chopped
2	tablespoons capers
1	can (14 ounce) artichoke hearts, quartered

- Cut chicken up into 2-inch pieces. Place between wax paper and pound thin. Dredge in flour.

- Sauté chicken in butter and olive oil until browned, about 1 minute each side. Place on a warm platter.

- Add wine and chicken stock to skillet. Reduce. Scrape up pan drippings. Add lemon juice. Cook until hot and bubbling.

- Add parsley, capers and artichoke hearts. Pour over chicken.

Serves 4

133

Chicken Angelo with Ziti

2 whole chickens
1 pound sweet Italian
   sausages
½ cup olive or vegetable oil
Salt and freshly ground
   pepper, to taste
1 cup butter, divided
4 cloves garlic, chopped,
   divided
2 large onions, sliced
2 shallots, crushed
12 medium-sized ripe
   tomatoes, 6 cut in chunks,
   6 cut in large slices
Pinch of dried oregano
½ cup plus 2 tablespoons of
   fresh parsley, chopped,
   plus additional parsley for
   garnish
2 cups homemade or canned
   chicken stock
Flour
2 cups dry white wine,
   divided
1 pound whole button
   mushrooms
1 can (8 ounce) artichoke
   hearts in water, reserve
   water and quarter hearts
1 pound large shells or ziti
1 bunch broccoli, cut into
   florets, stems discarded

• Preheat oven to 350 degrees.

• Cut chicken into small pieces. Cut sausages into bite-sized pieces.

• Heat the oil in a large skillet and fry the chicken and sausages until browned. Sprinkle generously with salt and pepper. Place chicken and sausage in a large baking pan.

• In the same skillet, melt ½ cup butter. Add 2 garlic cloves, the sliced onions and shallots. Sauté gently. Add the chopped tomatoes, salt and pepper to taste, oregano, and ½ cup chopped parsley. Toss lightly then pour over the meat in baking pan.

• In a large jar, shake the chicken stock with enough flour to make a thin paste. Pour into a small saucepan and cook over medium heat until slightly thickened. Add salt and pepper to taste.

• Reserve ½ cup of the thickened stock. Pour the remainder over the chicken and sausages, tossing lightly to coat. Bake for 25 minutes. Sprinkle with 1 cup of the wine and bake 15 minutes longer.

• In a large skillet, melt remaining butter. Add mushrooms, the sliced tomatoes, artichoke hearts, 2 tablespoons of parsley, and salt and pepper to taste. Sauté for 3 minutes and add reserved ½ cup of stock. Simmer gently for 10 minutes. Add more wine to keep sauce at desired consistency.

(continued on next page)

Chicken Angelo with Ziti continued

- Meanwhile, boil the pasta according to package directions. Drain, then toss with a little butter to keep from sticking.

- At the same time, sauté the broccoli with the remaining 2 garlic cloves in the juice from the artichokes and enough oil to cover the bottom of the pan. Combine the broccoli and pasta. Season to taste with salt and pepper.

- Place the broccoli and pasta on a large platter. Spoon the baked chicken and sausages on top. Cover with sauce. Sprinkle with chopped parsley and serve.

Serves 12

Chicken Breasts with Orange and Mustard

⅔ **cup sliced natural almonds**
3 **tablespoons butter, divided**
3 **whole chicken breasts, skinned, boned, and split**
½ **teaspoon salt, plus salt to taste**
¼ **teaspoon ground white pepper plus white pepper to taste**
1½ **cups heavy cream**
4 **teaspoons coarsely grained mustard**
2 **tablespoons orange marmalade**
⅛ **teaspoon cayenne pepper**

- Sauté almonds in 1 tablespoon butter until crisp. Set aside.

- Season chicken with salt and white pepper to taste. In 2 remaining tablespoons of butter, sauté chicken over medium-high heat for 30 seconds on each side.

- Add cream, mustard, marmalade, ½ teaspoon salt, ¼ teaspoon white pepper, and cayenne. Reduce over medium heat until chicken is tender and sauce thickens and coats the back of a spoon, about 10 minutes. Stir in almonds.

Serves 6

135

Chicken Breasts with Asparagus and Artichokes

6   whole boneless chicken breasts
6   large or 12 small fresh asparagus spears
6   slices (1½-ounces each) mozzarella cheese, cut in half and divided
6   large fresh mushrooms, sliced
1   can (14 ounce) artichoke hearts, drained and chopped
1   tablespoon pimiento, diced
½   teaspoon salt
¼   teaspoon pepper
1   cup flour
2   eggs, beaten
1   cup fine, dry bread crumbs
3   tablespoons butter
3   tablespoons vegetable oil

• Place chicken breasts between 2 sheets of wax paper. Flatten to ¼-inch thickness, using a meat mallet or rolling pin. Set aside.

• Snap off tough ends of asparagus. Remove scales from stalks with a knife or vegetable peeler.

• Arrange 1 large or 2 small asparagus spears, 1 cheese slice and 1 sliced mushroom on half of each chicken breast. Top with chopped artichoke heart and pimiento. Sprinkle with salt and pepper. Fold remaining half of each chicken breast over vegetable mixture. Secure with wooden picks. Dredge chicken in flour, dip in beaten egg and coat with bread crumbs.

• In a large skillet over medium heat, combine butter and oil until butter melts. Add chicken and cook 7 to 10 minutes on each side, or until browned. Remove chicken from skillet and drain on paper towels.

• Place chicken on a baking sheet. Top each with 1 remaining cheese slice. Bake for 15 minutes or until cheese melts and chicken is done.

Serves 6

Chicken Breasts with Garlic and Herb Sauce

1	**tablespoon cooking oil**
1	**red bell pepper, chopped**
2	**scallions including green tops, chopped**
1	**carrot, grated**
8	**ounces cream cheese, at room temperature**
1	**teaspoon salt, divided**
½	**teaspoon ground black pepper, divided**
4	**boneless chicken breasts, skin removed**

- Preheat oven to 425 degrees.

- In a medium frying pan, heat oil over moderate heat. Add pepper and cook, stirring occasionally, until starting to soften, about 3 minutes. Add the scallions and carrot and cook 2 minutes longer. Mix the vegetables with the cream cheese, ¾ teaspoon salt and ¼ teaspoon pepper.

- Sprinkle the chicken breasts with the remaining ¼ teaspoon salt and ¼ teaspoon pepper. Place the chicken breasts in a roasting pan and spread them with the cream cheese mixture. Bake the chicken about 20 to 25 minutes.

Serves 4

Substitute a 5½ ounce package of garlic and herb flavored cheese spread for the cream cheese.

Chicken Breasts with Pecan Crust

2   whole chicken breasts,
     boned, skinned and split
Coarse salt
Freshly ground pepper
10   tablespoons butter
3   tablespoons Dijon
     mustard, divided
8   ounces pecans, coarsely
     ground
⅔   cup sour cream

• Preheat oven to 400 degrees.

• Between wax paper, lightly flatten chicken breasts. Season with salt and pepper.

• Melt butter in saucepan, remove from heat and whisk in 2 tablespoons mustard. Dip chicken in butter mixture and roll in pecans.

• Place chicken in 9x12-inch greased baking dish. Bake 12 to 20 minutes, depending on size of chicken breasts.

• Combine sour cream with remaining tablespoon of mustard and bring to boiling point. Do not boil. Spoon sauce on four plates. Place a chicken breast on each plate and serve immediately.

Serves 4

Chicken Dijon in Phyllo

1½ cups mayonnaise
1   cup scallions, chopped
⅓   cup lemon juice
3   cloves garlic, minced
2   teaspoons fresh dill
1   tablespoon Dijon mustard
6   whole boneless, skinless
    chicken breasts, split
Salt and freshly ground
    pepper, to taste
24 sheets phyllo dough
1⅓ cups butter, melted
⅔   cup Parmesan cheese,
    freshly grated

- Preheat the oven to 375 degrees.

- Combine mayonnaise, scallions, lemon juice, garlic, dill and mustard to make a sauce. Lightly sprinkle chicken pieces with salt and pepper.

- To prevent the phyllo dough from drying out, keep it covered with plastic wrap and a damp cloth, removing only one sheet of dough at a time. Place a sheet of phyllo on working surface. Brush with melted butter. Place second sheet of dough on top of first and brush with butter. Spread about 1½ tablespoons of sauce on each side of a chicken breast. Place breast in one corner of buttered phyllo sheets. Fold corner over breast, then fold sides over and roll breast up in the sheet to form a package. Place in an ungreased baking dish. Repeat with remaining breasts and phyllo sheets. Brush packets with the rest of the butter and sprinkle with Parmesan cheese. (At this point, the dish may be tightly sealed and frozen. Thaw completely before baking.)

- Bake for 20 to 25 minutes or until golden. Serve hot.

Serves 12

For a quick alternative, instead of preparing the mayonnaise dill sauce, spread each chicken breast with 2 tablespoons of herbed cheese spread and 1 teaspoon finely chopped scallions before rolling in phyllo dough.

Chicken and Spinach in Phyllo

4   whole large chicken breasts, boned, skinned and split

Salt and freshly ground pepper, to taste, plus ½ tablespoon salt

8   tablespoons melted butter plus 4 tablespoons cold butter

2   cups spinach leaves, chopped

1   cup Swiss cheese, shredded

½   cup ricotta cheese

½   medium onion, chopped

2   hard-boiled eggs, chopped

1   clove garlic, crushed

2   heaping tablespoons green peppercorns, crushed

½   pound phyllo dough

Pink Madeira sauce (recipe follows)

- Preheat oven to 400 degrees. Pound chicken breasts to flatten. Sprinkle with salt and pepper.

- To make green peppercorn and spinach stuffing: In a very large bowl, mix until well blended the spinach, Swiss cheese, ricotta cheese, onion, eggs, garlic, green peppercorns and ½ tablespoon salt.

- Spread ⅓ cup stuffing on each chicken breast. Beginning at one end, roll up once and fold in sides.

- Place 1 sheet of phyllo on a damp towel. Keep remaining phyllo covered to prevent drying. Brush phyllo with butter. Fold in half along short side. Turn phyllo so that narrow end faces you. Place one rolled chicken breast 2 inches from end of phyllo. Top chicken with ½ tablespoon cold butter. Roll phyllo over chicken once and then fold in sides. Continue rolling to end of phyllo. Place on rimmed baking sheet, seam side down. Brush top with melted butter. Repeat with remaining chicken and phyllo.

- Place on baking sheets at least 1 inch apart. Bake for 25 to 30 minutes until golden. Serve on a platter, drizzled with Madeira sauce. Pass remaining sauce.

Serves 6 to 8

Phyllo rolls may be refrigerated overnight, covered with foil. They may also be frozen for up to 2 weeks. Freeze in single layer until solid, then wrap securely. Defrost on baking sheets and bring chicken to room temperature before baking.

(continued on next page)

Chicken and Spinach in Phyllo continued

Pink Madeira Sauce

2   **tablespoons butter**
2   **tablespoons flour**
2   **tablespoons Madeira wine**
1   **cup chicken broth**
2   **tablespoons tomato paste**
⅓   **cup sour cream**
⅓   **cup chives or green onion tops, chopped**
Salt and ground white pepper, to taste

- In medium saucepan, melt butter. Add flour and cook to golden. Remove from heat. Whisk in Madeira and chicken broth. Return to heat and cook, stirring until mixture boils and thickens.

- In a small bowl, mix tomato paste and sour cream. Add a little of the hot sauce to the bowl, mix thoroughly and return all of mixture to saucepan. Stir in chives, salt and pepper.

Sauce may be held at room temperature for several hours or refrigerated overnight. Place a piece of waxed paper directly on top to keep skin from forming. Reheat slowly. Do not boil. If desired, thin with Madeira or cream.

Chicken Florentine in Pastry with Herbed Cream Sauce

4   **whole chicken breasts, split, skinned and boned**

1½ **teaspoons salt, divided**

1¼ **teaspoons pepper, divided**

2   **packages (10 ounce) frozen spinach, thawed and drained**

6   **ounces Gruyère or Swiss cheese, shredded**

1   **dash ground nutmeg**

1   **cup prosciutto or cooked ham, finely chopped**

4   **frozen puff pastry sheets, thawed, (from two 17.5 ounce packages)**

2   **large eggs**

2   **teaspoons water**

12 **ounces whipping cream**

8   **ounces garlic-herb cheese**

Fresh parsley for garnish

- Preheat oven to 400 degrees.

- Place chicken between two sheets of heavy duty plastic wrap. Flatten to ⅛ inch thickness, using a meat mallet or rolling pin. Sprinkle with 1 teaspoon each of salt and pepper.

- Combine spinach, Gruyère cheese, remaining ½ teaspoon salt and ¼ teaspoon pepper, the nutmeg and ham. Shape into balls, one per chicken piece, and place in the center of chicken pieces. Fold chicken over balls.

- Roll each pastry sheet into a 12-inch square. Cut a 1-inch strip from each sheet and set aside. Cut sheets in half, making two 6x5½-inch rectangles. Place chicken in the center of each rectangle. Fold pastry over chicken. Make sure that there is not too much pastry on bottom or dough will not fully cook.

- Combine egg and water, stirring well. Use egg mixture to repair any tears in pastry. Brush edges of pastry and pinch seams to seal. Place bundles, seam side down, in a lightly greased pan.

- Cut decorative shapes from reserved pastry strips. Brush backs of shapes with egg mixture and arrange on bundles. Chill bundles and remaining egg mixture for 1 hour.

(continued on next page)

Chicken Florentine in Pastry with Herbed Cream Sauce continued

- Before placing bundles in oven, brush them with egg mixture. Bake for 25 minutes or until golden brown.

- Meanwhile, cook whipping cream and herbed cheese in a heavy saucepan over low heat, stirring constantly, until smooth. Spoon onto individual serving plates and top with chicken bundles. Garnish with fresh parsley.

Serves 6 to 8

Grilled Grecian Chicken

3   **whole chicken breasts, split**
3   **tablespoons olive oil**
¼   **cup lemon juice**
½   **teaspoon oregano**
1   **clove garlic, minced**

- Place chicken in a bowl. Mix olive oil, lemon juice, oregano and garlic. Pour over chicken. Cover. Place in refrigerator and marinate for several hours.

- Remove chicken from marinade and grill or broil until done, basting often.

Serves 6

Sliced Chicken Rolls with Artichoke and Prosciutto

1 cup artichoke hearts (fresh, canned or frozen), cooked and chopped

1 cup Parmesan cheese, grated

¼ cup mayonnaise

2 cloves garlic

3 tablespoons fresh basil, minced

3 whole boneless, skinless chicken breasts (about 1½ pounds), split

Salt, to taste

Ground white pepper, to taste

6 thin slices prosciutto (about ¼ pound)

2 tablespoons olive oil

- Preheat oven to 350 degrees.

- Place artichokes, cheese, mayonnaise, garlic and basil in food processor and purée until smooth.

- If breasts are large, slice in half horizontally. Place chicken breasts between 2 sheets of wax paper. Flatten to ⅛-inch thickness, using meat mallet or rolling pin. Season with salt and pepper.

- Top each chicken breast with a slice of prosciutto. Spread prosciutto with a thin layer of artichoke mixture. Roll jelly roll style and secure with toothpicks or string.

- Heat olive oil in skillet over medium heat. Add chicken rolls and cook turning frequently until lightly browned, about 5 minutes.

- Transfer chicken rolls to a baking dish. Bake for 20 minutes. Cool.

- Slice horizontally on diagonal ⅓-inch wide.

Serves 6

Stuffed Chicken Breasts with Three Cheeses

4   **whole boneless chicken breasts**
½   **teaspoon salt**
¼   **teaspoon pepper**
¼   **cup goat cheese, crumbled**
½   **cup Gouda cheese, grated**
½   **cup Port-Salut cheese, grated**
¼   **cup flour**
4   **tablespoons butter**
1   **tablespoon shallots, chopped**
6   **medium tomatoes, peeled, seeded, and chopped**
¼   **cup dry white wine**
1   **tablespoon fresh basil**

- Preheat oven to 400 degrees.

- Lay chicken breasts flat and pound to an even thickness. Sprinkle with salt and pepper.

- Combine goat, Gouda, and Port-Salut cheeses and divide evenly among breasts, placing cheeses in center. Fold breasts over completely enclosing cheeses. Secure with toothpicks.

- Dredge chicken in flour. Melt butter in a large frying pan. Sauté chicken until golden brown on both sides. Transfer chicken to an 8x10-inch baking dish. Bake for 15 to 20 minutes.

- Meanwhile, remove excess oil from frying pan. On medium high heat, sauté shallots until tender. Stir in tomatoes, wine and basil. Continue cooking until reduced to 3 cups. Place warm chicken breasts on platter. Top with sauce.

Serves 4

Chicken Scallops with Mustard Glaze

4   **whole chicken breasts, skinned, boned and split**
3   **tablespoons flour**
½   **teaspoon dried marjoram**
½   **teaspoon dried thyme**
½   **teaspoon ground pepper**
2   **tablespoons butter**
Non-stick spray
½   **cup dry vermouth**
1   **cup chicken broth**
2   **tablespoons Dijon mustard**
¼   **teaspoon lemon peel, grated**
3   **tablespoons whipping cream**
Thin lemon slices
Parsley

- Cut the chicken breasts in half again and pound thin.

- Combine flour, marjoram, thyme and pepper. Transfer 1 tablespoon of this mixture to a small bowl and reserve. Rub remainder of mixture on chicken.

- Spray skillet generously with non-stick spray. Add butter and melt. Add chicken and cook over medium heat until brown. Transfer to plate.

- Add vermouth to skillet and boil until reduced to glaze, about 5 minutes. Mix in broth, mustard and lemon peel. Boil 2 minutes.

- Mix cream into the 1 tablespoon of reserved flour mixture and whisk in ¼ cup of the hot broth. Return mixture to skillet. Simmer until thickened and smooth, about 3 minutes.

- Return chicken to skillet and cook until done. Garnish with lemon slices and parsley.

Serves 4

Kung Pao Chicken

1⅓ pounds boneless, skinless chicken breasts (about 4), cut into ½ inch pieces

5 tablespoons soy sauce, divided

2 tablespoons sherry, divided

1 tablespoon plus 2 teaspoons cornstarch

2 teaspoons sugar

2 tablespoons white wine-vinegar or rice vinegar

2 teaspoons Asian sesame oil

⅓ cup water

2 tablespoons cooking oil, divided

½ cup peanuts

4 scallions, white bulbs and green tops cut separately into ½-inch pieces

¼ teaspoon dried red-pepper flakes

• In a medium bowl, toss the chicken with 1 tablespoon of the soy sauce, 1 tablespoon of the sherry, and 1 tablespoon of the cornstarch.

• In a small bowl, combine the sugar, vinegar, sesame oil, water and the remaining 4 tablespoons of soy sauce, 1 tablespoon of sherry and 2 teaspoons cornstarch.

• In a wok or large frying pan, heat 1 tablespoon of the oil over moderately high heat. Add the peanuts and stir-fry until light brown, about 30 seconds. Remove peanuts from the pan. Set aside.

• Heat the remaining 1 tablespoon oil. Add the white part of the scallions and the red-pepper flakes to the pan and cook, stirring for 30 seconds. Add the chicken with its marinade and cook, stirring, 1 to 2 minutes. Add the soy-sauce mixture and the scallion tops and simmer until the chicken is just done, about 1 minute longer. Stir in the peanuts.

Serves 4

For Cashew Chicken, substitute ½ cup of cashews for the peanuts.

Mediterranean Chicken Tart

2   whole chicken breasts
2   teaspoons plus ½ teaspoon salt
¼   teaspoon black pepper
1   small onion, cut up and 1 medium onion, chopped
1   carrot, cut up
1   stalk celery, cut up
3   sprigs parsley
1   bay leaf
1½ cups chicken broth reserved from cooking chicken
1   cup butter, divided
¼   pound mushrooms, chopped
½   teaspoon thyme
3   tablespoons flour
2   tomatoes, peeled, seeded and diced
¾   cup pitted, sliced black olives
16   sheets phyllo dough
¾   cup Parmesan cheese, freshly grated

• Thaw the phyllo dough and have at room temperature.

• Place chicken breasts in a pan with water to cover. Add 2 teaspoons salt, pepper, the small onion, carrot, celery, parsley and bay leaf.

• Cover pan and simmer 40 minutes or until chicken is tender. Skin, bone and cube the chicken. Strain and reserve 1½ cups of the chicken broth.

• Preheat oven to 400 degrees.

• Melt ¼ cup butter in large skillet. Add 1 medium chopped onion and sauté 5 minutes until soft. Add mushrooms, ½ teaspoon salt, and the thyme. Stir over low heat for 5 minutes longer. Blend in flour. Add chicken broth and tomatoes. Cook and stir until slightly thickened. Add the cubed chicken and olives. Simmer 5 minutes. Cool.

• Melt ¾ cup butter. Brush bottom and sides of a 13x9-inch pan with some of the butter. Line pan with a sheet of phyllo. Brush with butter. Repeat until 8 sheets have been used. Spoon on chicken filling, spreading to corners. Sprinkle with Parmesan cheese. Top with remaining phyllo, brushing each sheet with butter. Trim edges of dough, using scissors.

(continued on next page)

Mediterranean Chicken Tart continued

- Bake for 10 minutes. Reduce oven temperature to 300 degrees and bake for 40 minutes longer. Brush with remaining melted butter several times during baking time.

- Let stand for 10 to 15 minutes before cutting into squares.

Serves 12

Mexican Chicken

1   chicken, or 3 to 3½ pounds chicken parts, cooked, skinned and boned
1   large onion, chopped
1   large green pepper, chopped
1   teaspoon chili powder
Garlic salt
1   can (10.5 ounce) condensed cream of chicken soup
1   can (10.5 ounce) condensed cream of mushroom soup
1   bag (13.5 ounce) nacho flavored tortilla chips, crushed
1   can (14.5 ounce) chopped tomatoes with green chilies, divided
½   pound Monterey Jack cheese, grated

- Preheat oven to 375 degrees. Cut chicken into bite-sized pieces.

- Sauté onion and green pepper until tender.

- Mix together chili powder, garlic salt, chicken and mushroom soups, and ½ the tomatoes.

- In a greased 9x12-inch baking dish, layer the tortilla chips and chicken. Pour the soup mixture over the chicken. Sprinkle top with cheese and remaining tomatoes.

- Bake for 30 minutes.

Serves 8 to 10

149

Rock Cornish Hens with Cranberry and Spice Stuffing

1	cup cranberries, chopped
3	tablespoons sugar
2	cups dry raisin bread cubes (4 slices)
1	teaspoon orange peel, grated
½	teaspoon salt plus salt, to taste
⅛	teaspoon ground cinnamon
2	tablespoons plus 3 tablespoons butter, melted
2	tablespoons plus ¼ cup orange juice
4	Cornish hens (1 to 1½ pounds)

- Preheat oven to 375 degrees.

- Combine cranberries and sugar. Add bread cubes, orange peel, ½ teaspoon salt and cinnamon. Toss lightly with 2 tablespoons butter and 2 tablespoons orange juice until well mixed.

- Salt cavity of birds and stuff each with the cranberry stuffing. Push drumsticks under band of skin at tail, or tie them to tail. Place birds on rack in shallow roasting pan. Cover loosely with foil and roast for 30 minutes.

- Meanwhile make a glaze by mixing 3 tablespoons melted butter with ¼ cup orange juice. Uncover birds and roast 60 minutes longer, brushing occasionally with orange glaze.

Serves 4

Rock Cornish Hens Stuffed with Grapes and Mushrooms

1½ cups Madeira wine

3 ounces dried Cèpe, Porcini or morel mushrooms

1½ cups seedless green or red grapes

12 tablespoons butter, at room temperature, divided

1½ cups seasoned dried bread crumbs

3 tablespoons fresh parsley, chopped

⅓ teaspoon dried thyme leaves

6 Cornish game hens

Salt and freshly ground pepper, to taste

- Bring Madeira to a boil in a small saucepan. Add mushrooms. Remove from heat and set aside.

- Preheat oven to 350 degrees.

- Combine grapes, 6 tablespoons of the butter, bread crumbs, parsley and thyme in a mixing bowl. Toss well.

- Rinse the hens well and pat dry. Fill the cavities with the bread crumb stuffing and bury 1 mushroom in each cavity. The mushroom must be buried to prevent it drying out. Reserve the Madeira.

- Place the stuffed birds in a roasting pan large enough so that they do not touch. Dot them with the remaining 6 tablespoons butter and sprinkle them with salt and pepper. Pour 3 tablespoons of the reserved Madeira on each bird. Roast for 1 hour, basting occasionally. Internal temperature should be at least 180 degrees.

- Heat remaining mushrooms and Madeira in a pan and cook over low heat until the liquid is slightly reduced, 8 to 12 minutes. Pour the sauce over the hens and serve.

Serves 6

Turkey, Sausage and Spinach Pie

1	**pound ground turkey**
½	**pound pork sausage**
6	**eggs**
2	**packages (10 ounce) frozen, chopped spinach, thawed and squeezed dry**
1	**package (16 ounce) mozzarella cheese, shredded**
8	**ounces ricotta cheese**
1	**teaspoon salt**
½	**teaspoon pepper**
Favorite pie crust recipe for 2 (9-inch) crusts	
2	**teaspoons water**

• Preheat oven to 350 degrees.

• Brown turkey and sausage together for 10 minutes. Pour off excess fat.

• Separate 1 egg. Set aside the yolk. In a large bowl, combine the remaining 5 whole eggs with the 1 egg white, the cooked turkey and sausage, spinach, mozzarella, ricotta, salt and pepper. Set aside.

• Prepare pie crust. Divide dough. Roll out enough dough to fit bottom and sides of a spring form pan. Place dough in pan. Trim edges. Roll out remaining dough to make a top crust. Set top crust aside. Spoon turkey mixture into crust.

• Mix reserved yolk and water. Brush edge of pastry. Cover with top crust. Cut hole in middle for steam. Press edges together. Brush top with egg mixture. Decorate with extra dough.

• Bake for 1¼ hours. Cool at least 10 minutes for easier slicing.

Serves 8 to 10

Turkey Scallops with Horseradish Sauce

4   **turkey scallops, about 1 pound of sliced boneless, skinless turkey breast**

6   **tablespoons dry unseasoned bread crumbs**

3   **tablespoons fresh horseradish root, peeled and grated**

½   **tablespoon fresh rosemary, finely chopped**

1   **tablespoon fresh tarragon, finely chopped**

1   **tablespoon fresh thyme, finely chopped**

2   **teaspoons Dijon mustard**

⅓   **cup dry white wine**

2   **tablespoons olive oil**

1   **tablespoon butter**

Salt and freshly ground black pepper, to taste

Horseradish sauce (recipe follows)

- Place the turkey between 2 sheets of plastic wrap and pound with a meat mallet or the bottom of a small, heavy saucepan until scallops are ¼ inch thick.

- On a plate, combine the bread crumbs, horseradish, rosemary, tarragon, and thyme. On another plate, combine the mustard and wine. Dip each turkey cutlet into the wine mixture and then into the bread crumb mixture.

- In a large sauté pan, heat the oil. When it is hot, add the butter. Swirl the pan just until the butter melts, then add as many turkey scallops as the pan will hold.

- Season the scallops with salt and pepper and cook for 4 minutes, turning them often, until they are golden brown. Repeat with remaining scallops.

- Set a scallop on each of 4 warm dinner plates. Serve at once with horseradish sauce.

Serves 4

Horseradish Sauce

2   **teaspoons Dijon mustard**

1   **tablespoon horseradish root, freshly grated**

Squeeze of lemon juice

½   **cup plain yogurt (regular or lowfat)**

½   **cup sour cream**

Salt and freshly ground black pepper, to taste

- In a small bowl, combine the mustard, horseradish, lemon juice, yogurt, sour cream, salt and pepper. Adjust the seasoning. Add more lemon juice if desired. Serve at once.

Filet Mignon with Mustard Cream Sauce

2   **filet mignons, 1¼-inch thick each**
Freshly ground black pepper
1   **tablespoon butter, divided**
½   **tablespoon vegetable oil**
Salt
1   **green onion, minced**
1   **tablespoon brandy**
⅓   **cup whipping cream**
½   **teaspoon Dijon mustard**
Parsley sprigs

• Grind pepper generously over both sides of steak and press in.

• In a heavy skillet over high heat, melt ½ tablespoon butter with the oil. Salt one side of steak. Place in skillet, salted side down. Cook 2 minutes. Salt second side and turn until two sides are brown.

• Reduce heat to medium and cook to desired degree of doneness (6 minutes for rare). Transfer steaks to heated plates. Discard drippings from skillet. Add remaining ½ tablespoon butter to skillet and cook over medium heat. Add onion. Stir and cook 1 minute.

• Remove from heat and add brandy. Return to heat and bring to a boil, scraping up any brown bits from bottom of the pan, until mixture begins to take on a glaze-like consistency. Add cream and boil until mixture thickens, about 1 minute. Stir in mustard and any juices from the steaks. Season to taste with salt and pepper. Spoon over steaks and garnish with parsley.

Serves 2

Roast Tenderloin of Beef

1 tablespoon vegetable oil
1 beef tenderloin,
   6 to 7 pounds
Salt and freshly ground black
   pepper, to taste
½ cup bourbon whiskey
1 tablespoon brown sugar
Tabasco sauce, to taste
12 carrots, peeled
1 bunch celery
24 medium red new potatoes
2 heads of garlic, separated
   into cloves and peeled

• Preheat oven to 400 degrees.

• In a large skillet, heat oil and quickly brown the tenderloin on all sides. Remove from pan and season with salt and pepper. Set aside.

• Pour whiskey into skillet. Cook over high heat to reduce liquid. Add brown sugar and Tabasco. Reduce further to the consistency of thick syrup. Place tenderloin in pan and turn to glaze on all sides.

• Cut carrots and celery into ¼-inch thick sticks, about 2 inches long. Place tenderloin in baking pan with carrots, celery, potatoes and garlic. Roast in oven for 25 to 30 minutes or until thickest part of roast reaches an internal temperature of 120 degrees. Allow to rest at room temperature for 20 minutes. Slice and serve with potatoes and vegetables.

Serves 10 to 12

Roast Beef with Shiitake Mushroom Sauce

1	**boneless rib roast, about 7 pounds, at room temperature**

Salt and freshly ground black pepper, to taste

4	**large onions, trimmed and quartered lengthwise**
1	**ounce dried shiitake mushrooms**
1	**tablespoon vegetable oil**
¼	**pound fresh mushrooms, sliced**
4	**cups beef stock or broth**
¾	**cup Madeira wine**
4	**teaspoons arrowroot**
2	**tablespoons cold water**

• Preheat oven to 500 degrees. Rub beef well with salt and pepper.

• Roast beef on a rack in roasting pan for 15 minutes. Reduce heat to 350 degrees and roast for 12 minutes more per pound for medium rare, or until a meat thermometer registers desired doneness. About 1 hour before roast is done, add onions to roasting pan and turn gently to coat in drippings. Baste onions several times during roasting.

• While beef is roasting, soak shiitake mushrooms in hot water to cover for 30 minutes. Drain. Discard stems and slice. In a large heavy skillet, heat oil until hot. Sauté the fresh mushrooms for 2 to 3 minutes. Add shiitake mushrooms and sauté 1 minute. Add stock, bring to a boil and reduce to about 2½ cups.

• When roast has reached desired temperature, remove from oven, transfer roast to cutting board and let stand 30 minutes. Remove onions from pan and keep warm.

• While roast is resting, pour off pan drippings. Add Madeira to roasting pan and deglaze over high heat, scraping bottom and sides of pan. Strain and add to sauce. Bring sauce to a boil. Stir in arrowroot dissolved in the cold water. Simmer 3 to 4 minutes, or until sauce thickens. Season with salt and pepper.

• Carve beef. Arrange on heated platter and surround with roasted onions. Serve with mushroom sauce.

Serves 8

Swedish Pot Roast

2 **tablespoons butter**
2 **tablespoons oil**
4 **pounds boneless beef pot roast**
1 **cup onion, finely chopped**
3 **tablespoons flour**
1 **tablespoon dark corn syrup or molasses**
2 **tablespoons white vinegar**
2 **cups beef stock**
1 **large bay leaf**
1 **teaspoon peppercorns**
Salt, to taste

• Preheat oven to 350 degrees.

• In a heavy casserole, melt butter and oil over moderate heat. When the foam subsides, add meat and brown on all sides, about 15 minutes. Remove meat from pan and set aside. Add chopped onions to casserole and let them cook over moderate heat until lightly browned.

• Remove pan from heat and add flour. Stir gently to dissolve. Add corn syrup, vinegar and beef stock. Add bay leaf and peppercorns. Return meat to casserole, cover and bring to a boil on top of stove.

• Place casserole in oven. Adjust temperature until liquid simmers. Bake for 3 hours.

• Transfer meat to a platter. Remove bay leaf from gravy. Season to taste. Pour gravy into sauceboat and serve with roast.

Serves 6 to 8

Basil Stuffed Beef

1	**boneless beef sirloin roast, 3 to 3½ pounds, 1¾ inches thick**
¼	**teaspoon salt**
¼	**teaspoon pepper**
2	**cups lightly packed fresh basil leaves, cut into strips**
8-10	**cloves garlic, minced**
2	**teaspoons olive oil**

Heavy string for tying roast

- Make five or six 5-inch long slits along the top of the roast, cutting almost through the roast. Sprinkle with salt and pepper.

- For filling, in a medium mixing bowl combine basil and garlic. Stuff the filling into the slits in the meat. Tie the meat with heavy-duty string to hold slits closed. Drizzle with olive oil.

- Roast using indirect grilling, quick oven-roasting, or slow oven-roasting method (directions follow). Roast to desired temperature (140 degrees for rare, 155 degrees for medium, 165 degrees for well-done). Let meat stand, covered, for 10 minutes before slicing. (Meat temperature will rise slightly upon standing). Slice across the grain.

Serves 10 to 12

Indirect Grilling Method

- In a covered grill, arrange coals around a drip pan. Place meat on grill rack over drip pan but not over coals, lower grill hood. Over medium-low heat, grill for 45 to 90 minutes, or until a meat thermometer registers desired temperature. Add more coals as necessary.

(continued on next page)

Basil Stuffed Beef continued

Slow Oven-roasting Method

• Place the roast on a rack in a shallow roasting pan. Roast, uncovered, in a 325 degree oven for 1½ to 1¾ hours or until the meat thermometer registers desired temperature.

Quick Oven-roasting Method

• Place roast on a rack in a shallow roasting pan. Insert a meat thermometer. Roast, uncovered, in a 425 degree oven for 15 minutes. Reduce oven temperature to 350 degrees. Roast for 35 to 45 minutes more or until thermometer registers desired doneness.

Spit Roasted Churrasco Beef

1	rolled, boneless sirloin tip or rump roast, 6 to 8 pounds
2	tablespoons onion, minced
2	teaspoons thyme
1	teaspoon marjoram
1	bay leaf, crushed
½	cup olive oil
1	cup wine vinegar
3	tablespoons lemon juice
1	clove garlic, minced

• Combine onion, thyme, marjoram, bay leaf, oil, vinegar, lemon juice and garlic. Pour over roast. Let stand at room temperature at least 2 hours, turning beef and basting with marinade occasionally. Refrigerate overnight.

• Remove roast from marinade and place on a spit. Roast on outdoor grill for 15 minutes per pound; on indoor grill, 15 to 18 minutes per pound for rare. Slice thinly. Spoon juices over slices and serve.

Serves 8 to 10

159

Italian Party Flank Steak

¼ **cup olive oil**

¼ **cup red wine vinegar**

2 **cloves garlic, finely chopped**

5 **tablespoons parsley, chopped and divided**

¼ **teaspoon coarse black pepper**

1 **flank steak, 1¼ pounds, ¾-inch thick, butterflied**

2 **red bell peppers**

6-8 **thin slices prosciutto or other cured ham**

24 **medium-sized fresh basil leaves**

2 **tablespoons Parmesan, grated**

Freshly ground black pepper to taste

1 **bunch watercress for garnish**

- Combine olive oil, vinegar, garlic, 2 tablespoons parsley, and ¼ teaspoon black pepper in a bowl. Add butterflied steak and marinate for 2 hours at room temperature.

- Preheat broiler. Halve peppers lengthwise. Remove seeds. Place, skin side up, on broiler tray, 4 inches from heat. Broil until skins are charred black. Seal peppers in a plastic bag for 15 minutes to steam. Remove charred skins.

- After 2 hours, remove steak from marinade and scrape off any excess. Lay meat opened on a long piece of aluminum foil on a flat surface. Reserve marinade.

- Preheat oven to 350 degrees.

- Place the 4 pepper halves on top of steak to cover. Sprinkle with 1 tablespoon of the parsley. Cover with prosciutto slices. Arrange basil leaves in a single layer over complete surface of prosciutto. Sprinkle with Parmesan and remaining 2 tablespoons parsley. Season with freshly ground black pepper.

- With the long side of the layered steak facing you, lift it from the foil and roll it tightly away from you. With 6 pieces of kitchen string, 8 inches long, tie the steak at 2 to 3 inch intervals. Slip the strings under and around the roll to secure.

(continued on next page)

Italian Party Flank Steak continued

- Place steak in shallow baking dish and pour marinade over the top. Bake for 30 minutes, basting twice. Let rest for 15 minutes before slicing.

- To serve, carefully cut into ½-inch slices, discarding string. Arrange on a serving platter garnished with watercress.

Serves 8

You may substitute a small jar of roasted red peppers for freshly roasted peppers.

To butterfly flank steak: with long end of the steak facing you, run a thin sharp knife through the middle thickness of the meat. Leave about ½ inch at the long opposite end to make a "hinge." Flip meat open to resemble a butterfly.

Flank Steak Gourmet

1   **pound flank steak**
½   **cup Cheddar cheese, grated**
½   **teaspoon Worcestershire sauce**
1   **teaspoon Dijon mustard**

- Score meat so that it will not curl.

- Mix together cheese, Worcestershire sauce and mustard.

- Broil steak 3 to 6 minutes on each side. For final 2 minutes, spread cheese mixture on one side of steak. Broil until bubbly and melted.

- Cut on diagonal and serve.

Serves 4

161

Sirloin Tips and Noodles

2 **pounds beef tips**
4 **tablespoons butter**
2 **tablespoons olive oil**
1 **teaspoon salt**
½ **teaspoon pepper**
Dash of sage
Dash of ground cumin
1 **pound fresh mushrooms,
   or 1 (16 ounce) can**
2 **cloves garlic, crushed and
   chopped fine**
2 **medium onions, diced**
2 **green peppers, diced**
½ **cup soy sauce**
2 **tablespoons apple cider
   vinegar**
2 **tablespoons tomato paste**
2 **medium-sized fresh
   tomatoes, cut in wedges**
1 **package (12 ounce) egg
   noodles, cooked**

• Slice beef into bite-sized pieces. Sauté quickly in butter and olive oil. Place in a baking dish and sprinkle with salt, pepper, sage and cumin. Toss to mix.

• Sauté mushrooms for 2 minutes. Add to meat. Sauté garlic, onions and peppers for 2 minutes. Add to baking dish and mix.

• Add soy sauce, vinegar and tomato paste to pan and bring to a boil. Pour into baking dish. Add tomatoes and cooked noodles and mix.

Serves 4 to 6

Beef Stroganoff

1½ cups cooked wild rice

4 cups cooked white rice

2 pounds beef sirloin

4 tablespoons butter, divided

1 cup onion, thinly sliced

1 clove garlic

½ pound fresh mushrooms, sliced

3 tablespoons flour

½ cup beef stock (or 6 beef bouillon cubes dissolved in ½ cup water)

1 tablespoon ketchup

½ teaspoon salt

⅛ teaspoon ground black pepper

¼ cup dry white wine

1 tablespoon fresh dill, snipped, or ¼ teaspoon dried dill (plus dill for garnish)

1½ cups dairy sour cream

- Combine wild and white rice and keep warm.

- Trim fat from beef. Cut steak crosswise into ½-inch thick slices. Slowly heat a large heavy skillet and melt 1 tablespoon butter. Add beef strips and brown, or sear quickly on both sides. Remove beef as it browns. Beef should be rare. Set beef and all meat juices aside.

- Melt the remaining 3 tablespoons of butter in the skillet. Add the onion, garlic and mushrooms and sauté until golden brown, about 5 minutes. Remove from heat. Add flour, stock, ketchup, salt and pepper. Stir until smooth. Return to heat and gradually bring to boil, stirring. Simmer 5 minutes more.

- Over low heat, add wine, dill and sour cream. Mix well and add beef and meat juices. Simmer until sauce and beef are hot. Serve over bed of rice and sprinkle with dill.

Serves 4 to 6

163

Beef Carbonnade

¼	**pound bacon**
1½-2	**pounds large yellow onions, peeled and thinly sliced**
1	**tablespoon granulated sugar**
1	**cup unbleached, flour**
1	**tablespoon dried thyme**
1	**teaspoon salt**
½	**teaspoon ground black pepper**
3	**pounds beef stew meat, cubed (chuck preferred)**

Vegetable oil, as necessary

2	**cups imported dark beer**

Parsley for garnish, chopped

- Preheat oven to 325 degrees.

- Coarsely dice the bacon and sauté in a large skillet until crisp and brown. Remove with a slotted spoon and set aside.

- Add the onions to the skillet and cook, covered, in the rendered bacon fat until tender, about 20 minutes. Uncover the skillet, raise the heat and sprinkle onions with the sugar. Toss and stir them until well browned. Transfer onions to a strainer set over a bowl and let stand.

- On a plate, stir together the flour, thyme, salt and pepper. Roll the cubes of meat in the mixture until well-coated. Shake off excess and set cubes on another plate.

- Press onions gently with the back of a spoon to extract as much of the cooking fat as possible. Heat fat in an oven proof casserole over high heat. When very hot, add 6 to 8 cubes of beef. Do not crowd. Turn the heat down slightly and brown beef on all sides. With a slotted spoon, transfer beef to a clean plate. Repeat with remaining beef, adding small amounts of vegetable oil as necessary to brown meat evenly.

- Pour beer into the oven proof casserole, stirring and loosening brown bits from bottom of the pan. Return beef, bacon and onions to the casserole. Bring to a simmer on top of the stove. Cover and place on middle shelf of the oven.

(continued on next page)

Beef Carbonnade continued

- Cook for 1½ hours, stirring occasionally, until liquid is reduced and thickened and meat is tender. Regulate temperature as needed to maintain a moderate simmer. Adjust seasoning. Transfer to a heated serving dish, garnish with parsley and serve immediately.

Serves 6

Boeuf Bourguignon

4   strips bacon, chopped
3   tablespoons butter
2   pounds lean beef, cut into chunks
4   tablespoons flour
1   teaspoon salt
Cracked pepper
½   bay leaf
1   bottle dry red wine
1   can (14 ounce) beef broth
15   small white onions, peeled
1   pound mushrooms, sliced
Parsley, chopped
Broad egg noodles, cooked according to package directions

- Preheat oven to 300 degrees.

- Sauté bacon. Remove from pan and set aside. Add butter to pan. Sauté beef until brown. Sprinkle meat with flour. Transfer to ovenproof dish. Add pan drippings, bacon, salt, pepper and bay leaf. In the ratio 3 parts wine to 1 part broth, add enough liquid to cover meat. Cover and cook for 1 hour.

- Add onions. Cook an additional ½ hour.

- Add mushrooms and cook ½ hour more.

- Serve over freshly cooked broad egg noodles and sprinkle with parsley.

Serves 4 to 6

165

Beef Trittini

2   pounds ground beef

2   medium onions, chopped

2   cans (6 ounce) tomato
    paste

2   cans (8 ounce) tomato
    sauce

2   teaspoons dried parsley

1   teaspoon dried oregano

¼   teaspoon garlic salt

Freshly ground pepper

3   packages (10 ounce) frozen
    chopped spinach

1½ pounds ricotta cheese, or
    creamed cottage cheese

1   package (8 ounce)
    shredded mozzarella
    cheese

• Preheat oven to 350 degrees.

• Brown ground beef and onions. Drain.
  Add tomato paste, tomato sauce, parsley,
  oregano, garlic, salt and pepper. Simmer
  uncovered for 10 minutes. Stir often.

• Cook spinach according to directions on
  the package. Cool and thoroughly squeeze
  water out of spinach. Mix spinach with
  ricotta cheese.

• Make 5 rows of even width across the
  bottom of a 9x13-inch baking dish, starting with the spinach/cheese mixture and
  alternating rows with the tomato/beef
  mixture. There will be 3 rows of spinach
  and 2 rows of tomato mixture. Sprinkle
  with half the mozzarella cheese. For the
  second layer, reverse the rows, having
  the tomato mixture on top of the spinach
  mixture. Top with remaining mozzarella
  cheese.

• Bake for 40 minutes.

Serves 4 to 6

Meatballs and Sausage Fiorentino

3 tablespoons olive oil

3 large cloves garlic, peeled

3 cans (6 ounce) tomato paste

4 cans (28 ounce) peeled Italian plum tomatoes

Salt and freshly ground black pepper, to taste

2 tablespoons dried parsley

1 tablespoon dried oregano

Basil, to taste

Meatballs and Sausages

7-8 eggs

¾-1 cup Italian bread crumbs

½ cup Parmesan cheese

3 cloves garlic, minced

2 pounds ground beef

Salt and freshly ground black pepper, to taste

Olive oil for browning

2 tablespoons water

1¾ pounds sweet Italian sausages

- Heat olive oil in 8-quart stockpot and sauté 3 whole peeled garlic cloves.

- Stir in tomato paste.

- Add tomatoes, salt, pepper, parsley, oregano, and basil. Stir. Bring to boiling point.

- Reduce heat and simmer for 2 hours, stirring frequently. Mash garlic cloves in the sauce after they become soft.

- Meanwhile, to make the meatballs, beat eggs. Add bread crumbs. Stir to moisten.

- Add cheese, minced garlic and bread crumb mixture to ground beef. Salt and pepper to taste.

- With your hands, mix the beef until all ingredients are well combined. Shape into 2-inch balls. Brown in oil.

- Brown sausages in 2 tablespoons water. If sausages are large, cut them into 2-inch lengths before browning.

- Add sausage and meatballs to sauce and simmer for approximately 1 hour.

Serves 8

Recipe makes enough for 2 pounds of pasta.

Meatloaf with Red Wine Sauce

1½ **pounds ground beef**
1   **cup bread crumbs**
1   **egg**
1   **small onion, chopped**
1   **can (8 ounce) tomato sauce, divided**
Salt and freshly ground black pepper, to taste
¾   **cup red wine**
¾   **cup water**
1   **beef bouillon cube**
1   **tablespoon cornstarch**
1   **tablespoon vinegar**
1   **teaspoon mustard**
2   **tablespoons brown sugar**

• Preheat oven to 350 degrees.

• Combine ground beef, bread crumbs, egg, onion and ½ can of the tomato sauce. Salt and pepper to taste. Mix well. Make into 3 or 4 loaves and place in baking pan. Bake for 30 minutes. Drain off fat.

• Meanwhile, combine the wine, water, bouillon cube, cornstarch, vinegar, mustard, brown sugar and remaining ½ can of tomato sauce in a saucepan. Bring to a boil.

• Pour over meatloaves and bake for an additional 30 minutes.

Serves 4 to 6

You may double the meatloaf recipe. There is enough sauce without doubling.

Blanquette de Veau

2   **pounds veal from breast, cut in pieces**
4   **cups boiling water**
2   **large carrots, cut up**
10 **small onions**
Salt and freshly ground black pepper, to taste
Bouquet garni of parsley, thyme and bay leaf
5   **tablespoons butter**
1   **tablespoon flour**
2   **egg yolks**
4   **tablespoons heavy cream or crème fraîche**
Juice of 1 lemon

- Place veal pieces in 4 cups boiling water. Skim fat. Add carrots, onions, salt, pepper, and bouquet garni. Cover and simmer 1½ hours.

- While veal is cooking, melt butter, add flour and stir for 3 minutes. Add 2 to 3 ladles of veal stock to make sauce. Remove from heat. Beat egg yolks with the heavy cream and juice of 1 lemon. Add to the sauce. Place veal pieces, carrots and onion on a serving platter and pour sauce over them.

Serves 4

Accompany with rice, boiled potatoes or noodles.

Hungarian Goulash

4　cups onion, chopped
2　tablespoons oil
2　tablespoons garlic, chopped
4　pounds beef or veal, cut in cubes
2-3 tablespoons paprika
2　tablespoons flour
2½ cups beef or chicken broth
1½ cups green pepper, chopped
Salt and freshly ground black pepper, to taste

• Preheat oven to 325 degrees.

• Cook onion in oil until tender. Add chopped garlic and meat. Sprinkle meat with 2 tablespoons paprika while stirring. Add additional paprika, salt and pepper to taste. Sprinkle meat with flour and stir. Add broth and bring to a boil. Bake in oven for 1½ hours. Add peppers in the last half hour.

• Serve over egg noodles.

Serves 8 to 10

Goulash may be cooked on top of stove instead of in the oven.

Veal Stew with Green Peas

1½ **pounds lean shoulder of veal, cut into 1-inch cubes**

Flour

2 **tablespoons olive oil**

2 **tablespoons butter**

½ **cup onion, finely chopped**

½ **cup carrot, finely chopped**

½ **cup celery, finely chopped**

1 **cup dry white wine**

Salt and freshly ground black pepper, to taste

1 **cup canned Italian plum tomatoes, chopped**

2 **cups beef broth**

2 **cups fresh or frozen petite green peas**

- Dip veal cubes in flour to coat.

- Heat oil in a skillet and sauté veal. Remove and add butter, onion, carrot, and celery. Sauté until tender. Return veal to pan. Add wine. Lower heat. Season with salt and pepper to taste.

- Add tomatoes and broth. Add green peas. Cover and cook gently for 1½ hours.

Serves 4 to 6

Serve veal stew with hot noodles.

Veal Stew with Asparagus and Arugula

2½-3 pounds veal stew meat, cut into 2-inch pieces

½ cup plus 2 tablespoons unbleached flour

Salt and freshly ground black pepper, to taste

8 tablespoons unsalted butter, at room temperature, divided

3½ cups chicken stock

1 cup dry white wine

3-4 veal bones

1 onion, quartered

2 carrots, broken in half

3 cloves garlic, quartered

Bouquet garni (2 bay leaves, 3 parsley sprigs, and 2 sprigs fresh thyme tied in cheesecloth)

1 pound white pearl onions

4 cups arugula leaves, cut into ¼-inch strips

½ cup heavy or whipping cream

Fresh thyme, to taste

8 ounces fresh wild mushrooms, well rinsed, patted dry, sliced

2 pounds asparagus, ends trimmed, cut diagonally into 1-inch pieces

• Toss the veal with ½ cup flour, seasoned with salt and pepper to taste. Melt 4 tablespoons of the butter in a Dutch oven over medium-high heat. Brown the veal, a few pieces at a time, in the butter.

• Pour the stock and wine over the veal. Add the bones, onion, carrots, garlic, and bouquet garni. Heat to boiling. Reduce heat and simmer, covered, until the meat is tender, about 1½ hours.

• While meat is simmering, cut a small X in the root of each pearl onion. Heat a pan of salted water to boiling, drop in the onions, and boil until tender, 10 to 15 minutes. Drain and plunge into cold water. When onions cool enough to handle, slip off the skins.

• Remove the veal from the Dutch oven and combine with the onions. Strain the cooking liquid and return to the pan. Cook until reduced by half.

• Make a beurre manié by mixing 2 tablespoons of the remaining butter and the 2 tablespoons flour in a small bowl until smooth. Stir in a few tablespoons of the reduced cooking liquid and then stir it into the remaining liquid in the Dutch oven. Cook, stirring constantly, for several minutes.

• Stir in the arugula and cook gently for 5 minutes. Stir in the cream and season to taste with salt, pepper and thyme. Return the veal and onions to the sauce.

(continued on next page)

Veal Stew with Asparagus and Arugula continued

- Sauté the mushrooms in the remaining 2 tablespoons butter and add to the veal. Heat until warmed through.

- At the same time, steam the asparagus until tender but still crisp. Stir into the stew and serve immediately.

Serves 6 to 8

The stew, without the asparagus, can be prepared up to 1 day in advance. Refrigerate, covered, and add asparagus just before serving.

Veal with Capers

8   **veal scaloppini, about 1½ to 2 pounds**
¾   **teaspoon salt**
¼   **teaspoon pepper**
Flour
4   **tablespoons butter, divided**
2   **tablespoons vegetable oil**
½   **pound fresh mushrooms, sliced**
2   **tablespoons water**
2   **tablespoons red or white wine vinegar**
2-4 **tablespoons capers, drained**
½   **cup chicken broth**
2   **tablespoons parsley, chopped**
4   **cups cooked vermicelli**

- Pound veal very thin. Season veal with salt and pepper and dredge in flour. Melt 2 tablespoons of the butter and the oil in a sauté pan. Sauté the veal 2 minutes on each side. In a different pan, melt the remaining 2 tablespoons of butter and sauté the mushrooms. Add water and vinegar to veal pan and deglaze. Add mushrooms, capers and chicken broth. Cook until a light syrup consistency. Add parsley. Pour sauce over veal and serve over vermicelli.

Serves 4

Bahamian Butterflied Lamb

1   **whole leg of lamb, boned and butterflied, excess fat removed**
½-¾ **cup olive oil**
2   **lemons**
2-3 **large cloves garlic, crushed**
1   **teaspoon salt**
Freshly ground pepper, to taste
½   **teaspoon oregano**
2   **cans (15 ounce) peach halves**
Butter, to taste
1   **jar (10 ounce) mint jelly**
Nutmeg or cinnamon

- Coat lamb with olive oil. Squeeze lemon over lamb, both sides.

- Place crushed garlic, salt, pepper and oregano on both sides. Marinate 2 to 3 hours.

- Preheat oven broiler.

- Place lamb under broiler for about 5 minutes on each side.

- Turn oven temperature to 325 degrees and cook lamb for 40 to 45 minutes more. Remove from oven.

- While lamb is resting, dot each peach half with butter and 1 teaspoon of mint jelly. Sprinkle with nutmeg or cinnamon.

- Place peaches under broiler until lightly browned.

- Serve lamb with peach halves.

Serves 10

174

Marinated Butterflied Leg of Lamb on the Grill

1   leg of lamb, 4 to 5 pounds,
     boned and butterflied

1½ tablespoons oregano

1   tablespoon crushed bay
     leaves

½   teaspoon ground black
     pepper

¼   cup red wine vinegar

4   cloves garlic, crushed

½   cup soy sauce

2   cups sweet vermouth

2   cups dry sherry

2   tablespoons vegetable oil

- Have a butcher bone and butterfly a leg of lamb.

- Remove all visible fat.

- Combine remaining ingredients and marinate all day or overnight in refrigerator.

- Grill over charcoal about 15 minutes for medium rare.

Serves 4 to 6

Moroccan Lamb with Oranges, Raisins and Almonds

2 cups onions, sliced
2 cloves garlic, minced
⅓ cup olive oil, divided
3 pounds boneless lamb, leg or shoulder, cut into 1-inch cubes
Salt and freshly ground pepper, to taste
1½ cups chicken stock or broth
1 cup dry white wine
1 tablespoon tomato paste
½ teaspoon saffron
½ cup golden raisins
3 oranges, peeled with pith and seeds removed, cut into sections
½ cup sliced almonds, lightly toasted

- Preheat oven to 325 degrees.

- In a heavy, large casserole, sauté onions and garlic in oil over low heat until softened.

- Transfer to a bowl using slotted spoon.

- In remaining oil over medium heat, brown lamb with salt and pepper to taste.

- Add sautéed onion and garlic, broth, wine, tomato paste, saffron and raisins.

- Bring mixture to a boil.

- Transfer to the oven and bake 1½ to 2 hours until lamb is tender.

- Remove from oven. Skim off fat.

- Add salt and pepper to taste. Stir in orange sections.

- Sprinkle almonds over top.

Serves 4 to 6

Almond-Crusted Roasted Boneless Pork Loin

¾	**cup plain yogurt**
2	**cloves garlic, minced**
2	**tablespoons olive oil**
1	**tablespoon fresh lemon or lime juice**
1	**teaspoon dry mustard**
½	**teaspoon ground black pepper**
1	**boneless center-cut pork loin roast (about 3 pounds)**
1	**cup almonds, finely chopped**
½	**cup fresh bread crumbs**
½	**teaspoon salt**

- In a small bowl, whisk together yogurt, garlic, olive oil, lemon juice, dry mustard and pepper.

- Place pork loin in shallow baking dish.

- Pour yogurt marinade over roast and roll to coat all sides. Cover and refrigerate 6 to 24 hours.

- When ready to cook, position a rack in center of oven. Preheat oven to 450 degrees.

- Mix together almonds, bread crumbs and salt.

- Scrape most of marinade off meat. Roll meat in almonds and bread crumb mixture, pressing crumbs into roast.

- Place roast in oven and roast 10 minutes.

- Reduce oven temperature to 250 degrees. Roast pork until a meat thermometer registers 150 to 155 degrees, about 60 minutes.

- Remove roast to a cutting board, cover loosely with foil and let stand for 15 minutes.

- Skim fat off pan juices.

- Slice pork and serve with warm pan juices.

Serves 6

177

Cuban Pork Roast

6   **cloves garlic**

4   **scallions, white bulbs and green stalks, minced**

½   **cup pine nuts**

1   **fresh jalapeño pepper, seeded and minced**

2   **cups fresh coriander leaves, minced**

⅔   **cup olive oil**

½   **cup plus 3 tablespoons fresh lime juice, divided**

⅓   **cup Niçoise or Greek olives, pitted and minced**

Salt and freshly ground pepper, to taste

1   **boneless pork loin roast (about 4 pounds)**

½   **cup fresh grapefruit juice**

½   **cup fresh orange juice**

½   **cup hot pepper jelly**

- The day before pork is to be served, prepare filling and marinade:

- Place garlic, scallions, pine nuts, jalapeño pepper and coriander in a food processor fitted with a steel blade.

- Process to form a thick paste.

- With machine running, pour olive oil in a thin, steady stream through feed tube until fully incorporated.

- Transfer to a small bowl. Stir in ½ cup lime juice, olives and salt and pepper.

- If roast is tied, untie it and roll it out flat.

- Spread ⅔ of garlic-coriander paste over meat. Reroll roast and tie.

- Stir grapefruit, orange juice and 3 tablespoons lime juice into remaining paste to make marinade.

- Make shallow incisions over surface of the roast with tip of a sharp knife.

- Place roast in shallow dish or pan and pour marinade over top.

- Let pork marinate 24 hours in refrigerator, turning occasionally.

(continued on next page)

Cuban Pork Roast continued

- Preheat oven to 375 degrees.

- Remove roast from marinade and place in roasting pan.

- Roast uncovered for 1¾ hours, basting occasionally with any left-over marinade.

- Remove roast. Brush all over with hot pepper jelly.

- Bake 15 minutes more, or until cooked to desired doneness.

- Remove roast. Let it rest 10 minutes.

- Carve into ½-inch slices and serve.

Serves 8

Pork Crown Roast with Apple Sausage Stuffing

For Roast

2	tablespoons vegetable or olive oil
4	teaspoons dried thyme
4	teaspoons ground allspice
2	teaspoons salt
1	teaspoon ground black pepper
1	pork crown roast (8 to 10 pounds)
½	cup Madeira or dry white wine
1½	cups chicken stock
2	tablespoons cornstarch
2	tablespoons cold water

Most butchers will prepare a crown roast to order. Make sure the roast is uniform in size so that it will cook evenly.

For Stuffing

1	pound bulk pork sausage
4	cups Granny Smith or other green apples, diced
1	package (14 ounce) bread stuffing mix

Pork Roast

- Position a rack in lower third of oven. Preheat oven to 450 degrees.

- Mix together oil, thyme, allspice, salt and pepper. Rub mixture over surface of roast and bake for 15 minutes.

- Reduce oven temperature to 250 degrees and roast 2 to 3 hours or until a meat thermometer inserted in thickest part registers 155 to 160 degrees.

- Remove roast to a cutting board, cover loosely with aluminum foil and let stand for 15 minutes.

- Skim fat off the pan juices.

- In same roasting pan, bring juices and wine to a simmer, scraping browned bits from bottom of pan.

- Remove to a saucepan and add chicken stock. Bring to a boil and continue cooking until mixture has reduced and flavor has concentrated.

- In a small bowl, mix cornstarch and water to form a paste.

- Reduce heat and add cornstarch mixture to juices, whisking until smooth.

- Return sauce to a boil until thickened. Adjust seasoning.

- Pass sauce separately.

(continued on next page)

Pork Crown Roast with Apple Sausage Stuffing continued

Bread Stuffing with Sausage and Apples

- In a large skillet over medium-high heat, cook sausage until no longer pink, about 8 to 10 minutes.

- Break meat up with a spoon as it cooks.

- Remove sausage to a paper towel-lined plate to drain.

- Pour off all but 2 tablespoons of fat. Add diced apples and cook until tender.

- Prepare bread stuffing mix according to directions on package.

- Toss with sausage and apples.

- Place stuffing in a casserole, cover, and bake with the roast for the last hour, or until stuffing is heated through.

Serves 10 to 12

Grilled Pork Tenderloin with Port, Plums and Apricots

1 **boneless pork loin, about 4 pounds, cut in half lengthwise**
4 **tablespoons olive oil**
Coarse (Kosher) salt
1½ **cups Port**
1 **cup fresh orange juice**
3 **tablespoons honey**
3 **tablespoons cider vinegar**
3 **shallots, minced**
3 **cloves garlic, halved**
½ **cup dried apricots**
8 **fresh prune plums, cut in half and pitted**
2 **tablespoons fresh rosemary, chopped**
Salt and freshly ground pepper, to taste

- Rub pork loin all over with oil and coarse salt. Place in a 5 to 6-inch deep bowl or pan.

- Place all remaining ingredients into a saucepan and heat to simmering. Simmer 5 minutes.

- Pour warm marinade over pork and let cool to room temperature.

- Cover and place in refrigerator for at least 4 hours, turning pork occasionally.

- Prepare coals or wood chips for grilling.

- When coals are hot, remove pork from marinade and sear a few inches from heat on all sides until nicely browned.

- Adjust grill rack so that pork roast is about 4 to 5 inches from coals.

- Cover and cook pork, turning occasionally to desired doneness, 35 to 45 minutes.

- Boil marinade in saucepan, 1 to 2 minutes.

- Cut pork into ½-inch slices and spoon warm marinade over top.

Serves 6 to 8

Honey-Sesame Boneless Pork Tenderloin

½   **cup soy sauce**
2   **cloves garlic, minced**
1   **tablespoon fresh ginger, grated (or 1 teaspoon dried)**
1   **tablespoon sesame oil**
2-2½ **pounds boneless pork tenderloin**
¼   **cup honey**
2   **tablespoons brown sugar**
4   **tablespoons sesame seeds**

• Combine soy sauce, garlic, ginger and sesame oil.

• Pour over pork tenderloin.

• Marinate in refrigerator for at least 2 hours.

• Preheat oven to 400 degrees.

• Mix honey and sugar on a shallow plate.

• Roll marinated pork in the honey-sugar mixture and then in sesame seeds.

• Line shallow pan with foil. Place pork in pan and roast for 20 to 30 minutes or to an internal temperature of 160 degrees.

• Slice thinly to serve.

Serves 4 to 6

If using a pork loin roast, cook 30 minutes per pound at 350 degrees.

Marinated Cubed Pork Tenderloin on the Grill

3-4 pounds pork tenderloin
¾ teaspoon salt
¾ teaspoon freshly ground
pepper
1 tablespoon brown sugar
1 tablespoon coriander
1 tablespoon cumin
½ cup olive oil
4 tablespoons soy sauce
½ cup onions, sliced
Dash ground ginger
Mushroom caps
Green pepper, in chunks
Red pepper, in chunks
Cherry tomatoes
Onions, quartered
Juice of 2 limes, freshly
squeezed at serving time

• Cut pork into 1½-inch cubes.

• Make marinade using salt, pepper, sugar, coriander, cumin, olive oil, soy sauce and sliced onions.

• Pour marinade over pork and refrigerate for at least 6 to 8 hours.

• When ready to grill, alternate meat cubes and vegetables on skewers.

• Grill 15 to 20 minutes, turning and basting with marinade as they cook.

• Remove meat and vegetables to a heated serving platter. Squeeze juice of 2 limes over pork and vegetables before serving.

Serves 6 to 8

Pesto-Stuffed Grilled Pork

3   pounds boneless pork loin
⅔   cup packed, coarsely
     chopped basil leaves
⅓   cup Parmesan cheese,
     grated
2   tablespoons pine nuts or
     walnuts
½   teaspoon salt
⅜   teaspoon ground pepper,
     divided
⅓   cup olive oil
2   cloves garlic, divided
1   cup white wine
½   cup honey
½   cup Dijon mustard
¼   cup vegetable oil
1½ teaspoons dried rosemary
     (or 3 tablespoons fresh
     rosemary, chopped)

• Butterfly pork roast.

• To make pesto, combine basil, cheese, pine nuts, salt, ⅛ teaspoon pepper and olive oil.

• Mince 1 garlic clove and add to pesto.

• Place in a blender or food processor and purée.

• Spread pesto evenly on inside of roast. Roll and tie.

• To make marinade, crush 1 garlic clove.

• Combine garlic, wine, honey, mustard, vegetable oil, rosemary and ¼ teaspoon pepper. Combine well.

• Pour over stuffed roast. Refrigerate for at least 6 hours.

• Grill covered for 30 minutes per pound or until an internal temperature of 150 degrees is reached. Baste occasionally.

• Bring remaining marinade to a boil. Reduce heat and simmer 5 minutes. Serve with roast.

Serves 6

Roast can be baked in a 350 degree oven. Roast 20 to 30 minutes per pound or until internal temperature reads 150 degrees.

Gingered Pork Chops with Apricots

1   tablespoon vegetable oil

4   pork chops, 1-inch thick, trimmed of fat

2   shallots, chopped

1   clove garlic, minced

1   tablespoon fresh ginger, minced

¼   cup sherry

½   cup chicken stock

2   ounces dried apricots, cut in strips

¼   teaspoon dried sage

¼   teaspoon dried coriander

1   2-inch strip lemon zest

Salt and freshly ground pepper, to taste

- Heat the oil in a large skillet over medium-high heat. Brown chops on both sides, about 5 minutes. Remove pork from skillet.

- Soften shallots in the pan juices, cooking until they begin to brown.

- Add garlic, ginger and sherry. Deglaze pan, stirring to dissolve any sediment.

- Return pork to pan with chicken stock, apricots, sage, coriander and lemon zest.

- Over low heat, braise chops until just cooked through but still moist and tender inside, 15 to 20 minutes.

- Place chops on a serving platter and keep warm.

- Turn up the heat and cook liquid a few minutes to reduce to a sauce.

- Discard lemon zest and season to taste with salt and pepper.

- Spoon apricots and sauce over pork chops when ready to serve.

Serves 4

Fantastic Pork Fajitas

1   **pound lean boneless pork**

2   **cloves garlic, minced**

1   **teaspoon seasoned salt**

2   **tablespoons orange juice**

2   **tablespoons vinegar**

Dash Tabasco sauce

1   **tablespoon oil, divided**

1   **medium onion, peeled and sliced**

1   **green pepper, seeded and thinly sliced**

4   **flour tortillas**

Green onion tops, sliced, for garnish (optional)

Lettuce, shredded, for garnish (optional)

Salsa for garnish (optional)

- Slice pork across grain into ⅛-inch strips.

- Make marinade by combining garlic, seasoned salt, orange juice, vinegar and Tabasco sauce.

- Marinate pork strips for 10 minutes in marinade.

- Heat heavy griddle or skillet until hot.

- Add ½ tablespoon oil, onions and green pepper. Sauté. Remove from skillet.

- Add remaining ½ tablespoon oil and pork strips, sautéing until pork is no longer pink, about 2 minutes.

- Return vegetables to skillet and heat through.

- Serve with flour tortillas, green onion, lettuce and salsa.

Serves 4

Baby Back Ribs with Rhubarb Glaze

**3-3½   pounds pork loin back
            ribs**
½   teaspoon onion salt
½   teaspoon ground pepper
**¾-1   cup Rhubarb Glaze
            (recipe below)**

• Cut ribs into serving-sized pieces and place ribs in a Dutch oven.

• Add enough water to cover ribs. Bring to a boil and reduce heat.

• Cover and simmer 30 minutes.

• Drain ribs. Cool slightly. Season with onion salt and pepper.

• Place ribs on grill over medium heat. Cover and grill for 45 to 50 minutes until tender and no pink remains.

• Brush ribs with rhubarb glaze often during last 10 minutes of grilling.

• Heat any remaining glaze on grill or stove top until bubbling. Serve with ribs.

Serves 4

Rhubarb Glaze

**4   cups fresh or frozen
        rhubarb, sliced**
**¾   cup (6 ounces) frozen
        cranberry-apple juice
        cocktail concentrate**
2   tablespoons cornstarch
2   tablespoons water
⅓   cup honey
2   tablespoons Dijon mustard
1   tablespoon wine vinegar

• Combine rhubarb and cranberry-apple juice concentrate in a 2-quart saucepan.

• Bring to a boil and reduce heat.

• Cover and simmer for 15 minutes, or until rhubarb is tender.

• Strain mixture into a 2-cup liquid measure, pressing out liquid with back of a spoon.

(continued on next page)

Baby Back Ribs with Rhubarb Glaze continued

- Add water to equal 1¼ cups liquid. Discard pulp.

- In same saucepan, combine cornstarch with 2 tablespoons water. Stir in rhubarb liquid.

- Cook, stirring until thickened and bubbly. Cook for 2 minutes longer.

- Stir in honey, Dijon mustard and wine vinegar. Heat through.

Yield: 1¾ cups

Sauce may be kept refrigerated up to 5 days.

Vegetable Stuffed Pork Tenderloin

4   pounds boneless pork
    tenderloin or loin roast
½   cup butter
1   green pepper, chopped
1   medium onion, chopped
2   celery stalks, chopped
2   cloves garlic, minced
2   teaspoons ground black
    pepper
2   teaspoons salt
1   teaspoon ground white
    pepper
1   teaspoon cayenne pepper
1   teaspoon paprika
1   tablespoon fresh thyme,
    chopped, or 1 teaspoon
    dried thyme
½   teaspoon dry mustard

• Preheat oven to 325 degrees.

• If roast is tied, untie and unfold. Otherwise, cut a lengthwise slit in roast to make a long pocket. Set aside.

• In a hot skillet, melt butter and sauté green pepper, onion, celery and garlic until vegetables are soft, not brown.

• Stir in black pepper, salt, white pepper, cayenne, paprika, thyme and mustard.

• Fill pocket or place filling in center of roast, roll up and retie.

• Roast 20 to 30 minutes per pound or until internal temperature reads 150 degrees.

Serves 8 to 10

Fish & Seafood

Walden Pond

Walden Pond

In his final essay "Walking" published posthumously in 1862, Thoreau wrote, "Life consists with wildness. The most alive is the wildest. Not yet subdued to man, its presence refreshes him...In short, all good things are wild and free..." Thoreau may be one of the wildest, free spirits Concord ever produced. Thoreau often declared his life-long love of the place in which he was born and lived out his life. His good friend Emerson called Thoreau "The man of Concord," but the ripples of Thoreau's Concord life define so much more in American thought today. While Emerson talked about going out and truly seeing life with his "transparent eyeball," Thoreau actually lived the life that transcended daily, mundane dreariness and embraced the natural wildness of things. Emerson believed in and wrote about man's need to be "self-reliant," while Thoreau lived a life relying on and trusting in his own sure-footedness. Beyond Concord society and parlors, Thoreau searched for ways "...to live deep and suck out all the marrow of life..." Graduating from Harvard at age twenty, Thoreau determined that if he worked "...six weeks a year, I could meet all the expenses of living. The whole of my winters, as well as most of my summers, I had free and clear for study..." To that end, he worked as a land surveyor, drafting the boundaries of the Alcott and Hawthorne properties among many others. He was a periodic caretaker and gardener at the Emerson house. Having earned his support and accumulated free time, he spent his days walking four to six hours. Making a careful distinction between walking and what he called "sauntering," Thoreau literally defined the importance of "stopping to smell the roses" in daily American life. Of his retreat to Walden Pond, Thoreau wrote in Walden (1854), "I went to the woods because I wished to live deliberately..." There, he joined a purified society of trees, plants, sky, water, wind, critters, and land, and he declared they were all good company. Louisa May Alcott wrote upon his early death at age forty-four, "Our Pan is dead...(he) made one small spot a continent..." "The man of Concord" embraced his wild and free, self-reliant, deliberate life in the "small spot" of Concord and opened our minds to a "continent" of ideas and limitless possibilities.

Fish and Seafood

192

Fish in Crazy Water

2   pounds white-fleshed fish
    fillet (striped bass, sea
    bass, snapper)
2   cups mineral or filtered
    water
2   cups white wine
1   cup extra-virgin olive oil
12 red cherry tomatoes, firm
    and ripe, halved
2   fresh or dried hot chili
    peppers
2   cloves garlic, sliced
1   yellow onion, thickly sliced
6   sprigs of parsley
Salt and ground white or black
    pepper, to taste
Fresh herbs for garnish (basil,
    oregano, parsley, etc.)

Garlic Bruschetta
8   small slices French bread,
    toasted or grilled
1   clove garlic, split in half

• Rinse fish under cold water. Place fish in a large frying pan or stockpot and pour in water, wine, and oil to cover fish half way.

• Add tomatoes, peppers, garlic, onion, parsley, and salt and pepper to taste.

• Bring crazy water to a boil, reduce to simmer and partially cover.

• Cook for 20 to 25 minutes, basting fish occasionally with cooking liquid. To test fish, insert a fork in the thickest part of the fish and twist the fork. The flesh should be thoroughly opaque white and juicy. Remove from heat.

• To make garlic bruschetta, rub each piece of toast with the garlic.

• Place 2 garlic bruschetta on bottom of each serving bowl. Divide fish fillets into four portions and place on top of bruschetta. Ladle some of crazy water and vegetables over the fish. Garnish with fresh herbs as desired.

Serves 4

Island Fish

4 tablespoons plain yogurt
4 tablespoons mayonnaise
Zest of fresh lime
Juice of fresh lime
1 tablespoon fresh mint
  leaves, chopped
4 firm, fresh fish fillets
  (sole, mahi mahi),
  6 to 8 ounces each
½ cup croutons, crumbled
¼ cup slivered almonds
½ cup green seedless grapes,
  halved

- Preheat oven to 425 degrees.

- Mix together yogurt, mayonnaise, lime zest, lime juice, and mint.

- Place fish in ovenproof dish and cover with yogurt mixture. Sprinkle croutons and almonds on top.

- Bake for 8 to 10 minutes.

- Sprinkle grapes on top and serve.

Serves 4

Pan Seared Chilean Sea Bass with Orange Basil Cream

4   **portions Chilean sea bass, 6 to 8 ounces each**

Salt and freshly ground pepper, to taste

4   **tablespoons pure olive oil**

2   **medium shallot, diced**

2   **large cloves garlic, diced**

2   **tablespoons butter**

2   **cups dry white wine**

Juice of 2 oranges

2   **pinches of ground cumin seed**

12 **large fresh basil leaves, thinly sliced, stems removed and saved**

12 **ounces heavy cream**

Fresh lemon juice, to taste

- Preheat oven to 400 degrees.

- Pat sea bass dry and sprinkle with salt and pepper. Heat the olive oil until just smoking. Sear the fish in the hot oil for 2 to 3 minutes on each side until golden and crispy.

- Place the fish in an ovenproof dish and bake for approximately 8 minutes, or until done to taste.

- In a stainless steel pan, sauté the shallot and garlic in the butter until they are just beginning to brown. Add the wine and orange juice and reduce until syrupy.

- Add a pinch of ground cumin, the reserved basil stems and the heavy cream. Simmer gently until reduced by $1/3$. Adjust the sauce with salt and pepper and a few drops of lemon juice. To avoid curdling, be sure sauce has been reduced before adding lemon juice.

- Strain sauce and serve over fish, sprinkled with basil leaf slices.

Serves 4

195

Striped Bass with Beurre Blanc

4 **fresh striped bass fillets, 6 ounces each**

1 **tablespoon butter, softened**

4 **tablespoons shallot, minced, divided**

¾ **cup plus 2 tablespoons dry white wine or vermouth, divided**

1 **cup fish stock (or fish bouillon cubes to make 1 cup)**

⅓ **cup white wine vinegar**

2 **tablespoons heavy cream**

Salt and ground white pepper, to taste

1 **cup unsalted butter, cut into 16 pieces**

¼ **cup julienne carrots, blanched**

¼ **cup julienne celery, blanched**

¼ **cup julienne zucchini, blanched**

- Preheat oven to 400 degrees.

- Cut a piece of parchment paper to fit a large ovenproof skillet. Butter one side of the paper and set aside.

- Butter the skillet and sprinkle with 1 tablespoon of shallots. Arrange the bass fillets, seasoned with salt and pepper, in the pan in one layer.

- Add ¾ cup white wine and fish stock. Cover with the parchment paper, buttered side down, and bring the liquid just to a simmer on the stovetop.

- Place the skillet in the oven and poach the fish for 7 to 9 minutes. Transfer the fish with a slotted spatula to a plate and cover with foil to keep it warm.

- Combine 3 tablespoons shallot, the vinegar and 2 tablespoons wine in a heavy-bottomed saucepan. Cook over medium-high heat until the liquid is reduced to 2 tablespoons.

- Add the heavy cream and season with salt and pepper. Reduce to 2 tablespoons of liquid.

- Reduce the flame to low and whisk in 2 pieces of butter. When butter is just incorporated, whisk in another piece of butter and continue until all butter is added. Do not allow the sauce to become too hot. The sauce should be thick and

(continued on next page)

Striped Bass with Beurre Blanc continued

thoroughly combined. Remove the pan from the heat.

- Arrange the striped bass fillets on warm plates. Briefly reheat the julienne carrots, celery and zucchini in boiling water. Drain and sprinkle vegetables over the fillets.

- Pour the beurre blanc sauce around and over the fish and serve immediately.

Serves 4

Grilled Fresh Bluefish

½   **cup mayonnaise**
¼   **cup Dijon mustard**
2   **large fresh bluefish fillets, 6 to 8 ounces each**
Juice of 1 lemon

- Mix mayonnaise and mustard.

- Heavily coat skin side of fillets with mayonnaise mixture. Squeeze lemon juice over fillets.

- Place on grill, skin side down, at medium heat. Cook for about 5 minutes. Turn and cook for another 5 minutes. Carefully remove from grill.

Serves 2

Nantucket Grilled Bluefish

3   **pounds bluefish fillets**
5   **tablespoons extra-virgin olive oil**
Salt and freshly ground pepper, to taste
2   **tablespoons fresh rosemary, chopped**
1½ **tablespoons fresh lavender leaves, chopped**
2   **teaspoons fennel seeds, lightly crushed**
1   **teaspoon ground cumin**
Lemon wedges

• Place the bluefish fillets in a shallow bowl. Brush all over with the oil and sprinkle lightly with salt and pepper.

• Combine the rosemary, lavender, fennel and cumin. Sprinkle over the top of the fish fillets. Marinate at room temperature for 30 minutes.

• Prepare charcoal or wood chips for grilling.

• When the coals are ready, grill the fish, skin side down, a few inches from the heat, for about 5 minutes. With a large spatula, flip the fillets over and grill several minutes longer, until the fish is done.

• Serve immediately, garnished with lemon wedges.

Serves 6

Grilled Cod with Red Onion and Dill

¼   **cup mayonnaise**
2   **teaspoons Dijon mustard**
⅓   **cup red onion, finely chopped**
1   **tablespoon fresh lemon juice**
2   **tablespoons fresh dill, chopped**
Salt and freshly ground pepper, to taste
1   **pound cod fillets**

• In a small bowl, stir together the mayonnaise, mustard, onion, lemon juice, dill, salt and pepper.

• On a piece of aluminum foil, with edges rolled up, spread some of the mixture. Place the cod on the foil and spoon remaining mixture over the fillets.

• Cook in a covered grill for approximately 10 minutes or until fish flakes easily.

Serves 2

Cod Cakes with Scallions and Herbs

¾ **teaspoon salt, divided**
2 **pounds cod fillets**
1½ **cups dry bread crumbs, divided**
¼ **cup mayonnaise**
¼ **cup lemon juice**
1 **egg, beaten**
½ **red bell pepper, finely chopped (optional)**
4 **scallions, including green tops, minced**
2 **tablespoons fresh basil, chopped (optional)**
2 **tablespoons flat-leaf parsley, chopped**
Pinch cayenne
⅛ **teaspoon ground black pepper**
Cooking oil for frying

Lemon Mayonnaise
½ **cup mayonnaise**
2 **teaspoons lemon juice**
⅛ **teaspoon freshly ground black pepper**

- Place 1 inch of water in a large frying pan. Add ¼ teaspoon of salt and bring to a simmer. Place cod in the pan. Cook, covered, until just done, about 6 minutes.

- Remove the cod from the water and let cool. Pour out water and wipe the pan.

- With your fingers, flake the fish into a large bowl, removing any bones as you go.

- Add ¾ cup of bread crumbs, the mayonnaise, lemon juice, egg, bell pepper, scallions, basil, parsley, cayenne pepper, remaining ½ teaspoon salt and black pepper. Stir until well combined.

- Divide the cod mixture into 12 portions and shape into patties. Coat the patties with the remaining ¾ cup bread crumbs and pat off the excess.

- In the frying pan, heat ¼ inch of oil over moderate heat. Working in batches if necessary, fry the cakes until golden brown and crisp, about 2 minutes. Turn and fry until golden brown on the other side, about 2 minutes longer. Drain on paper towels.

- For Lemon Mayonnaise, in a small bowl, stir mayonnaise, lemon juice and black pepper together. Serve the cod cakes with the lemon mayonnaise.

Serves 4

199

Spicy Codfish Cakes Rémoulade

3 **pounds codfish fillets, poached in water until just tender and drained**
1 **small red onion, minced**
4 **scallions, bulbs and stalks, chopped**
2 **ribs of celery, minced**
2 **red bell peppers, seeded and diced**
½ **cup fresh parsley, minced**
8 **cups fresh bread crumbs, divided**
3 **tablespoons Dijon mustard**
1 **teaspoon dried thyme**
1½ **teaspoons cayenne pepper**
½ **teaspoon Worcestershire sauce**
4 **large eggs, divided**
1 **cup mayonnaise**
Salt and freshly ground pepper, to taste
1 **cup unbleached flour, seasoned lightly with salt and pepper**
½ **cup light cream**
3 **tablespoons unsalted butter, more if needed**
Rémoulade Sauce (recipe follows)
Lemon wedges for garnish
Sprigs of parsley for garnish

- Flake the codfish in a large mixing bowl using a wooden spoon. Add the onion, scallions, celery, peppers and parsley and toss to combine.

- Add 3 cups of the bread crumbs, the mustard, thyme, cayenne, and Worcestershire sauce. Toss to combine thoroughly.

- Beat 2 of the eggs into the codfish mixture until well blended. Fold in the mayonnaise and season the mixture with salt and pepper.

- Place the seasoned flour in a small bowl. Beat the remaining 2 eggs with the light cream in a second bowl. Place remaining 5 cups of bread crumbs in a third bowl.

- Using hands, form codfish mixture into patties 3 inches in diameter. Dip each patty lightly but thoroughly in the flour mixture, then in the egg mixture, and finally in the bread crumbs, being sure they are coated all over. Place the patties in a single layer on a flat tray as they are formed. There should be about 16 codfish cakes.

- Melt the butter in a large frying pan over medium heat. Add as many codfish cakes as will comfortably fit in the pan and fry, turning once, until golden brown on both sides, about 4 or 5 minutes per side. Keep the codfish cakes warm while cooking the rest. Add more butter to the pan as needed.

(continued on next page)

Spicy Codfish Cakes Rémoulade continued

Serve the codfish cakes with a generous dollop of the Rémoulade Sauce. Garnish with lemon wedges and sprigs of parsley.

Serves 8

Rémoulade Sauce

1 **large egg**
2 **large egg yolks**
6 **anchovy fillets, drained**
2 **tablespoons capers, drained**
4 **cornichons, minced**
2 **cloves garlic, minced**
2 **tablespoons Dijon mustard**
⅓ **cup fresh parsley, minced**
2 **tablespoons fresh tarragon, minced, or 1 tablespoon dried tarragon**
2 **tablespoons balsamic vinegar**
2 **tablespoons fresh lemon juice**
1¾ **cups olive oil**
Salt and freshly ground pepper, to taste

• Place egg, egg yolks, anchovies, capers, cornichons, garlic, mustard, parsley, tarragon, vinegar and lemon juice in a food processor fitted with a steel blade to combine, 15 seconds. With the machine running, pour the oil through the feed tube in a thin, steady stream to make a thick mixture. Season the sauce with salt and pepper to taste. Store in the refrigerator for up to 1 week.

Yield: 2½ cups

Sesame Cod

¼ **cup fresh orange juice**
1 **tablespoon brown sugar**
2 **tablespoons ketchup**
2 **tablespoons soy sauce**
1 **tablespoon lemon juice**
1 **teaspoon vegetable oil**
¼ **teaspoon ground pepper**
4 **cod (4 ounces each) or other fish fillets**
1 **tablespoon sesame seeds, toasted**

• Place orange juice, brown sugar, ketchup, soy sauce, lemon juice, oil and pepper in a small bowl. Stir well to combine.

• Arrange fillets in a single layer in a baking dish.

• Pour orange juice mixture over fillets, cover and marinate fillets in refrigerator 2 hours, turning once.

• Remove fillets from marinade, reserving marinade.

• Pour marinade into a small saucepan. Bring to a boil, reduce heat, and simmer 5 minutes. Set half of marinade aside.

• Place fillets on a lightly greased rack in a shallow roasting pan. Broil fillets 6 inches from heat for 10 to 12 minutes or until fish flakes easily when tested with a fork. Baste occasionally with marinade.

• Transfer fillets to a serving platter. Sprinkle toasted sesame seeds evenly over fillets. Serve fillets with reserved marinade.

Serves 4

Camembert Crab Soufflé

¼ **cup celery, finely chopped**
2 **tablespoons green onion, chopped**
1 **small clove garlic, minced**
3 **tablespoons butter or margarine**
3 **tablespoons flour**
1 **teaspoon dry mustard**
¾ **teaspoon salt**
Dash of pepper
1 **cup milk**
5 **ounces Camembert cheese, rind removed, cubed**
1 **can (6 ounce) crabmeat, drained, flaked, cartilage removed**
5 **egg yolks**
7 **egg whites**

- Butter one side of a foil strip 3 or 4 inches wide and long enough to circle a 2-quart soufflé dish. Secure strip around top edge of dish, extending it 2 inches above edge.

- Cook celery, onion and garlic in butter until tender.

- Blend in flour, mustard, salt and pepper.

- Add milk all at once and cook until bubbly.

- Add cheese and crab. Stir to melt cheese. Remove from heat.

- Beat egg yolks 5 minutes, or until lemon colored. Add cheese mixture to yolks, stirring constantly. Wash beaters.

- Beat egg whites to stiff peaks. Stir ¼ of the egg whites into the yolk mixture. Gently fold in the rest of the whites, until well mixed.

- Turn into the prepared ungreased soufflé dish. Trace a 1-inch deep circle through the mixture, 1 inch from the edge.

- Bake for 40 minutes or until a knife inserted in the center comes out clean. Remove foil collar. Serve immediately.

Serves 6

Do not butter soufflé dish. Eggs will climb up sides of ungreased dish.

Crab Cakes with Salsa and Lemon Butter

Salsa

2   cups plum tomatoes, diced
½   cup yellow onion, diced
¼   cup fresh cilantro, chopped
1   tablespoon garlic, minced
¼   cup fresh lemon juice
2   tablespoons fresh lime
     juice
1   teaspoon salt
½   teaspoon ground black
     pepper

Lemon Butter

1   lemon, peeled and
     quartered
1   shallot, minced
¼   cup white wine
1   bay leaf
1½   teaspoons whole black
     peppercorns
1   cup unsalted butter, cut
     into pieces
¾   teaspoon salt
⅛   teaspoon ground white
     pepper

Salsa

- Combine tomatoes, onion, cilantro, garlic, lemon juice, lime juice, salt and pepper in a small bowl. Cover and chill.

Lemon Butter

- Combine lemon quarters, shallot, wine, bay leaf and peppercorns in a heavy saucepan. Cook over low heat, reducing liquid to approximately a tablespoon. Strain liquid. Reserve. Discard bay leaf, peppercorns and lemon quarters.

- Over low heat, whisk butter, one piece at a time, into strained liquid, melting butter before adding more pieces. Do not allow mixture to boil. Add salt and pepper. Set aside and keep warm.

(continued on next page)

Crab Cakes with Salsa and Lemon Butter continued

Crab Cakes

5   tablespoons extra-virgin olive oil, divided

½   cup red bell pepper, diced

½   cup green bell pepper, diced

½   cup yellow bell pepper, diced

2   tablespoons garlic, minced

2   tablespoons Creole mustard or other coarse grain mustard

2   tablespoons Worcestershire sauce

Pinch cayenne pepper

1   teaspoon salt

½   teaspoon ground black pepper

½   cup bread crumbs

2   large eggs, lightly beaten

1½   pounds cooked fresh lump crabmeat, shells removed

½   cup green onions, minced

3   tablespoons unsalted butter

Crab Cakes

- Heat 2 tablespoons of olive oil in a large skillet. Add bell peppers, onion and garlic. Sauté until tender.

- Add mustard, Worcestershire sauce, cayenne pepper, salt and black pepper. Stir to combine.

- Add bread crumbs and sauté 1 to 2 minutes. Remove from heat. Place mixture in a large bowl.

- Fold in eggs, stirring to blend.

- Stir in crabmeat and green onions. Mix well. Chill 30 to 40 minutes.

- Shape mixture into 12 small cakes, about ⅓ cup each.

- Heat 1 tablespoon olive oil and 1 tablespoon butter in large skillet. Sauté crabmeat cakes on both sides until golden brown, 4 cakes at a time. Repeat with remaining crab cakes, adding additional olive oil and butter as needed.

- Spoon lemon butter onto serving plate. Place crab cakes on the butter and top each with a dollop of salsa.

Serves 4

Crabmeat and Mushrooms in Wine

1   **pound fresh lump crabmeat**
¼   **cup butter or margarine**
¼   **pound mushrooms, sliced**
2   **tablespoons flour**
½   **cup milk**
½   **cup white wine**
½   **teaspoon dry mustard**
¼   **teaspoon tarragon**
¼   **teaspoon salt**
Dash of pepper
½   **cup cut pimiento (optional)**

- Preheat oven to 350 degrees. Grease casserole.

- Flake crabmeat. Remove membranes. Set aside.

- Melt butter in saucepan and sauté mushrooms for 5 minutes.

- Stir in flour. Gradually add milk and wine. Cook over low heat, stirring constantly until thickened and smooth. Stir in mustard, tarragon, salt, pepper, crabmeat and pimiento.

- Turn into casserole. Bake for 30 minutes.

Serves 4

Tidewater Crab Cakes

2	**large eggs**
½	**cup celery, finely chopped**
1	**cup saltine crackers, crushed**
1	**tablespoon Dijon mustard**
1	**teaspoon Old Bay seasoning**
½	**teaspoon red pepper flakes**
2	**teaspoons Worcestershire sauce**
3	**tablespoons parsley, chopped**
½	**cup scallions, finely chopped**
	Salt and freshly ground pepper, to taste
1	**pound lump crabmeat, cartilage removed**
½	**cup fresh bread crumbs**
2	**tablespoons unsalted butter**
2	**tablespoons vegetable oil**

- Combine eggs, celery, saltines, mustard, Old Bay seasoning, pepper flakes, Worcestershire sauce, parsley, scallions, salt and pepper. Blend well.

- Fold in crabmeat very gently.

- Divide the crabmeat mixture into 8 to 10 equal portions. Shape into flat patties.

- Dredge patties in bread crumbs and place on foil-lined cookie sheet. Cover and refrigerate for at least 30 minutes.

- Heat the butter and oil in a large, non-stick skillet. Add patties and sauté over medium-high heat for 2 to 3 minutes on each side, or until golden and lightly crisped. Drain on paper towel.

Serves 4 to 5

Herb Grilled Salmon with Vidalia Relish

¾   **cup tomatoes, peeled, seeded and chopped**

2   **tablespoons fresh basil, chopped**

2   **teaspoons white wine vinegar**

2   **teaspoons olive oil**

¼   **teaspoon salt**

⅛   **teaspoon pepper**

⅛-¼ **teaspoon Tabasco sauce**

6   **salmon steaks, 6 ounces each**

Vegetable cooking spray

Vidalia Relish (recipe follows)

• Place tomatoes, basil, vinegar, oil, salt, pepper, and Tabasco sauce in a food processor and process until smooth.

• Pour into a shallow dish. Add salmon, turning to coat.

• Cover and marinate in refrigerator for 30 minutes, turning occasionally.

• Remove salmon, reserving marinade.

• Prepare grill.

• Place salmon on grill rack coated with cooking spray and grill 8 minutes on each side, or until fish flakes easily when tested with a fork. Baste occasionally with reserved marinade.

• Serve with Vidalia relish.

Serves 6

(continued on next page)

Herb Grilled Salmon with Vidalia Relish continued

Vidalia Relish

3   cups Vidalia or other sweet
      onions, ¼-inch sliced
      Olive oil cooking spray
1   cup tomatoes, seeded and
      diced
2   tablespoons fresh basil,
      thinly sliced
1½ tablespoons jalapeño
      pepper, seeded and
      chopped
2   teaspoons extra-virgin
      olive oil
2   teaspoons white wine
      vinegar
⅛   teaspoon salt
⅛   teaspoon pepper

- Preheat oven to 400 degrees.

- Arrange onion slices in a single layer on a jelly-roll pan coated with cooking spray. Bake for 15 minutes.

- Turn over the onion slices and bake an additional 25 minutes or until tender and lightly browned. Let cool.

- Coarsely chop onion. Combine chopped onion, tomatoes, basil, jalapeño, olive oil, vinegar, salt and pepper in a bowl. Stir well.

- Let stand at room temperature 20 minutes before serving.

Serves 6 (⅓ cup each)

Pan Seared Salmon Malaysian Style with Ginger Sauce

7	**ounces dried mushrooms, divided**
3	**cups fish stock**
5	**tablespoons peanut oil, divided**
4	**tablespoons garlic, chopped**
4	**tablespoons shallots, chopped**
6	**tablespoons fresh ginger, chopped**
½	**cup rice wine or dry sherry**
5	**tablespoons cornstarch**
8	**(6 ounce) salmon fillets**

Salt and freshly ground pepper, to taste

- Soak dried mushrooms overnight in fish stock and keep refrigerated.

- When ready to prepare sauce, drain mushrooms in a strainer and press all remaining juice out of mushrooms. Reserve stock and mushrooms separately.

- Cut one third of the mushrooms into julienne strips and set aside.

- Preheat oven to 375 degrees.

- In a heated saucepan, add 2 tablespoons peanut oil. Add garlic, shallots and ginger and sauté until moist.

- Add uncut mushrooms and all of the reserved stock to the pan and simmer for 5 minutes.

- Remove from heat and add julienned mushrooms. Adjust seasoning.

- Mix cornstarch with wine until smooth. Add to stock, stirring constantly, until slightly thickened.

- Remove sauce from heat and keep warm.

- Season fillets with salt and pepper.

(continued on next page)

Pan Seared Salmon Malaysian Style with Ginger Sauce continued

- Add remaining 3 tablespoons peanut oil to a heated oven proof sauté pan. Pan sear salmon on both sides until lightly brown.

- Remove salmon from heat and finish cooking in the oven for 3 to 5 minutes.

- Serve salmon with sauce.

Serves 8

Bay Scallops with Lemon and Dill

Non-stick vegetable oil spray
2 tablespoons butter
⅔ cup dry vermouth
½ teaspoon grated lemon peel
¼ teaspoon fresh ground pepper
1½ pounds bay scallops
1 tablespoon fresh lemon juice
¼ cup fresh dill, chopped, or ½ teaspoon dried dill, or more to taste

- Coat skillet generously with spray. Add butter and melt.

- Add scallops and stir until almost pink, about 2 minutes. Transfer to bowl.

- Add vermouth, lemon peel and lemon juice to skillet and heat until reduced to a thick glaze, about 5 minutes. Add any juices exuded from the scallops and boil until reduced to a glaze.

- Return scallops to skillet and stir until coated with glaze.

- Mix in dill and pepper. Serve immediately.

Serves 4

211

Baked Salmon with Creole Mustard Sauce

1   **cup whipping cream**
¾   **cup Creole mustard or other coarse grained mustard**
4   **teaspoons Worcestershire sauce**
1   **tablespoon Dijon mustard**
¾   **teaspoon ground black pepper**
¼   **teaspoon ground white pepper**
½   **teaspoon dried basil or 1 tablespoon fresh, chopped basil**
¼   **teaspoon cayenne pepper**
2   **center-cut salmon fillets, 1½ pounds each (or one 3 pound fillet)**
¼   **cup unsalted butter, melted**
3   **tablespoons golden brown sugar**
3   **tablespoons soy sauce**
2   **tablespoons fresh lemon juice**
2   **tablespoons dry white wine**
1   **cup sour cream**

- In a small saucepan, combine cream, Creole mustard, Worcestershire sauce, Dijon mustard, black and white peppers, basil, and cayenne pepper. Simmer, stirring frequently, until very thick, about 5 minutes. Cover and refrigerate.

- Line a large baking pan with foil. Arrange fish, skin side down, in single layer on foil.

- Mix butter, brown sugar, soy sauce, lemon juice and wine in a bowl. Pour over fish. Cover and refrigerate at least 1 hour, up to 6 hours.

- Preheat oven to 400 degrees.

- Uncover fish and bake until just cooked through, basting occasionally with pan drippings, about 18 minutes.

- Meanwhile, rewarm sauce over low heat, stirring constantly. Add 1 cup sour cream and whisk just until heated through. Do not boil. Season sauce to taste with salt.

- Arrange salmon on platter. Serve sauce separately.

Serves 8

Sauce can be prepared up to 1 day in advance.

Bayside Enchiladas

1	cup sour cream
½	cup salsa
6	soft flour tortillas
½	pound uncooked medium shrimp, shelled and deveined
½	pound bay scallops
8	ounces Monterey jack cheese, shredded
¼	cup cottage cheese
¼	cup milk
2	tablespoons Parmesan cheese, grated
¼	cup scallions, chopped
6-8	pitted black olives, sliced

- Preheat oven to 350 degrees.

- Combine sour cream and salsa.

- Place tortillas on a flat surface. Spoon 3 to 4 tablespoons of sour cream mixture on each tortilla.

- Place shrimp and scallops across middle of the tortilla. Sprinkle 3 to 4 tablespoons of shredded cheese over seafood and roll up the tortillas.

- Lightly grease a 9x13-inch baking dish and place the filled tortillas seam side down in the dish.

- Blend the cottage cheese, milk and Parmesan cheese in a processor. Pour over tortillas.

- Sprinkle with chopped scallions and olives. Bake for 30 minutes.

Serves 4 to 6

New England Shellfish Stew

4 tablespoons olive oil

2 cups yellow onions, finely chopped

2 red peppers, stemmed, seeded and coarsely diced

1 green pepper, stemmed, seeded and coarsely diced

6-8 cloves garlic, peeled and finely chopped

2 cups fish stock (or bottled clam juice or fish bouillon cubes to make 2 cups)

2 cups hearty red wine

1 can (35 ounce) peeled plum tomatoes, drained

1½ tablespoons dried basil

1 teaspoon dried thyme

1 bay leaf

Salt and freshly ground pepper, to taste

Red pepper flakes, to taste

1 can (6 ounce) tomato paste

8 mussels

8 small clams, Little Necks or Cherrystones

8 large shrimp, peeled and deveined

¾ pound bay scallops

1 cup flat-leaf parsley, chopped

• Heat the oil in a large soup kettle. Add the onions, red and green peppers and garlic. Cook over low heat, covered, until vegetables are tender, about 25 minutes.

• Add fish stock, wine and tomatoes and raise the heat. Stir in the basil, thyme and bay leaf, and season to taste with salt, pepper and red pepper flakes. Add tomato paste.

• Bring the soup to a boil, reduce heat and simmer, partially covered, for 30 minutes. Stir occasionally, crushing the tomatoes with the spoon. Taste and correct the seasoning. Soup may be made to this point the day before. It improves with refrigeration.

• Scrub the mussels and clams well and debeard the mussels. Place them in the bottom of a heavy kettle, add an inch of water, cover, and set over high heat. As they steam open, remove them one by one with a slotted spoon and reserve.

• Rinse the shrimp and scallops and pat dry.

• Five minutes before serving the stew, bring the tomato and wine mixture to a boil. Drop in shrimp and scallops, then clams and mussels in their shells. Add the parsley, stir well, and remove from heat. Let stand, covered, for 1 minute.

(continued on next page)

New England Shellfish Stew continued

- Ladle the stew into heated bowls, dividing the seafood evenly.

Serves 4

You can vary the shellfish, adding lobster, squid, Dungeness crab or other favorites.

Freeze the shellfish juices for your next batch of fish stock.

Provençal Shrimp Sauté

2	teaspoons olive oil
1	pound uncooked shrimp, shelled and deveined
2	tablespoons slivered almonds, toasted
4	cloves garlic, minced
1	tablespoon capers, drained
2	tomatoes, cored and chopped
1	tablespoon fresh parsley, minced
¼	teaspoon salt

Freshly ground pepper, to taste

- Heat a large heavy, non-stick skillet over medium heat until hot. Add the olive oil.

- Add the shrimp and sauté 1½ minutes.

- Add the almonds and garlic and sauté until shrimp are cooked.

- Stir in the capers, tomatoes and parsley. Cook for 1 minute. Stir in salt and pepper.

Serves 4

Shrimp Curry

1   **large onion, chopped**
1   **green apple, cored and chopped, skin on**
2   **large stalks celery, chopped**
5   **tablespoons butter**
1-2 **tablespoons curry powder**
½   **teaspoon paprika**
Dash of nutmeg
4   **tablespoons flour**
1   **cup chicken broth**
Dash of Worcestershire sauce
1   **cup light cream**
3   **cups cooked shrimp**
Salt and freshly ground pepper, to taste

• Sauté onions, apple and celery in butter until transparent.

• Add curry, paprika and nutmeg and cook 3 to 4 minutes.

• Add flour and cook 2 to 3 minutes, stirring constantly.

• Add broth and Worcestershire sauce, stirring until thickened.

• Add cream. Stir until thickened and smooth. Add shrimp.

• Heat through and add salt and pepper to taste.

Serves 4

Serve over rice with bowls of condiments: raisins, chopped parsley, chutney, flaked coconut, chopped peanuts, bacon bits, or chopped hard-boiled egg.

Shrimp with Water Chestnuts

⅓ cup salad oil

1 **pound uncooked shrimp, shelled and deveined**

1 **clove garlic, minced**

1 **large onion, chopped**

½ **pound mushrooms, sliced**

1 **can (8 ounce) water chestnuts, drained and thinly sliced**

2 **tablespoons cornstarch**

2 **tablespoons pale dry sherry**

½ **teaspoon sugar**

1 **teaspoon salt**

1 **tablespoon soy sauce**

1 **can (13.5 ounce) chicken broth**

4 **cups cooked rice**

• Place the oil in a large skillet over medium-high heat. Add the garlic, onion and mushrooms and cook 2 to 3 minutes. Add water chestnuts.

• In a small bowl, combine cornstarch and sherry. Stir until dissolved. Stir in sugar, salt, soy sauce and chicken broth.

• Pour mixture over vegetables. Stir over medium heat 2 to 3 minutes until thickened. Add shrimp. Cook until just pink. Serve over rice.

Serves 4

Spicy Shrimp

½   **cup olive oil**

2   **tablespoons Cajun or Creole seasoning**

2   **tablespoons fresh lemon juice**

2   **tablespoons fresh parsley, chopped**

1   **tablespoon honey**

1   **tablespoon soy sauce**

Pinch of cayenne pepper

1½ **teaspoons dry mustard**

1   **pound uncooked large shrimp, shelled and deveined**

Lemon wedges

1   **pound fresh asparagus, cooked**

1   **pound pasta, cooked**

• Combine olive oil, Creole seasoning, lemon juice, parsley, honey, soy sauce, cayenne pepper and dry mustard in a 9x13-inch baking dish.

• Add shrimp. Toss to coat. Refrigerate 1 hour.

• Preheat oven to 450 degrees.

• Bake until shrimp are cooked through, stirring occasionally, for about 10 minutes.

• Add fresh cooked asparagus.

• Serve shrimp over your favorite pasta. Garnish with lemon wedges.

Serves 4

Sole Stuffed with Crabmeat

¼ **cup onion, finely chopped**
¼ **cup celery, finely chopped**
6 **tablespoons butter, divided**
1 **can (7.5 ounce) crabmeat, flaked**
½ **cup fresh bread crumbs or ¼ cup dried crumbs**
1 **egg, slightly beaten**
6 **sole fillets**
½ **cup white wine**
½ **cup heavy cream**
½ **pound mushrooms, sliced**

- Preheat oven to 350 degrees.

- Sauté onions and celery in 2 tablespoons of the butter. Add crabmeat, bread crumbs and egg.

- Divide breadcrumb stuffing in 6 portions. Wrap each fillet around a portion of stuffing and place in a buttered baking dish.

- Pour wine over the fish and dot with 2 tablespoons butter.

- Bake for 10 to 15 minutes, or until fish is cooked through.

- While fish is baking, sauté the mushrooms in 2 tablespoons of butter in the same pan used for the onions and celery. Set aside.

- When fish is cooked, place fillets on warm platter. Mix cream into liquid in baking dish. Transfer liquid to a saucepan and add sautéed mushrooms. Reduce by boiling for 5 to 10 minutes. When sauce has thickened, pour over fillets and serve.

Serves 6

219

Grilled Swordfish -Turkish Style

3   **pounds fresh swordfish, cut into 1-inch chunks**

¾   **cup fresh lemon juice**

½   **cup olive oil**

2   **cloves garlic, finely minced**

1   **medium red onion, cut into thin rings**

Salt and freshly ground black pepper, to taste

36   **bay leaves**

2   **yellow bell peppers, seeded and cut into ¾ inch chunks**

- Place the swordfish in a shallow bowl.

- Whisk the lemon juice and oil together in a small bowl. Stir in garlic and onion. Season to taste with salt and pepper.

- Pour the marinade over the swordfish. Cover the bowl and marinate, tossing occasionally, in the refrigerator for 6 hours.

- Prepare charcoal or wood chips for grilling.

- Cover the bay leaves with boiling water in a small bowl. Let stand for 10 minutes to soften. Drain thoroughly.

- Thread the swordfish chunks alternately with the bay leaves on 6 metal skewers. Every third piece or so, thread a bell pepper chunk on the skewer.

- Grill the swordfish skewers a few inches from medium-hot coals, basting occasionally with the marinade and turning the skewers every 5 minutes or so, until just cooked through, about 15 minutes.

Serves 6

Oriental Swordfish

1 tablespoon butter
1 tablespoon honey
1 tablespoon brown sugar
2 tablespoons soy sauce
3 tablespoons Dijon mustard
1 tablespoon olive oil
1 teaspoon fresh ginger, mint or garlic
2 pounds swordfish

- In a small saucepan, heat butter, honey, sugar, soy sauce, mustard, olive oil and ginger until blended. Cool.

- Pour over fish and marinate 30 minutes.

- Grill fish. Brush marinade on fish while grilling.

Serves 4 to 6

May substitute fish of your choice.

Grilled Tuna Vera Cruz

2 pounds fresh tuna steaks
½ cup vegetable oil, divided
¼ cup lime juice
2 onions, sliced
3 cloves garlic, minced
4 large tomatoes, peeled and quartered
½ cup green olives, sliced
Salt and freshly ground pepper, to taste

- Brush tuna with ¼ cup oil and sprinkle with lime juice. Cook on hot grill until thickest part of fish is done.

- Meanwhile, make sauce by heating ¼ cup vegetable oil in a saucepan. Sauté onions and garlic until tender.

- Add tomatoes and olives. Cook over medium heat 6 to 8 minutes or until sauce is slightly thickened. Season with salt and pepper. Pour over grilled tuna.

Serves 4 to 6

Tuna Steaks with Wasabi Butter

¼	cup Oriental sesame oil
½	cup vegetable oil
¼	cup rice wine vinegar
2	tablespoons sweet vermouth
1	tablespoon brown sugar
¼	cup soy sauce
2	tablespoons fresh ginger, chopped
3	cloves garlic, minced
3-3½	pounds tuna steaks, about 1½-inch thick
½	cup unsalted butter
1½	teaspoons wasabi paste (or more to taste)
3	tablespoons fresh coriander, chopped

• At least 4 hours before grilling the tuna, whisk the sesame oil, vegetable oil, vinegar, vermouth, brown sugar and soy sauce together in a small bowl. Stir in the ginger and garlic.

• Pour the marinade over the tuna steaks in a shallow bowl. Cover and marinate in the refrigerator at least 4 hours, turning the fish occasionally.

• Meanwhile, prepare the wasabi butter by beating the butter and wasabi paste together in a small bowl until creamy. Beat in the coriander until well blended. Store in a cool place.

• Prepare charcoal or wood chips for grilling

• When the coals are hot, remove the tuna steaks from the marinade and grill a few inches from the heat just until cooked through, 5 minutes on each side. Baste occasionally with the marinade to keep it moist.

• When the tuna is cooked, cut it into serving portions and top each serving with a heaping tablespoon of the wasabi butter.

Serves 6

Wasabi paste is available at most specialty food stores.

Creole Seafood Supreme Casserole

8   ounces cream cheese
½   cup butter, divided
1½ pounds uncooked shrimp, peeled
6-7 green onions, sliced
1   small red bell pepper, seeded and chopped
3   ribs celery, thinly sliced
2-3 cans (10.75 ounce) condensed cream of mushroom soup, undiluted
6   ounces mushrooms, sliced
1   teaspoon Tabasco sauce
1   teaspoon garlic salt, or to taste
1   teaspoon Worcestershire sauce
½   teaspoon cayenne pepper
2   pounds crabmeat
1   tablespoon lemon juice
4-5 cups cooked rice
2   cups Cheddar cheese, grated
Cracker crumbs
Paprika

- Preheat oven to 350 degrees.

- Melt cream cheese and 6 tablespoons butter in the top of double boiler or in microwave oven. Set aside.

- Sauté shrimp, green onions, bell pepper, celery and mushrooms in remaining 2 tablespoons butter until soft.

- In large bowl, combine mushroom soup, Tabasco, garlic salt, Worcestershire sauce and cayenne pepper.

- Add cream cheese mixture, sautéed vegetables and shrimp. Stir to combine.

- Sprinkle crabmeat with lemon juice. Stir crabmeat carefully into shrimp mixture. Stir in cooked rice.

- Spoon into greased 3-quart casserole dish. Top with Cheddar cheese, then sprinkle with cracker crumbs and paprika.

- Bake 30 minutes, or until heated through and bubbly.

Yield: Serves 10 to 12

New England Seafood Casserole

1½ pounds fresh or frozen
uncooked jumbo shrimp
(fresh preferred), shelled
and deveined
½ pound fresh or canned
crabmeat
1 pound fresh lobster meat,
cut into bite-sized pieces
1 cup celery, finely chopped
½ cup green pepper, finely
chopped
1 tablespoon Worcestershire
sauce
1 small onion, finely chopped
1 cup mayonnaise
Fresh bread crumbs, enough to
cover top
½ cup butter, melted

• Preheat oven to 350 degrees.

• In a large bowl, mix together shrimp, crab-meat, lobster, celery, green pepper, Worcestershire sauce, onion and mayonnaise.

• Place in buttered casserole dish. Sprinkle top with bread crumbs. Drizzle with melted butter.

• Bake for 30 minutes, until bubbling and slightly browned.

Serves 8

Serve over rice.

Lobster Newberg

1¼ **cups butter, divided**
½   **cup flour**
4   **cups whole milk**
4   **cups heavy cream**
4   **teaspoons salt**
2   **teaspoons paprika**
4   **cups lobster (about 2 pounds), cooked and cubed**
½   **cup sherry**
1   **cup Swiss cheese, shredded**
1   **cup mushrooms, sliced**

- Melt ½ cup butter in 4-quart saucepan over moderate heat.

- Blend in flour.

- Gradually add milk and cream.

- Cook and stir constantly until smooth and thickened.

- Add salt and paprika.

- Melt additional ½ cup butter in large skillet over low heat and add lobster.

- Add sherry and cook about 5 minutes until liquid is absorbed.

- Stir lobster into cream sauce.

- Melt ¼ cup butter in small skillet and sauté sliced mushrooms.

- Stir mushrooms and Swiss cheese into prepared lobster newberg.

- Heat gently just before serving.

Serves 8 to 10

Steamed Clams

8   **dozen steamer or small soft-shell or long-neck clams**

4   **tablespoons butter, cut into ½-inch bits, plus ½ pound butter, melted**

½   **cup fresh parsley, finely chopped**

3   **cups water**

Cheesecloth

• Wash clams thoroughly under cold running water, discarding any with broken shells as well as those whose necks do not retract when prodded gently with a finger.

• In an 8 to 10-quart steamer or casserole, melt 4 tablespoons butter bits over moderate heat.

• When foam begins to subside, add onions. Cook, stirring constantly, 5 minutes or until onions are translucent.

• Stir in parsley and water. Bring to a boil over high heat.

• Add clams, cover tightly and steam 5 to 8 minutes, turning them in the pot once or twice with a slotted spoon. Discard any clams that remain closed.

• With tongs or a slotted spoon, transfer clams to a deep heated platter or serving bowl.

• Strain broth through a sieve lined with a double thickness of damp cheesecloth set over a bowl.

(continued on next page)

Steamed Clams continued

- Pour broth into 4 heated soup cups. Pour melted butter into 4 separate cups.

Serves 4

To eat a steamed clam, remove it from shell with a small fork or fingers. Remove skin from neck of clam. Dip clam into broth to moisten and remove any trace of sand. Then immerse it in the melted butter.

Although steamers taste best when fresh, they can be safely kept in the refrigerator for 2 or 3 days. Place them in a bowl or pan and store them uncovered so clams can breathe. Do not wash them until you are ready to steam them.

New England Traditional Clambake

6   cups water
Wet celery, lettuce or spinach
3   chickens, split
6   ears corn, soaked in salted
    water 1 hour
48 small clams, cleaned
6   lobsters, 1-pound each
1   baking potato
Several packages cheesecloth

- Place water in 24-quart steamer. Place a large layer of greens on bottom.

- Wrap chicken in cheesecloth. Tie at ends and place on greens.

- Wrap corn in cheesecloth. Place on chicken.

- Wrap clams in cheesecloth, 12 clams to a bundle. Place on corn.

- Wrap lobsters in cheesecloth and place on top of clams.

- Cover lobsters with thick layer of greens.

- Place 1 potato on top of greens.

- Steam 1 to 1½ hours. When potato is cooked, clambake is ready.

Serves 6

Vegetables

the Emerson House

The Emerson House

Ralph Waldo Emerson's hats and walking sticks still stand by the side door of the home he bought for his family in 1835. The four Emerson children were born here, and Mr. Emerson called the large white house "home" until his death there forty-seven years later in 1882. When not on tour or lecturing, his homelife was regulated and ordered. He rose early, breakfasted with his family, set out on the one mile walk to town, visited the grocer, butcher, and post office, and stopped along the way for greetings and conversation. Returning home, he went to his study to write and think before dinner at one o'clock; afternoons would typically find him in his study once again. The house's location was ideal for this private public man; it was in the village of Concord, but away from the center of town. It afforded wide meadow views and a buffer of grass and trees from the town, while providing large parlors and gathering spots for the continual stream of visitors coming to talk with Mr. Emerson. Among those many guests were Concord neighbors Bronson Alcott, Nathaniel Hawthorne, Henry David Thoreau, and their families. Thoreau was a periodic resident and caretaker in the Emerson House. Emerson offered generosity, hospitality, and shelter. Emerson's friendship to many was returned to him when his home caught fire on July 24, 1872. The fire caused the roof to collapse and threatened to destroy all the papers and books representing a lifetime of contemplation, writing, and study. At home at the time, Emerson had awakened and run out into the yard; his calls for help were answered by his neighbors and fireman who somehow managed to save most of Emerson's library and papers, along with a large amount of the furnishings. While the walls were still standing, the smoke-filled spaces were not inhabitable, so the Emerson's took up residence once again in The Old Manse. Uprooted and despondent, Emerson was adrift and became ill; friends sent Emerson and his daughter Ellen to Europe and set about rebuilding the house in his absence. With the house rebuilt and his precious study restored by his friends, Emerson was welcomed back at the Concord train station with a band playing "Home Sweet Home." Throughout his long years at home in Concord, Emerson welcomed all into the large downstairs rooms where the great thinkers of the times gathered along with his Concord neighbors to "converse." Emerson loved to talk and listen to divergent ideas. In Nature, he expressed his hope "...to look at the world with new eyes..." and to discover that "The invariable mark of wisdom is to see the miraculous in the common."

Vegetables

230

Baked Acorn Squash with Spinach and Pine Nuts

3-4 acorn squash (3.5 inch diameter)
4 tablespoons butter, divided
½ teaspoon salt, divided
½ teaspoon ground pepper, divided
½ teaspoon freshly ground nutmeg, divided
3 tablespoons pine nuts
3 pounds fresh spinach

- Preheat oven to 375 degrees.

- Cut squash in half and remove seeds.

- Melt 1 tablespoon butter and brush all cut surfaces.

- Season squash with ¼ teaspoon each of salt, pepper and nutmeg.

- Cover with foil and bake, cut side up, for 35 minutes or until tender when pierced with a fork. Remove from oven and set aside.

- Meanwhile, sauté pine nuts in 1 tablespoon butter until golden brown. Drain on paper towels.

- Wash spinach to remove grit. Remove coarse main stem.

- Cook spinach in deep skillet over medium-high heat in the water that clings to the leaves after washing until just wilted. Drain well.

- Add remaining 2 tablespoons butter, ¼ teaspoon each of salt, pepper, nutmeg and 3 tablespoons pine nuts. Heat through.

- Spoon spinach mixture into center of squash.

Serves 6 to 8

231

Vegetables

Artichokes in Lemon Herb Butter

½ **cup onion, finely chopped**
½ **clove garlic, minced**
2 **tablespoons butter**
¾ **cup chicken broth**
2 **pounds canned artichoke hearts**
3 **tablespoons lemon juice**
1½ **teaspoons salt**
1 **teaspoon oregano**
¼ **teaspoon lemon rind, grated**

- Sauté onion and garlic in butter until tender.

- Add chicken broth, artichoke hearts, lemon juice, salt, oregano and lemon rind.

- Simmer about 10 minutes until artichokes are tender and heated through.

Serves 6

Great with chicken or fish

Chinese Asparagus

2 **pounds asparagus, cut diagonally into 2-inch pieces**
4 **teaspoons soy sauce**
1 **teaspoon sugar**
2 **teaspoons sesame seed oil**

- Parboil asparagus pieces 1 minute.

- Drain and run under cold water. Pat dry with paper towels.

- Prepare dressing, mixing soy sauce, sugar and oil.

- Toss with cooked asparagus and serve at room temperature.

Serves 4

232

Asparagus with Roasted Shallot and Seasame

2½ **pounds asparagus, trimmed**
1½ **tablespoons olive oil**
2 **tablespoons shallot, minced**
2 **tablespoons sesame seeds, lightly toasted**
Fresh lemon juice, to taste
Salt and freshly ground pepper, to taste

- Preheat oven to 500 degrees.

- Place asparagus in large shallow baking dish.

- Toss asparagus with olive oil, coating completely.

- Bake for 6 to 8 minutes, or until almost al dente, shaking dish every 2 minutes.

- Sprinkle asparagus with the shallot and sesame seeds.

- Bake for 1 minute or until it is al dente.

- Sprinkle with lemon juice, salt and pepper to taste.

Serves 8

New England Crock Pot Baked Beans

2   pounds beans (pea, navy or great northern)
1½   cups sugar
1   scant teaspoon ground ginger
2   teaspoons dry mustard
1   teaspoon salt
¼   cup molasses
2   onions, peeled
6   slices salt pork

- Wash and pick over beans. Place beans in a crock pot and cover with water to soak overnight. (Water should be 2 inches above beans.)

- After soaking, do not drain. Mix sugar, ginger, dry mustard, salt and molasses with enough water to make a paste.

- Pour over beans.

- Place onions and salt pork on top of beans.

- Turn crock pot on high and cook for 9 to 10 hours.

Serves 8 to 10

Vermont Baked Beans

2 **pounds dried yellow eyed, soldier or navy beans**
1 **teaspoon baking soda**
2 **cups maple syrup**
1 **teaspoon ground ginger**
1 **teaspoon ground pepper**
1 **teaspoon dry mustard**
2 **teaspoons salt**
1 **onion**
¼ **pound salt pork**

- Place beans in large saucepan, cover with water and soak overnight.

- To cook, pour off water. Add baking soda and enough water to cover beans.

- Simmer uncovered about 50 minutes or until tender. Drain, reserving liquid.

- Preheat oven to 300 degrees.

- Stir together the maple syrup, ginger, pepper, mustard and salt. Set aside.

- Slice onion and place in bottom of 2-quart bean pot.

- Alternate layers of beans and syrup. Add reserved liquid to almost cover beans.

- Score fat side of salt pork and place on top of beans with rind side up.

- Cover and cook in oven 6 to 8 hours.

Serves 12

Vegetables

Black Beans with Tomatoes and Cilantro

1½ tablespoons peanut, corn
    or safflower oil
1   medium onion, chopped
1   teaspoon garlic, chopped
6   fresh plum tomatoes,
    peeled, seeded and
    chopped
1   can (16 ounce) black beans,
    drained and rinsed
½ teaspoon Tabasco sauce
½ teaspoon salt, or to taste
2   tablespoons cilantro,
    chopped, divided

• Heat oil in a small skillet over medium-high heat. Add onion and garlic.

• Sauté, stirring constantly, until onion is almost translucent but still firm, about 2 minutes.

• Add tomatoes and cook, stirring frequently, for 2 minutes more.

• Add black beans, Tabasco and salt. Stir to combine.

• Cover skillet and cook until beans are heated through, about 2 minutes.

• Remove from heat and stir in 1 tablespoon of cilantro.

• Transfer to serving dish and sprinkle with remaining 1 tablespoon cilantro.

Serves 4

Harvard Beets

⅓ cup sugar
1½ tablespoons flour
¼ cup vinegar
2   tablespoons vegetable oil
¼ cup water or beet juice
12 small beets, cooked and cut
    into cubes
8   whole cloves

• Mix sugar, flour, vinegar, oil and water.

• Boil 5 minutes.

• Add Beets and cloves. Simmer over low heat for 30 minutes.

Serves 4

236

Sautéed Broccoli with Bread Crumbs

3 **pounds broccoli**
¼ **cup extra-virgin olive oil**
2 **cloves garlic, minced**
3 **tablespoons coarse plain bread crumbs**
Juice of 1 lemon
Salt and freshly ground pepper, to taste

- Steam broccoli until slightly soft but still firm.

- Heat olive oil in skillet.

- Add garlic and bread crumbs. Sauté until lightly browned.

- Add cooked broccoli, lemon juice, salt and pepper.

- Cover and cook 5 minutes.

Serves 6

Brussels Sprouts with Mustard Cream

2 **pints Brussels sprouts (1½ pounds)**
1 **tablespoon unsalted butter**
¼ **cup whipping cream**
1 **tablespoon Dijon mustard**
¼ **teaspoon ground thyme**
¼ **teaspoon salt**

- Trim Brussels sprouts and cut a shallow "x" into the stem of each.

- Cook sprouts in large amount of rapidly boiling water until tender, 8 to 9 minutes. Drain. Refresh under cold running tap water to stop further cooking.

- Melt butter in skillet. Add cream, mustard, thyme and salt and cook over high heat, stirring often, until thickened, about 4 minutes.

- Add sprouts and toss to coat.

- Cook until heated through.

- Serve immediately.

Serves 6

Brussels sprouts may be boiled a day in advance and refrigerated. Finish preparation just before serving.

237

Caramelized Onions and Pecan Brussels Sprouts

1	**large onion**
1	**pound Brussels sprouts**
¼	**cup butter**
1	**cup pecan pieces**
1	**teaspoon salt**
½	**teaspoon ground pepper**

- Cut onion in half and thinly slice.

- Cut Brussels sprouts in half and cut each half crosswise into thin slices.

- Place onions and Brussels sprouts in separate plastic bags. Close bags and chill 8 hours.

- Melt butter over medium heat. Add pecans and sauté 5 minutes or until toasted. Remove.

- Add onions to pan and cook 15 minutes or until caramel color.

- Add pecans and sprouts and cook 3 minutes on high heat, being careful not to let mixture burn.

- Season with salt and pepper.

Serves 8

Shredded Brussels Sprouts with Prosciutto and Parmesan

½ **cup unsalted butter**

6 **cloves garlic, minced**

4 **ounces prosciutto, thinly sliced and cut into thin slivers**

2 **pounds Brussels sprouts, trimmed and shredded by cutting each into several thin slices**

3 **tablespoons flour**

1½ **cups heavy or whipping cream**

1 **cup light cream**

¼ **cup sweet Marsala**

1 **teaspoon nutmeg, grated**

Salt and freshly ground pepper, to taste

1½ **cups Parmesan cheese, freshly grated, divided**

- Preheat oven to 350 degrees.

- Melt butter in a large sauté pan or skillet over medium-high heat. Add garlic and prosciutto and cook, tossing with a spoon, for 4 minutes.

- Add Brussels sprouts and continue to cook, tossing constantly, for another 4 minutes.

- Stir in flour and toss to coat.

- Gradually stir in heavy cream, light cream and Marsala.

- Reduce heat and simmer until Brussels sprouts are just tender, about 5 minutes.

- Add nutmeg and season to taste with salt and pepper.

- Stir in 1 cup of the Parmesan cheese and cook just until cheese is melted.

- Remove from heat. (The gratin may be prepared to this point one day in advance. Refrigerate, covered. Bring the gratin to room temperature before baking.)

- Transfer mixture to a shallow 9-inch square gratin dish. Top with remaining ½ cup Parmesan cheese.

- Bake the gratin until bubbly and top is slightly browned, about 20 minutes. Serve hot.

Serves 10 to 12

Carrot Casserole

2 pounds carrots, peeled
½ cup butter, melted
2 tablespoons minced dried onion
¼ cup flour
1 teaspoon salt
½ teaspoon dry mustard
⅛ teaspoon ground black pepper
¼ teaspoon celery salt
2 cups whole milk
10 ounces sharp white Cheddar cheese, sliced
Fresh bread crumbs

- Preheat oven to 350 degrees.
- Slice and cook carrots until tender. Drain and set aside.
- Combine butter, onion, flour, salt, mustard, pepper, celery salt, and milk. Set aside.
- In a 2-quart buttered casserole dish, layer carrots with cheese slices, ending with carrot layer.
- Pour sauce over top and sprinkle with bread crumbs.
- Bake 25 minutes.

Serves 8

Do not leave casserole warming in oven too long, sauce will thin out.

Carrots Chablis

6-8 medium carrots, peeled and sliced
½ cup Chablis wine
2 tablespoons butter
⅛ teaspoon ground thyme
1 tablespoon parsley, chopped
Salt and freshly ground pepper, to taste

- Cook carrots in boiling water until tender, 10 to 15 minutes.
- Drain and return to pan.
- Pour wine over carrots and boil rapidly until wine is reduced to 2 tablespoons.
- Add butter, thyme, parsley and salt and pepper to the pan.
- Stir to mix and heat gently until butter is melted.

Serves 4

Cauliflower with Raisins and Pine Nuts

1   **ounce seedless raisins**

1   **cauliflower head, about 1½ pounds**

⅓   **cup extra-virgin olive oil**

2   **teaspoons garlic, finely chopped**

1   **ounce pine nuts**

Salt and freshly ground pepper, to taste

2   **tablespoons fresh parsley, chopped**

- Soak raisins in hot water for 15 to 20 minutes.

- Trim cauliflower and drop head into 4 quarts boiling water. After water returns to a boil, cook cauliflower for 6 to 7 minutes or until there is resistance when pricked with a fork.

- Drain and cut into 1½-inch slices.

- Drain raisins and gently squeeze out excess water.

- Heat oil and garlic in a large sauté pan until garlic is golden.

- Add cauliflower, raisins, pine nuts, salt and a generous amount of pepper.

- Cover pan, turn heat to low and cook for 8 to 10 minutes, stirring occasionally until cauliflower feels tender when tested with a fork.

- Pour into serving dish. Sprinkle with parsley.

- Serve hot.

Serves 4 to 6

Gratinée of Cauliflower

6 tablespoons unsalted butter

4 cloves garlic, minced

4 ounces prosciutto, thinly sliced and cut into thin strips

Florets of 1 large head cauliflower, cut into ¼-inch lengthwise slices

2 tablespoons flour

1½ cups heavy or whipping cream

Pinch cayenne pepper

Salt and freshly ground pepper, to taste

1½ cups Swiss cheese, grated

½ cup parsley, chopped

- Preheat oven to 350 degrees.

- Melt butter in a large skillet over medium heat.

- Add garlic and sauté 2 minutes.

- Stir in prosciutto and sauté 2 minutes longer.

- Add cauliflower and cook just until it begins to lose its crispness, 3 to 4 minutes.

- Stir in the flour and then the cream. Blend well. Season with cayenne, salt and pepper.

- Heat to boiling and remove from heat immediately.

- Pour cauliflower into a shallow au gratin dish. Top with cheese and parsley.

- Bake until top is lightly browned and bubbling, about 30 minutes. Serve immediately.

Serves 6 to 8

Celery Almondine

¾ cup slivered almonds, divided

1 bunch celery, washed, trimmed and cut diagonally into 1-inch pieces

¼ cup butter

¼ cup flour

½ teaspoon salt

Dash freshly ground pepper

1 jar (2 ounce) pimentos, chopped (optional)

3 green onions, thinly sliced

1 cup chicken broth

1 cup half-and-half

1 cup Swiss cheese, grated, divided

- Preheat oven to 350 degrees

- Toast almonds in oven until golden.

- Meanwhile, cook celery, covered, in boiling salted water for 5 minutes. Drain.

- Melt butter. Blend in flour, salt and pepper.

- Add pimentos, onions, chicken broth, half-and-half and ½ cup Swiss cheese.

- Cook, stirring constantly, until sauce is thickened and smooth.

- Mix celery and half of the almonds. Place in casserole dish.

- Top with sauce and ½ cup Swiss cheese.

- Sprinkle with remaining almonds.

- Bake 15 minutes.

Serves 6 to 8

Eggplant Parmigiana

Olive oil as needed
3   large green peppers,
**   chopped**
1   large onion, chopped
2   large eggplants
3-5 eggs
Salt and freshly ground
**   pepper, to taste**
Italian bread crumbs as
**   needed**
3-4 cups pasta sauce of your
**   choice**
Parmesan cheese, to taste

• Preheat oven to 350 degrees.

• Heat ¼ inch of olive oil in large frying pan.

• Sauté peppers and onion until soft but not mushy. Remove peppers and onions and set aside. Retain oil in pan for frying eggplant.

• Peel eggplant and slice ¼ inch thick.

• Beat eggs with salt and pepper in a bowl suitable for dipping eggplant.

• Place bread crumbs on a plate. Dip eggplant slices in egg, then in bread crumbs.

• Reheat olive oil in pan. Add more to ¼ inch if necessary. Brown eggplant slices on both sides until lightly browned.

• Place light layer of sauce in a 13x9-inch casserole dish. Place a layer of peppers and onions, then eggplant, then more sauce. Sprinkle with Parmesan cheese. Repeat layers, ending with sauce and Parmesan cheese.

• Cover with aluminum foil and bake 30 minutes.

Serves 8 to 10

Escarole with Pine Nuts

2   **pounds escarole**
¼   **cup extra-virgin olive oil**
3   **cloves garlic, minced**
**Salt and freshly ground
   pepper, to taste**
½   **cup pine nuts**

- Trim escarole and cut each bunch into quarters. Wash well and dry.

- Heat oil in skillet. Add garlic and brown lightly.

- Add escarole. Season with salt and pepper.

- Cover and reduce heat, cooking until very tender.

- Remove from heat. Toss with pine nuts. Serve hot.

Serves 4

Leeks Sautéed in Wine

3   **slices uncooked bacon,
   chopped**
4   **large leeks (1-inch or more
   in diameter), halved
   lengthwise and leaving any
   green that looks fresh and
   edible**
1   **cup dry vermouth or white
   wine**
½-1**cup Jarlsberg or Gruyère
   cheese, thinly grated**

- In 10 to 13 inch skillet, begin to fry bacon over very low heat.

- Add leeks, flat side down.

- Sauté for 10 to 15 minutes, covered, until leeks become soft.

- Add wine as leeks begin to stick to skillet.

- Turn leeks flat side up. Sprinkle cheese over top. Cover with lid until cheese melts.

- Serve immediately.

Serves 4

Vegetables

Apples Stuffed with Mushrooms

4   **large baking apples, such
    as Cortland, Gravenstein
    or Granny Smith**
½   **lemon**
3   **tablespoons unsalted
    butter**
2   **cloves garlic, minced**
8   **ounces white mushrooms,
    cleaned and thinly sliced**
¼   **cup crème fraîche or heavy
    cream**
¼   **cup fresh flat-leaf parsley,
    chopped**
**Salt and freshly ground black
    pepper, to taste**
½   **cup chicken stock or water**

• Preheat oven to 350 degrees.

• Butter a small shallow baking dish or
  9-inch pie plate.

• Cut off ¼ inch from top of each apple.
  With a grapefruit or paring knife, hollow
  out apples, forming a thin but sturdy cup.
  Reserve inside flesh.

• Moisten apple cups with cut lemon to
  prevent browning.

• Discard cores and seeds from the hol-
  lowed out flesh. Finely chop remainder.
  There should be about 1 cup of chopped
  apple.

• In a large skillet, melt butter over moderate heat. Add garlic and stir for 1 minute.

• Add chopped apple and mushrooms.

• Cook over medium-high heat, stirring
  frequently, about 5 to 8 minutes.

• Stir in crème fraîche, parsley, salt and
  pepper to taste.

• Simmer for a few minutes, or until most
  of liquid has evaporated.

• Season apple cups with salt and pepper.
  Spoon mixture into apples, mounding
  slightly. (Apples can be prepared to this
  point a few hours ahead and refrigerated.)

(continued on next page)

Apples Stuffed with Mushrooms continued

- Place apples in prepared baking dish and pour the stock around them.

- Bake uncovered for 45 to 60 minutes, or until tender when pierced with a knife. (Time will vary based on thickness and variety of apple.) If apples begin browning during cooking, cover with foil.

- Serve hot or warm.

Serves 4

Baked Vidalia Onions

½	**cup water**
½	**cup butter**
½	**cup brown sugar**
¼	**cup cider vinegar**
5	**Vidalia onions, sliced**

- Preheat oven to 350 degrees.

- Bring water to boil.

- Add butter, sugar and vinegar. Stir well. Set aside.

- Place onions in casserole. Pour water and butter mixture over onions.

- Bake uncovered for 1 hour.

Serves 5

Vegetables

Grilled Caramelized Vidalia Onions

4 large Vidalia onions, peeled
4 teaspoons butter
4 beef bouillon cubes

- Cut a slice from top and bottom of onions to create flat surfaces.
- Quarter each onion, keeping quarters together.
- Place each quartered onion on a sheet of aluminum foil.
- Place a teaspoon of butter and a bouillon cube on flat top of each onion.
- Wrap in foil.
- Grill for 25 to 30 minutes on high.

Serves 4

Onions can also be baked. Place foil wrapped onions in baking dish with water. Bake at 350 degrees for 25 to 30 minutes.

Stir-Fried Parsnips

1 pound parsnips, peeled and cut into 2-inch long strips
2 tablespoons butter
1 tablespoon fresh ginger, grated
Salt and freshly ground pepper, to taste
3 scallions, chopped

- Heat butter in wok or frying pan
- Add parsnips and toss until they begin to brown.
- Add ginger and cook for about 5 minutes. If parsnips become too brown before they are tender, add enough water to keep from browning and cook until tender.
- Remove from heat and add salt, pepper and scallions.
- Serve hot.

Serves 4

Three Onion Casserole

3   tablespoons unsalted butter, divided
2   large yellow onions, thinly sliced
2   large red onions, thinly sliced
4   medium-sized leeks, well rinsed, dried and thinly sliced
Salt and freshly ground black pepper, to taste
1½ cups Havarti cheese, grated
2   packages (5 ounce) herbed cheese spread, crumbled
1½ cups Gruyère cheese, grated
½   cup dry white wine

- Preheat oven to 350 degrees.

- Butter an 8-cup baking dish with 1 tablespoon butter.

- Make a layer in baking dish, using a third each of the yellow onions, red onions and leeks. Season with salt and pepper.

- Top with Havarti cheese.

- Make a second layer of yellow onions, red onions and leeks. Season with salt and pepper.

- Top with herbed cheese spread.

- Layer remaining yellow onions, red onions and leeks. Top with Gruyère cheese.

- Dot top with remaining 2 tablespoons butter.

- Pour wine over all.

- Bake for 1 hour. Cover top with aluminum foil if it browns too quickly.

- Serve immediately.

Serves 6

Vegetables

Mashed Red Potato Cakes with Fontina Cheese

1 **pound red potatoes, quartered**
2 **cloves garlic, peeled**
2 **cups whole milk**
2 **cups water**
Salt, to taste, divided
½ **cup Fontina cheese, shredded**
¼ **cup chives, chopped**
1 **small onion, finely chopped**
Freshly ground pepper, to taste
½ **cup dry white bread crumbs**
4 **tablespoons vegetable oil, divided**
2 **tablespoons butter, divided**

- In a saucepan, combine potatoes, garlic, milk, water and salt.

- Bring to a boil, lower heat and cook for 20 minutes or until potatoes are almost falling apart.

- Set strainer over a bowl. Drain potatoes into the strainer, reserving cooking liquid.

- Transfer potatoes to a bowl. Add 2 tablespoons of cooking liquid and mash well.

- Continue adding liquid, 1 tablespoon at a time, until potatoes hold together.

- Stir in cheese, chives, onion, salt and pepper.

- Preheat oven to 350 degrees.

- Place bread crumbs on a plate. Have on hand a bowl of water.

- Dipping hands into water, shape potato mixture into 3-inch cakes.

- With dry hands, roll each potato cake in bread crumbs, patting them to make sure crumbs stick.

- In a large heavy skillet, heat 2 tablespoons of oil.

- Add 1 tablespoon of butter to the hot oil.

(continued on next page)

Mashed Red Potato Cakes with Fontina Cheese continued

- When butter is foamy, add enough cakes to make one uncrowded layer. Cook them over medium-high heat until browned on one side. Turn them over and brown other side.

- Remove cakes from pan and transfer them to a heat-proof dish. Keep them warm in the oven.

- Add remaining 2 tablespoons oil and 1 table-spoon butter to the pan. Fry remaining cakes in the same manner. Serve at once.

Serves 6

Four-Cheese Potatoes

12　medium-size red potatoes (about 4 pounds), unpeeled and cut into 1-inch cubes
3　cups shredded Cheddar cheese, divided
2　cups shredded mozzarella cheese
2　cups ricotta cheese
8　ounces sour cream
⅓　cup Parmesan cheese, grated
¼　cup green onions, finely chopped
3　tablespoons fresh parsley, chopped
2　cloves garlic, crushed
1　teaspoon dried basil
¼　teaspoon ground pepper

- Preheat oven to 350 degrees.

- Cook potatoes in boiling water to cover for 10 minutes. Drain well and set aside.

- In a large bowl, combine 1½ cups Cheddar cheese, mozzarella cheese, ricotta cheese, sour cream, Parmesan cheese, onions, parsley, garlic, basil and pepper. Stir well.

- Gently stir in potato cubes.

- Spoon mixture into a greased 13x9x2-inch baking dish. Sprinkle with remaining 1½ cups Cheddar cheese. Bake, uncovered, for 30 minutes or until potatoes are tender.

Serves 8 to 10

251

Oven-Fried Sweet Potatoes

1 **medium sweet potato per person, peeled and cubed (½-inch pieces)**
1 **tablespoon virgin olive oil per potato**

• Preheat oven to 450 degrees.

• Parboil potatoes in boiling salted water for 3 minutes. Drain well and place in large bowl.

• Drizzle olive oil over potatoes and toss to coat on all sides.

• Arrange in single layer on baking sheet.

• Bake for 30 minutes, turning frequently to brown. (Potatoes will be crispy and caramelized on the outside with soft centers.)

Sweet Potato Soufflé

2 **cans (33 ounce) yams**
4 **eggs, separated**
½ **cup pecans, broken**
½ **cup sugar**
½ **cup milk**
¼ **cup dry sherry**
1 **tablespoon orange rind, grated**
1 **teaspoon salt**
½ **teaspoon nutmeg, grated**
¼ **cup melted butter**

• Preheat oven to 400 degrees.

• In electric mixer, beat yams thoroughly. Add egg yolks one at a time, beating thoroughly after each addition. Add sugar, milk, sherry, orange rind, salt and nutmeg.

• In a separate bowl, beat egg whites until they hold stiff peaks. Fold into yam mixture.

• Fold in pecans.

• Place in buttered 2-quart casserole dish.

• Bake in a water bath for 45 to 60 minutes. Soufflé is done when a knife inserted in the middle comes out clean.

Serves 6 to 8

Oven-Roasted Potatoes with Rosemary and Garlic

¼ **cup extra-virgin olive oil**

12 **large cloves garlic, slightly crushed**

1½ **pounds yellow potatoes, peeled and cut into 1-inch cubes**

8 **sprigs fresh rosemary or 2 tablespoons dried**

Salt and freshly ground pepper, to taste

Boiling water

- Preheat oven to 475 degrees.

- In a metal baking dish, heat oil and garlic over low heat for 1 to 2 minutes. Remove from heat.

- Place potatoes in boiling water for 10 seconds to help prevent breakage during roasting. Drain immediately and pat dry.

- Place potatoes in the baking dish in a single layer.

- Add rosemary and toss to thoroughly coat potatoes with oil.

- Place potatoes in center of oven and reduce heat to 425 degrees.

- Bake for 50 to 60 minutes, stirring 2 to 3 times. Potatoes are done when golden brown with crisp edges and showing no resistance when pierced with a fork.

- Season with salt and pepper and serve immediately.

Serves 4

Use sweet potatoes, garlic and rosemary optional. Bake at 450 degrees for 30 minutes.

Green Bean Bundles

2 pounds small fresh green beans, trimmed

1 quart water

2-3 small red or yellow sweet peppers

½ cup cashews, coarsely chopped, plus ¼ cup whole cashews for garnish

½ cup melted butter

½ teaspoon lemon peel, freshly grated

2 teaspoons fresh lemon juice

2 tablespoons green onions, sliced

2 tablespoons fresh parsley, chopped

• Blanch beans in boiling water for 4 to 5 minutes or until tender-crisp. Drain.

• Plunge into cold water. Drain.

• Divide beans into 8 bundles.

• Slice peppers into eight ¼-inch rings.

• Secure each bundle of beans with pepper ring.

• Arrange on baking sheet. Chill, covered, overnight.

• Sauté cashews in butter in skillet until lightly browned. Remove from heat.

• Add lemon peel, lemon juice, green onions and parsley.

• (Cashew butter may be chilled, covered for up to 24 hours.)

• Let cashew butter and beans stand for 30 minutes.

• Preheat oven to 350 degrees.

• Spoon butter over beans. Bake, covered, for 10 minutes or until heated through.

• Baste with pan juices.

• Garnish with whole cashews.

Serves 8

Oriental Snow Peas

½   **pound fresh snow pea pods**
1   **tablespoon vegetable oil**
1   **teaspoon soy sauce**
1   **medium clove garlic, minced**
1   **can (5 ounce) bamboo shoots, drained**
1   **can (5 ounce) water chestnuts, drained and sliced**
1   **chicken bouillon cube**
¼   **cup boiling water**
1   **teaspoon cornstarch**
1   **teaspoon cold water**

• Wash and remove tips and strings from pea pods.

• In preheated wok or skillet, place oil, soy sauce and garlic.

• Cook over low heat until garlic is soft.

• Add peas, bamboo shoots and water chestnuts.

• Toss and cook over high heat for 1 minute.

• Dissolve bouillon cube in ¼ cup boiling water and add to peas.

• Cover and cook over medium heat for 2 minutes.

• Combine cornstarch and 1 teaspoon cold water.

• Stir into pea pod mixture. Cook uncovered over high heat until thickened, about 1 minute.

Serves 4

Spanakopita
Greek Spinach and Cheese Pie

½   **pound phyllo dough**
1   **medium onion, diced**
1   **cup butter, divided**
3   **packages (10 ounce) frozen spinach, thawed and squeezed dry**
4   **eggs**
½   **pound feta cheese, crumbled**
1   **cup ricotta cheese**
¼   **cup parsley, chopped**
1   **teaspoon dried dill or 2 tablespoons fresh dill**
1   **teaspoon salt**
⅛   **teaspoon ground pepper**
Juice of ½ lemon

- Preheat oven to 450 degrees.

- Warm phyllo dough to room temperature.

- Sauté onion until soft in ¼ cup butter. Remove from heat and add spinach. Set aside.

- Beat eggs. Add feta cheese, ricotta, parsley, dill, salt, pepper and juice of ½ lemon. Add spinach.

- Melt ¾ cup butter.

- Brush 9x13-inch pan with a little butter.

- Layer 8 phyllo leaves, brushing each with melted butter. Spread with spinach mixture. Layer and brush 8 more leaves with butter. Trim uneven edges with a knife. Cut rectangle into 12 squares.

- Bake for 10 minutes, then reduce heat to 350 degrees and bake for 45 minutes longer. Let cool at least 10 minutes before serving.

Serves 12

Zucchini Primavera

6   **tablespoons unsalted butter at room temperature**

1   **clove garlic, peeled and minced**

1   **cup fresh parsley leaves, chopped**

6   **medium zucchini, unpeeled and cut into julienne strips**

1   **medium carrot, peeled and cut into julienne strips**

1   **package (10 ounce) frozen tiny peas, thawed**

2   **teaspoons fresh lemon juice**

½   **teaspoon dried basil**

½   **teaspoon dried oregano**

1   **teaspoon salt**

Freshly ground pepper, to taste

- Melt butter in pan over medium-high heat.

- Add garlic, parsley and zucchini. Cook for 3 to 5 minutes or until zucchini is barely heated through, shaking pan occasionally to prevent sticking.

- Add carrots, peas, lemon juice, basil, oregano, salt and pepper.

- Toss gently with two rubber spatulas and cook 2 minutes longer.

- Serve immediately.

Serves 6

257

Zucchini Stuffed with Corn and Cheese

2   **zucchini or yellow squash, 6 to 7 inches long and narrow**
1   **cup corn kernels**
½-⅔   **cup ricotta cheese**
1-2   **tablespoons chives, snipped (optional)**
Salt and freshly ground black pepper, to taste
¾   **cup Cheddar cheese, grated**

- Preheat oven to 350 degrees.

- Blanch squash in boiling, salted water for 5 minutes. Place under cold water and drain.

- Halve squash and scoop out seeds, forming cavities.

- Coarsely purée corn and ricotta cheese in a food processor or food mill.

- Add chives and season with salt and pepper.

- Fill squash halves with mixture, mounding slightly, and cover with Cheddar cheese.

- Place in a buttered casserole and bake for 15 minutes.

- Uncover and bake 20 to 25 minutes longer, until squash is tender and topping is browned.

Serves 4

Pasta & Rice

Wayside

The Wayside

Purchasing Bronson Alcott's house called Hillside in 1852, Nathaniel Hawthorne and his family returned to Concord and the broadening circle of American literary luminaries who called Concord home. In the first ten years of marriage, the Hawthornes had moved five times. Hawthorne's earlier Concord sojourn had produced some measure of happiness and *Mosses from an Old Manse,* and while living in Salem, he had achieved his greatest fame in 1850 with *The Scarlet Letter.* In its shadowy Puritan setting where witches could walk among us at the Devil's beckoning and with its themes examining the whole repertoire of human frailties and failings, Hawthorne offered a counter-balance to Emerson's common, good man who sees and understands all. *The Scarlet Letter's* success provided the means of at last settling down and buying the house just down the road from Mr. Emerson and the Alcotts. Hawthorne renamed the house The Wayside and was said to be happy paying so little ($1,500) for such a large house. Sophia set to work having the house decorated, and he found the study located away from the road and the common areas of the house suited his solitary nature. With Hawthorne barely settled in at The Wayside, President Franklin Pierce, his old Bowdoin College friend, appointed him as the new Consul to Liverpool. Upon their Concord return seven years later, the Hawthornes set about renovating The Wayside with a new front parlor, entryway, second floor bedroom, and a writing tower-study. Sadly, Hawthorne did not seem to feel at home at The Wayside, and from all reports, the renovations did not improve his comfort level inside its walls. While Sophia was active in Concord affairs and a welcoming presence in her home, Bronson Alcott described Hawthorne as "...a foreigner...his moats wide and deep, his drawbridges...up on all sides..." In spite of the shared love and devotion between Hawthorne, Sophia, and their children, Hawthorne found little comfort beyond the intimacy of his family circle. Returning from England, he found Concord a political hotbed of conflicting thought and argument. Abolitionist causes were gathering steam, and the Civil War would erupt 10 months after his return. Long walks and boat rides with his friend Thoreau could not offer a sustainable comfort, and while Emerson welcomed Hawthorne into his wide circle, Hawthorne did not possess the natural ease Emerson embodied. He had trouble writing, and his own health began to break down. Increasingly, he sat in his tower and waited for the ideas to form; when he died in 1864, he left four unfinished novels. The Wayside was the only home Hawthorne ever owned.

Pasta & Rice

Pasta

Rice

Chinese Banquet Noodles

1 whole chicken breast, boneless, skinless, poached, cooled and cut into thin julienne strips

5 ounces boiled or baked ham, sliced and cut into thin julienne strips

1 bunch scallions, cut into 2-inch lengths, then julienned. (Include tops)

½ cup walnuts, coarsely chopped

1 pound thin vermicelli, angel hair or Chinese rice stick noodles, cooked according to package directions, drained and cooled under running water

1½ cups vegetable oil

2½ tablespoons Asian sesame oil

2 tablespoons sesame seeds

3 tablespoons ground coriander

¾ cup soy sauce

1 teaspoon hot chili oil, or to taste

- Combine chicken, ham, scallions and walnuts in large mixing bowl. Add noodles.

- Heat vegetable and sesame oils and sesame seeds in small saucepan over medium heat just until the sesame seeds turn light brown. Remove from heat. Stir in coriander and soy sauce. (Stand back as you do this, as the mixture will crackle and sizzle.) Stir in chili oil.

- Pour hot dressing over noodle mixture and toss to coat evenly. Transfer noodles to a serving bowl. Refrigerate until cold, about 3 hours.

Serves 6 to 8

Creamy Bowties with Chicken and Spinach

4 quarts water

1½ teaspoons salt, divided

¾ pound bowtie pasta

2 teaspoons olive oil

2 teaspoons unsalted butter

1 small onion, chopped

¾ pound boneless, skinless chicken breasts, cut into 1-inch chunks

½ teaspoon black pepper

1 bag (10 ounce) spinach, cleaned, stems removed and coarsely chopped

½ cup heavy cream

½ cup Parmesan cheese, grated

• Bring 4 quarts of water with 1 teaspoon of salt to a boil. Add the bowtie pasta. Cook following package directions. Drain.

• Meanwhile, heat together the oil and butter in a large skillet over medium-high heat until butter melts. Add onion and sauté, stirring often until onion is tender, about 3 minutes.

• Add chicken and sprinkle with the remaining ½ teaspoon salt and the pepper. Sauté, stirring constantly, until chicken is lightly browned.

• Add the spinach to the skillet. Continue cooking and stirring until the spinach is wilted.

• Add the heavy cream. Bring to a rapid boil. Boil gently until the mixture is slightly thickened.

• Combine cooked bowties, chicken mixture and Parmesan cheese in a large bowl. Toss gently to mix well. Serve immediately.

Serves 4

This has a great flavor, is quick and easy to prepare and kids love it too!

Fettuccine with Ham and Artichoke Hearts

½ **pound fettuccine**
4 **tablespoons olive oil, divided**
3 **scallions, chopped**
1 **large clove garlic, minced**
1 **can (14 ounce) artichoke hearts, drained and cut into quarters**
½ **cup ham, cubed**
1 **teaspoon lemon zest**
⅓ **cup Fontina cheese, grated**
3 **tablespoons Parmesan cheese, grated, plus additional Parmesan cheese as a garnish**
4 **tablespoons parsley, chopped**
Salt and freshly ground pepper, to taste

• Cook fettuccine in boiling, salted water until it is *al dente*.

• In a large skillet, heat 2 tablespoons olive oil and sauté scallions and garlic for about 2 minutes. Add artichoke hearts, ham and lemon zest and toss to heat through. Add Fontina cheese, Parmesan cheese and parsley. Toss. Salt and pepper to taste.

• Toss cooked fettuccine with the remaining 2 tablespoons olive oil and top with artichoke mixture to combine. Serve with extra Parmesan cheese on the side.

Serves 4

Fettuccine with Spectacular Red Sauce

1   **medium onion, coarsely chopped**

¼   **pound sweet Italian sausage, casing removed**

½   **cup butter (or ½ cup olive oil)**

¼   **pound prosciutto, diced**

¼   **pound mushrooms, diced**

¼   **cup brandy**

Salt and freshly ground pepper, to taste

1   **can (8 ounce) whole plum tomatoes**

½   **pound egg fettuccine**

½   **pound spinach fettuccine**

¼   **cup fresh basil, chopped**

¼   **cup Parmesan or Romano cheese, grated**

• Sauté onion and sausage in butter. Add prosciutto and mushrooms. Sauté 10 minutes.

• Add brandy, salt, pepper and tomatoes. Mash tomatoes with a fork. Simmer 20 minutes.

• Cook fettuccine, drain and toss with half of the sauce. Sprinkle with basil.

• Serve in individual bowls. Add spoonfuls of remaining sauce and top with cheese.

Serves 4

Fettuccine with Shrimp, Tomatoes and Artichoke Hearts

2	tablespoons olive oil
⅓	cup carrot, chopped
⅓	cup onion, chopped
⅓	cup celery, chopped
4	tablespoons garlic, minced
6	tablespoons flour
1	(28 ounce) and 1 (16 ounce) can Italian plum tomatoes, drained and chopped
4	cups low salt chicken broth
1	cup dry white wine
2¼	teaspoons dried basil
¼	teaspoon dried crushed red pepper
1	package (9 ounce) frozen artichoke hearts, thawed
1½	pounds large shrimp, uncooked, peeled and deveined
1¼	pounds fettuccine
6	tablespoons fresh basil leaves, sliced
6	ounces Parmesan cheese, shaved

• Heat olive oil in large Dutch oven. Add chopped onion, carrot and celery and sauté 2 minutes. Add garlic and sauté 1 minute. Sprinkle flour over vegetables and stir 2 minutes.

• Stir in chopped tomatoes, chicken broth, wine, basil and red pepper. Bring to a boil. Reduce heat and cook until thickened to a thin sauce, about 4 to 5 minutes. Add artichoke hearts and cook until tender. Add shrimp to sauce and simmer until shrimp are cooked through.

• Cook pasta until tender but still firm. Drain and toss with sauce. Add fresh basil and shaved Parmesan cheese. Serve at once.

Serves 6

Pasta Primavera Seafood Salad for a Crowd

1 **pound fettuccine, broken into 2-inch pieces**	• Drop pasta into 8 quarts boiling, salted water. Boil rapidly until pasta is *al dente*. Drain, rinse with cold water, and drain again.
1 **teaspoon salt**	
⅓ **cup light olive oil**	
¼ **cup white wine vinegar**	• Transfer to a large bowl. Add oil, wine vinegar and sherry. Toss lightly. Season to taste with salt and pepper. Toss again.
1 **tablespoon sherry**	
Salt and freshly ground pepper, to taste	
	• May be prepared up to 3 days in advance. Cover and refrigerate until serving time.

You may substitute wine vinegar or balsamic vinegar for the sherry.

Vegetables

16 **thin asparagus, trimmed and cut into 1½-inch lengths**	• Separately steam asparagus and broccoli until crisp-tender. Do not overcook. Rinse with cold water.
2-3 **cups broccoli florets, cut into bite-sized pieces**	
2-3 **cups fresh peas (or frozen peas)**	• Steam fresh peas. Rinse with cold water. If using frozen peas, thaw.
4-6 **green onions, minced**	• Store asparagus, broccoli and peas in plastic bags in refrigerator until ready to use.
1 **pint cherry tomatoes, cut in half**	
1 **pound fresh young spinach leaves for platter garnish**	• Combine green onions with cherry tomatoes in a small bowl and refrigerate.
	• Rinse spinach leaves, discarding any that are bruised or wilted. Wrap in plastic and chill.

Vegetables may be prepared up to 2 days in advance.

(continued on next page)

266

Pasta Primavera Seafood Salad for a Crowd continued

Basil Cream

⅓ **cup cider vinegar or white wine vinegar**

2 **tablespoons Dijon mustard**

½ **cup tightly packed fresh basil leaves**

1-2 **large cloves garlic**

⅓ **cup vegetable oil**

1 **cup sour cream**

½ **cup whipping cream**

3 **tablespoons fresh parsley, minced (gives pale green color)**

Salt and freshly ground black pepper

• Combine vinegar, mustard, basil and garlic in a food processor or blender and mix until almost smooth.

• With machine running, drizzle in the oil. Add sour cream, whipping cream and parsley and purée until smooth. Season to taste with salt and pepper.

• May be prepared up to 2 days in advance. Refrigerate until shortly before serving. Stir thoroughly before pouring into serving bowl.

Yield: 3 cups

If using dried basil, increase amount of parsley to 7 tablespoons to give sauce a pale green color.

Seafood

2 **pounds bay or sea scallops**

2 **pounds large shrimp, uncooked**

⅓ **cup olive oil**

3 **tablespoons wine vinegar**

3 **tablespoons sherry**

1 **clove garlic, minced**

2 **green onions, minced**

Salt and freshly ground black pepper

• If using sea scallops, cut in half. Gently poach scallops in simmering water until barely firm, about 2 minutes. Drain. Rinse with cold water.

• Poach shrimp in their shells in simmering water for exactly 2 minutes. If using all shrimp, poach in batches, no more than 2 pounds at a time. You may use plain water or a poaching stock (see index for recipe). Rinse with cold water. Drain shrimp and remove to a platter to cool.

(continued on next page)

Pasta & Rice

Pasta Primavera Seafood Salad for a Crowd continued

- Shell and devein shrimp and cut in half. Transfer to a large bowl. Add oil, vinegar, sherry and garlic and toss. Seafood may be prepared to this point and refrigerated for up to 1 day.

- About 30 minutes before serving, arrange spinach leaves around edge of large platter. Gently toss pasta with asparagus, broccoli, peas and onion-tomato mixture. Arrange pasta in center of platter with spinach leaves as border. Make a well in center of pasta. Drain seafood. Toss with minced green onion and season to taste with salt and pepper. Mound in center of pasta. Serve with basil cream.

Serves 12 to 16 in a buffet or
8 to 10 as a main course

You may substitute shrimp for the scallops, using a total of 4 pounds of shrimp.

This recipe seems long but is broken down into easy steps that can be done in advance. It is a delicious company recipe that is well worth the effort.

268

Pasta Puttanesca

2	cans (2 pound 3 ounce) plum tomatoes
¼	cup olive oil
1	teaspoon oregano
⅛	teaspoon red pepper flakes, or to taste
½	cup black niçoise olives
¼	cup drained capers
4	cloves garlic, peeled and chopped
8	anchovy fillets, coarsely chopped
½	cup flat-leaf parsley, chopped, plus additional for garnish
2	tablespoons salt
1	pound spaghetti, linguine or other thin pasta

- Drain tomatoes, cut into halves crosswise and squeeze out as much liquid as possible.

- Combine tomatoes and olive oil in a skillet and bring to a boil. Keep the sauce at a full boil and add, one at a time, stirring after each addition, the oregano, red pepper flakes, olives, capers, garlic, anchovies, parsley and salt. Reduce heat and continue to cook until the sauce has thickened to your liking.

- Cook pasta in boiling, salted water until *al dente*. Drain and toss with sauce. Serve immediately. Garnish with additional chopped parsley.

Serves 4

Pasta with Shrimp, Tomato and Feta Cheese

4	scallions
1	tablespoon fresh thyme (or 1 teaspoon dried)
6	ounces feta cheese
9	ounces low or nonfat cottage cheese
12	ounces ripe, peeled, seeded tomatoes
12	ounces uncooked shrimp, shelled and deveined
12	ounces angel hair pasta

- Chop scallions with fresh thyme in a food processor. Add feta and cottage cheeses and process to make a creamy sauce. Remove from processor and add coarsely chopped tomato to cream sauce.

- Heat a large pot of water to boiling. Add shrimp and cook approximately 3 to 5 minutes, depending on size. Remove from water and add to cream sauce.

- Return water to hard boil and add pasta. Cook until *al dente*. Drain and mix with shrimp and cream sauce.

Serves 4

269

Seafood Linguini with Artichokes

1½ cups dry white wine or vermouth

20 medium shrimp, uncooked with shells

¾ pound bay scallops

2 tablespoons butter

1 clove garlic, minced

2 cups heavy cream

3 tablespoons Parmesan cheese, freshly grated

12 artichoke bottoms, quartered

1 pound fresh spinach linguine

2 ounces fresh spinach leaves, cut in ribbons

Salt and white pepper, to taste

- For the Seafood: In a non-aluminum skillet, bring the wine to a simmer. Add the shrimp and poach 1 minute. Add the scallops and poach with the shrimp for 1½ minutes. Do not overcook.

- Transfer the shrimp and scallops to a bowl and reduce the wine to ¼ cup. Set aside.

- Peel and devein the shrimp when cool. Reserve the shrimp shells for the sauce.

- For the Sauce: Melt the butter in a small saucepan over medium heat and sauté the shrimp shells for about 5 minutes. Add the garlic and cook another 2 minutes. Do no allow the garlic to brown.

- Add the heavy cream and cook over medium-high heat until reduced in volume by half. Strain the sauce and discard the shrimp shells at this point.

- Return the sauce to the pan and add the wine-poaching liquid and the Parmesan cheese. Cook over medium heat for another 5 to 7 minutes or until thickened. Remove from the stove and add the artichoke bottoms.

- For the Pasta: Cook the linguine until *al dente*. Drain and return to the pot.

(continued on next page)

Seafood Linguini with Artichokes continued

- Add the spinach ribbons and toss the mixture well. Next add the shellfish and the cream sauce and stir to combine. Season with salt and pepper to taste and reheat if necessary.

- Serve immediately on warm plates.

Serves 4

Farmer's Market Pasta

1 can (28 ounce) peeled tomatoes, chopped
¼ cup fresh basil, chopped
¼ cup fresh oregano, chopped
¼ cup fresh chives, chopped
½ red onion, thinly sliced
1 clove garlic, finely chopped
2 tablespoons balsamic vinegar
4 tablespoons virgin olive oil
2 tablespoons capers
1 tablespoon sugar
Salt and freshly ground pepper, to taste
½ pound sugar snap peas, blanched with pod strings removed
Parmesan cheese, shaved, to taste
1 pound fettuccine, spaghetti or angel hair pasta

- In a large bowl, toss together tomatoes, basil, oregano, chives, red onion and garlic. Drizzle on the vinegar and olive oil. Sprinkle with capers, sugar, salt and pepper. Toss gently. Set aside 30 minutes to marinate.

- Meanwhile, cook the pasta and refresh under cold water. Toss pasta with the tomato sauce, sugar snap peas and shaved Parmesan. Serve immediately.

Serves 6

271

Pasta with Salmon and Sun-Dried Tomatoes

1	cup water
1	tablespoon vinegar
1	bay leaf
1	salmon (8 ounce) fillet
1	cup lowfat cottage cheese
2	tablespoons skim milk
⅛	teaspoon nutmeg, grated
8	ounces fettuccine (spinach, mushroom, or plain)
⅔	cup sun-dried tomatoes, sliced
1	tablespoon Romano cheese, grated

- In a large skillet, combine water, vinegar and bay leaf. Bring to a boil. Reduce heat to low and add the salmon. Cover and cook 4 to 6 minutes or until pink. Discard bay leaf.

- Remove the salmon with a slotted spoon and let cool. Break into 1-inch chunks and set aside.

- In a blender, combine cottage cheese, milk and nutmeg. Process until smooth.

- In a large pot of salted water, boil noodles until just tender. Drain and transfer to a large serving bowl.

- Add the tomatoes, Romano cheese and half the cottage cheese mixture. Toss to combine. Add the salmon and remaining cheese mixture. Toss gently and serve.

Serves 4

Pasta with Apricots and White Wine

¾ **cup extra-virgin olive oil**

15 **cloves garlic, 6 minced and 9 cut into thin slivers**

1 **cup dry white wine**

1 **tablespoon fresh rosemary, (or 1½ teaspoons dried rosemary)**

¾ **cup dried apricots, cut into slivers**

Salt and freshly ground pepper, to taste

1 **pound linguine**

½ **cup fresh parsley, chopped**

- Heat the olive oil in a skillet over medium heat. Add the minced and slivered garlic and sauté just until browned.

- Stir in the white wine. Reduce the heat and simmer uncovered for 5 minutes. Add the rosemary and apricots. Season with salt and pepper to taste. Simmer 5 to 10 minutes longer.

- Meanwhile, cook the pasta in boiling, salted water until tender but still firm. Drain.

- Place the pasta, sauce and parsley in a serving bowl and toss to coat. Serve immediately.

Serves 4 to 6

Fusilli with Zucchini, Plum Tomatoes, Basil and Parsley

3	tablespoons olive oil, divided
4	tablespoons Parmesan cheese, grated, divided
½	pound small zucchini, cut into ¼-inch pieces
½	pound plum tomatoes, diced (or 1¼ cups drained diced canned tomatoes)
⅓	cup fresh parsley, chopped
¼	cup fresh basil, chopped (or 2 teaspoons dried basil), plus fresh basil leaves for garnish
2	medium shallots, chopped
2	cloves garlic, chopped
½	teaspoon dried marjoram
½	teaspoon salt
½	teaspoon pepper
½	pound fusilli pasta
¼	cup chicken broth
1	tablespoon fresh lemon juice

• Place 2 tablespoons of the olive oil on one small plate and 3 tablespoons of the Parmesan cheese on another. Dip one side of each zucchini slice in the oil, then in the cheese. Arrange cheese side up on a broiler pan.

• Combine tomatoes, parsley, basil, shallots, garlic, marjoram, salt, pepper and 1 tablespoon olive oil in a bowl. Preheat broiler.

• Cook fusilli in a large pot of boiling water until just tender. Drain. Rinse with cold water and drain thoroughly. Add to tomato mixture. Mix in chicken broth and lemon juice.

• Broil zucchini until bubbly and golden brown, about 3 minutes. Add to pasta and toss.

• Garnish with basil leaves and sprinkle with remaining 1 tablespoon of cheese. Serve at room temperature.

Serves 2 to 3

Linguine with Roasted Peppers, Basil, Pine Nuts and Niçoise Olives

1   **large yellow bell pepper, roasted, peeled and seeded**
1   **large red bell pepper, roasted, peeled and seeded**
½   **cup virgin olive oil, divided**
Balsamic vinegar, to taste
3   **cloves garlic, peeled and minced, divided**
Salt and freshly ground pepper, to taste
¼   **cup pine nuts**
⅓   **cup niçoise olives**
1   **small bunch fresh basil**
1   **pound linguine**
Parmesan cheese, freshly grated, to taste

- Slice roasted and peeled bell pepper into ¼-inch wide strips. Place in a dish with ¼ cup of the olive oil. Sprinkle lightly with balsamic vinegar, half of the garlic, salt and pepper to taste. Marinate for at least 20 minutes, or overnight.

- Preheat oven to 375 degrees. Place pine nuts on a baking sheet and toast until they turn golden, about 5 minutes.

- Pit and coarsely chop the olives. Strip basil leaves from stems and chop, or bundle together and slice into thin ribbons.

- Cook linguine in boiling, salted water until *al dente*. Do no overcook. Drain pasta and combine with bell peppers, remaining ¼ cup olive oil, remaining minced garlic, toasted pine nuts and chopped olives. Season to taste with salt, pepper and a little balsamic vinegar.

- Serve with a sprinkle of Parmesan cheese.

Serves 4

Pasta Primavera

Cream Sauce

2	cloves garlic
1	tablespoon olive oil
1	cup ricotta cheese
½	cup milk
¼	cup fresh basil leaves, chopped
½	teaspoon salt
¼	teaspoon ground pepper

Tomato Sauce

2	tablespoons olive oil
1	bunch scallions, sliced
4	cloves garlic, minced
4	large tomatoes (or 12 plum tomatoes), skinned, seeded and chopped
½	teaspoon salt
¼	teaspoon ground pepper

Vegetables

1	bunch fresh asparagus
3-4	tablespoons olive oil
1	bunch scallions, sliced
4	cloves garlic, minced
2	medium zucchini, chopped
2	medium yellow squash, chopped
1	red bell pepper, chopped
1	cup broccoli florets
6	shiitake mushrooms, sliced
½	cup fresh peas

Parmesan cheese, freshly grated, for garnish

Fresh basil leaves for garnish

1½ pounds linguine

- For the cream sauce: In a small skillet, sauté the garlic in the olive oil until tender but not browned. Drain.

- In a blender or food processor, combine the garlic, ricotta, milk, basil, salt and pepper. Cover and blend until smooth. Set aside.

- For Tomato Sauce: In a medium skillet, heat the olive oil and sauté the scallions and garlic until the garlic is tender but not browned.

- Stir in the tomatoes, salt and pepper, then sauté for 10 minutes. Cover and keep warm while preparing the vegetables and pasta.

- For Vegetables: Snap off the tough bottom ends of the asparagus, discarding the ends. Chop the asparagus.

- In a large skillet, heat the oil and sauté the scallions and garlic for 2 minutes.

- Stir in the asparagus, zucchini, yellow squash, red pepper, broccoli, mushrooms and peas. Cook until crisp-tender, about 8 to 10 minutes.

- Cook the pasta in boiling, salted water according to package directions until *al dente*. Drain.

- Return the drained pasta to the pan, add the cooked vegetables and cream sauce and toss well.

- Serve the pasta on heated serving plates. Top each serving with the tomato sauce, Parmesan cheese and basil leaves.

Serves 8

Pasta with Hot Chili-Fresh Tomato Sauce

1	**cup extra-virgin olive oil**
2	**tablespoons dried hot chili pepper flakes**
4	**cloves garlic, peeled and crushed**
6	**ripe tomatoes, peeled, seeded and chopped**
	Salt
8	**ounces penne rigati**
1	**tablespoon fresh parsley, chopped**
	Pecorino cheese, freshly grated

- Combine olive oil and chili flakes. Bring to a boil. Cool and add garlic cloves. Marinate for at least 30 minutes and strain.

- In a saucepan, heat 4 tablespoons of strained chili-garlic oil with tomatoes. Add salt to taste. Keep warm over low heat.

- Cook pasta in boiling, salted water until *al dente*. Drain well. Toss in saucepan with oil, tomatoes and parsley. Serve with freshly grated Pecorino cheese.

Serves 4

Chili-garlic oil will keep under refrigeration for a week or more.

Pasta with Swiss Chard and Cannellini Beans

3	**cloves garlic, minced**
¼	**cup olive oil**
2	**bunches Swiss chard, washed, stems removed, leaves chopped**
2	**cans (14 ounce) chicken broth**
1	**can (19 ounce) cannellini beans**
	Salt and freshly ground pepper, to taste
¾	**pound shell pasta, cooked** *al dente*

- Sauté garlic in oil until golden brown. Add Swiss chard leaves. Stir thoroughly. Add chicken broth. Cover pan and let come to a boil. Lower heat and cook until leaves are wilted. Add beans. Season with salt and pepper to taste.

- Add cooked pasta. Mix well and serve.

Serves 4

Fresh spinach may be substituted for the Swiss chard.

Penne with Tomatoes and Asparagus

6   tablespoons extra-virgin olive oil, divided
4   cloves garlic, minced
2   carrots, peeled and minced
1   red bell pepper, seeded and minced
1   leek, rinsed, dried and minced
2   ripe large tomatoes, seeded and diced
1½ cans (28 ounces each) whole tomatoes, drained
½   cup dry red wine
3   tablespoons fresh fennel tops, chopped
1   tablespoon fresh tarragon, chopped
4   tablespoons fresh basil, chopped
Salt and freshly ground pepper, to taste
1½ pounds penne
1½ pounds fresh thin asparagus
2   large egg yolks
1   large whole egg
1   cup heavy or whipping cream
2   cups Parmesan cheese, freshly grated, divided

• Heat 4 tablespoons of the olive oil in a large saucepan over medium-high heat. Add the garlic, carrots, bell pepper and leek. Sauté, stirring occasionally for 10 minutes. Stir in the fresh tomatoes and cook 2 minutes. Add drained tomatoes to the sauce and mash with the back of a wooden spoon. Add the wine, fennel, tarragon and 2 tablespoons of the basil. Season with salt and pepper to taste. Simmer uncovered, stirring occasionally, over low heat for 45 minutes.

• Heat a large pot of water to boiling. Add pasta and cook until *al dente*. While pasta is cooking, slice the asparagus stalks on a diagonal into 2-inch pieces. Heat the remaining 2 tablespoons oil in a sauté pan over high heat. Add the asparagus and stir-fry until barely tender. Set aside.

• When pasta is almost ready, whisk the egg yolks, whole egg and cream together in a small bowl.

• Add the asparagus and remaining 2 table-spoons of the basil to the tomato sauce and heat through.

• Drain the pasta and toss with the tomato sauce.

• Quickly stir in the egg mixture and 1 cup of the Parmesan. Toss well and serve at once. Pass the remaining Parmesan.

Serves 6

Tagliatelle with Peas and Asparagus

1   **tablespoon olive oil**

1   **clove garlic, crushed**

6   **scallions, sliced**

2   **cups frozen peas, thawed**

1   **pound fresh asparagus, divided**

2   **tablespoons fresh sage, chopped, plus whole sage leaves for garnish**

Rind of 2 lemons, finely grated

1¾ cups vegetable broth

1   **pound tagliatelle pasta**

4   **tablespoons lowfat plain yogurt**

- Heat the oil in a large skillet. Add the garlic and scallions and cook for 2 to 3 minutes.

- Add the peas and 4 ounces of the asparagus, together with the sage, lemon rind and broth. Bring to a boil, reduce heat and simmer for 10 minutes until tender. Cool slightly. Pour into food processor or blender and process until smooth.

- Cut remaining asparagus into 2-inch lengths, trimming off any fibrous stems. Blanch in boiling water for 2 minutes.

- Cook tagliatelle in plenty of boiling, salted water until *al dente*. Drain well.

- Add the cooked asparagus to the sauce and reheat. Stir in the yogurt. Toss with tagliatelle. Garnish with additional sage leaves if desired and serve immediately.

Serves 4

Vegetable Lasagna

1½ cups onion, chopped

2 large cloves garlic, minced

6 ounces mushrooms, coarsely chopped

3 tablespoons sherry

3 tablespoons butter

2 large head broccoli, chopped (4 cups)

½ pound spinach, chopped

½ teaspoon herb mix (recipe below), or Italian seasoning

16 ounces lowfat cottage cheese

4 ounces part skim mozzarella cheese, shredded

3 tablespoons Parmesan cheese, freshly grated, plus Parmesan cheese to taste for topping

¼ cup parsley, chopped, (or 1 tablespoon dried parsley)

2 eggs

¼ teaspoon salt

¼ teaspoon ground black pepper

30 ounces tomato sauce

8 ounces lasagna noodles, cooked *al dente*

- In a large skillet, sauté onion, garlic and mushrooms in sherry and butter until vegetables are soft.

- Add chopped broccoli, spinach and herb mix (see below). Stir to combine the ingredients. Reduce heat, cover skillet and simmer for 5 minutes or until broccoli is tender-crisp.

- In a medium bowl, combine cottage cheese, mozzarella, Parmesan, parsley, eggs, pepper and salt.

- In a 13x9x2-inch baking pan, spread ½ cup of sauce on bottom. Layer ingredients as follows: 3 strips noodles, ½ cheese mixture, ½ vegetable mixture and 1 cup sauce. Repeat, ending with layer of noodles topped with sauce. Sprinkle top with additional Parmesan cheese.

- Bake at 375 degrees for 30 minutes. Let stand 10 minutes.

Serves 8 to 10

(continued on next page)

Vegetable Lasagna continued

Herb Mix

½   teaspoon cayenne pepper
1   tablespoon garlic powder
1   teaspoon dried basil
1   teaspoon dried thyme
1   teaspoon dried parsley
1   teaspoon savory
1   teaspoon dried mace
1   teaspoon onion powder
1   teaspoon black pepper
1   teaspoon dried sage

• Mix all ingredients together.

Tofu Stuffed Jumbo Shells

6   cups spaghetti sauce, divided
1   box (12 ounce) jumbo shells, cooked
2   pounds tofu
6   ounces Monterey Jack cheese, shredded
2   egg whites
¾   cup fresh parsley, chopped
1   tablespoon onion powder
2   teaspoons salt
1   teaspoon garlic powder
1   teaspoon basil
1   cup Parmesan cheese, grated, divided

• Spread 3 cups of the spaghetti sauce on the bottom of a 9x13-inch pan.

• Mix together the tofu, Monterey Jack cheese, egg whites, parsley, onion powder, salt, garlic powder, basil and ½ cup Parmesan cheese.

• Spoon tofu mixture into the cooked shells, about ⅓ cup per shell, and arrange shells in pan. Pour remaining sauce on top of shells. Top with remaining ½ cup Parmesan cheese.

• Bake at 350 degrees until the sauce is bubbly and shells are hot, about 30 minutes.

Serves 4 to 6

281

Wild Mushroom Lasagna

Mushroom Sauce

2   **cups boiling water**
1   **ounce dried porcini mushrooms**
1   **tablespoon olive oil**
½   **cup carrot, finely chopped**
½   **cup celery, finely chopped**
½   **cup onion, finely chopped**
3-4 cloves garlic, chopped
2   **pounds white mushrooms, coarsely chopped**
2   **cans (28 ounce) crushed tomatoes**
1   **cup red wine**
2   **tablespoons dried parsley**
2   **teaspoons salt**
Pepper, to taste

White Sauce

½   **cup unsalted butter**
½   **cup flour**
½   **teaspoon salt**
¼   **teaspoon nutmeg**
2   **cups milk**
24 **ounces lasagna noodles**
1   **pound fresh mozzarella cheese, cubed**
¾   **cup Parmesan cheese, freshly grated**

- In a small bowl, combine boiling water and dried porcini mushrooms and set aside.

- In an 8-quart saucepan, heat oil over medium heat. Add carrots, celery and onion and sauté, stirring constantly until just tender. Add garlic and sauté for another minute.

- Stir in chopped white mushrooms, then tomatoes, wine, parsley, salt and pepper. Heat to boiling over high heat, stirring constantly.

- Reduce heat to low and cook 45 minutes, stirring occasionally. Cool slightly.

- In a heavy 2-quart saucepan, melt butter over medium heat. Using a whisk, stir in flour, salt, nutmeg and cook until bubbly.

- Gradually stir in milk and heat to boiling, stirring constantly. Cool slightly.

- Preheat oven to 375 degrees.

- Cook lasagna noodles, drain, and cover with cold water.

- Butter a deep 9x13-inch baking pan. Spread just enough mushroom sauce to cover bottom of pan. Remove noodles from cold water as needed and place on a clean cotton towel to drain.

(continued on next page)

Wild Mushroom Lasagna continued

- Place a layer of noodles over mushroom sauce. Add a layer of white sauce and sprinkle with mozzarella and Parmesan cheeses.

- Add another layer of noodles, sauces and cheeses, ending with noodles topped with mushroom sauce.

- Bake 45 minutes or until heated thoroughly. Check after 30 minutes and cover with foil if browning too quickly.

- Serve hot. Pass extra mushroom sauce.

Serves 8 to 10

May be assembled a day ahead. Bake day to be served.

Perfect Rice Every Thyme

1½ **tablespoons butter**
¼   **cup onion, finely chopped**
1   **cup rice**
1½ **cups chicken broth**
1   **bay leaf**
¼   **teaspoon dried thyme**
½   **tablespoon fresh parsley, chopped**
Fresh parsley sprigs

• Preheat oven to 400 degrees.

• Melt butter in ovenproof baking dish with lid. Add onion and sauté until translucent. Add rice and cook until grains are pink and slightly browned. Pour in chicken broth. Season with bay leaf, thyme and parsley. Stir and bring to a boil. Remove from heat, cover and place in oven. Bake for exactly 17 minutes. Remove from oven, toss and garnish with sprigs of fresh parsley.

Serves 4

This dish may be cooked entirely on top of the stove by reducing heat after reaching a boil, and simmering, covered, for 17 minutes.

Red Onion Rice Casserole

3   **red onions, chopped**
½   **cup butter**
1   **cup white rice**
2   **cans (10.75 ounce) undiluted beef consommé**

• Preheat oven to 425 degrees.

• Sauté onions in butter until yellow and soft. Combine onions, rice and consommé in a casserole dish.

• Bake uncovered for 1 hour. Onions will rise to the top.

Serves 4 to 6

Good buffet dish and goes well with almost anything.

284

Saffron Risotto

½ **cup butter, divided**
½ **cup onion, minced**
2 **cups Arborio rice**
1 **cup dry white wine**
6 **cups chicken broth, divided**
¼ **teaspoon saffron**
¼ **cup Parmesan cheese, freshly grated**

• Sauté onion in ¼ cup butter in a large saucepan. Add rice, stirring until well coated with butter. Add wine and simmer, stirring, until wine has evaporated. Add 1 cup of broth and simmer, stirring, until broth is almost absorbed. Reserve 1 tablespoon of broth and add remaining broth, one cup at a time, stirring, letting rice absorb each cup before adding more.

• Cook the rice an additional 15 minutes or until tender. Dissolve saffron in the reserved tablespoon of hot broth in a small dish. Add to the rice. Add Parmesan cheese and blend with a fork. Serve immediately.

Serves 8

Variations

Add ¼ pound sautéed porcini or shiitake mushrooms, zest of 1 lemon, and ¼ cup chopped Flat-leaf parsley.

Add 1 pound sautéed shrimp or chicken.

Add steamed vegetables of your choice.

Sour Cream Pilaf

½	cup slivered almonds
1	tablespoon plus ⅓ cup butter
1½	cups rice
3	cups chicken broth
1	tablespoon onion, grated
1	tablespoon fresh lemon juice
1-1½	teaspoons salt
¼	teaspoon pepper
1	bay leaf
1	cup sour cream
1	can (4 ounce) button mushrooms, drained
¼	cup fresh parsley, minced

• Sauté almonds in 1 tablespoon of the butter in a small skillet until lightly browned. Remove from heat and set aside.

• In a large saucepan, combine rice, chicken broth, ⅓ cup butter, grated onion, lemon juice, salt, pepper and bay leaf. Bring mixture to a boil, cover, reduce heat, and simmer 20 to 25 minutes or until rice is tender and liquid is absorbed. Remove from heat. Remove bay leaf and discard.

• Add sour cream and mushrooms to rice mixture, stir well. Transfer rice mixture to a serving dish. Sprinkle with almonds and parsley. Serve immediately.

Serves 6 to 8

Desserts

Orchard House

Orchard House

Even today, Louisa May Alcott's "mood pillow" still sits stationed in the front parlor of Orchard House and announces her willingness to receive guests. The pillow standing on end meant Miss Alcott would welcome your company and conversation; a pillow sitting flat meant quiet and solitude were the order for the day. Miss Alcott's pillow symbolizes her life-long independent spirit and command of her surroundings, no matter how much her fame threatened to intervene. She defined her spaces and her moods, but she also helped define the Alcott family and proved herself to be a devoted daughter and sister. In 1858, she came with her family to Orchard House, which she nicknamed "Apple Slump," when she was twenty-six. The family had called many places "home" before Orchard House, while Bronson Alcott moved to run various schools and experiment with communal living and her mother worked as a social worker to bolster the always lacking family budget. Mr. Emerson and a group of friends bought Orchard House for the Alcott family, and it was purchased under Mrs. Alcott's family name to shelter it from creditors. It was the first and only house Bronson and Abba Alcott ever owned, but it would be Louisa who would pay the bills and provide the financial security her beloved father's philosophy and theories could not. Miss Alcott wrote *Little Women* on a wooden desk her father had built for her in her upstairs bedroom. Stationed between two windows, Louisa May Alcott looked out on Lexington Road, and at age fifty she reflected on her own childhood. She said when she was fifteen she walked out into the countryside and said, "...I will do something by-and-by. Don't care what, teach, sew, act, write, anything to help the family; and I'll be rich and famous and happy before I die..." Her dedication to family and her talent with words paid for Orchard House's re-roofing, heating, running water, and finally settling all old family debts. She wrote "...the girl of fifteen found herself a woman of fifty with her...dream beautifully realized, her duty done, her reward greater than she deserved..."

Desserts

Cakes

Cookies

Pies

Desserts

Desserts

Apricot Cheesecake

1   cup dried apricots
1   cup gingersnap crumbs
3   tablespoons unsalted
    butter, melted
Zest of 1 orange, grated
1½ pounds cream cheese, at
    room temperature
¾   cup sugar
4   large eggs
½   cup sour cream

- Simmer the apricots in water to cover for 30 minutes. Drain.

- Preheat oven to 350 degrees. Butter an 8 or 9-inch springform pan.

- Toss the gingersnap crumbs with the melted butter in a small mixing bowl. Press the crumbs over the bottom and 1 inch up the side of the pan. Set aside.

- Purée the apricots with the orange zest in a food processor fitted with a steel blade.

- In a large mixing bowl, beat the cream cheese and sugar until smooth and creamy. Beat in the eggs, one at a time, beating well after each addition. Using a spatula, gently fold in the sour cream and apricot purée until completely blended. Pour the batter into the springform pan.

- Bake until the center is firm when touched lightly, 50 to 60 minutes. Cool the cake on a wire rack, and then refrigerate until thoroughly chilled.

- Top with a fruit topping, if desired.

Serves 10 to 12

In season, top with fresh, simmered and sweetened cranberries.

Kona Coffee Cheesecake

Crust

2   **cups chocolate wafer crumbs (about 8 ounces)**

6   **tablespoons unsalted butter, melted**

Filling

3   **packages (8 ounces each) cream cheese, room temperature**

1¼ cups sugar

¼   **teaspoon salt**

2   **tablespoons flour**

2   **tablespoons instant coffee granules, crushed to a powder**

4   **large eggs**

⅔   **cup whipping cream**

¼   **cup coffee liqueur**

Topping

½   **cup sour cream**

1½ tablespoons coffee liqueur

2   **teaspoons instant coffee granules, crushed to a powder**

1   **cup confectioners' sugar**

Whipped cream and chocolate-coated coffee beans for garnish

- Lightly grease sides of a 10-inch springform pan. Mix crumbs and butter in a large bowl. Press crumbs firmly onto sides and bottom of pan. Place crust on cookie sheet and refrigerate until firm.

- Place rack in center of oven. Preheat oven to 350 degrees.

- Using an electric mixer, beat cream cheese, sugar and salt until light. Blend in flour and coffee granules.

- Add eggs one at a time, beating well after each addition. Add whipping cream and coffee liqueur and blend thoroughly.

- Pour into crust. Bake until edges are set and center still moves when pan is shaken, about 1¼ hours. Let cake cool 10 minutes.

- Increase oven temperature to 375 degrees.

- Mix sour cream, coffee liqueur, coffee granules and powdered sugar in medium bowl. Spread over cheesecake. Bake just until set, about 10 minutes.

- Transfer to rack and cool. Cover and refrigerate overnight.

- Before serving, spoon whipped cream into a pastry bag fitted with a medium star tip. Pipe cream decoratively over cake. Garnish with chocolate-coated coffee beans.

Serves 10 to 12

May be prepared up to 2 days in advance.

The Best Cheesecake

1½ **cups graham cracker crumbs**
¼ **cup sugar**
6 **tablespoons butter, melted**
½ **teaspoon cinnamon**
5 **packages (8 ounce each) cream cheese**
1 **tablespoon vanilla**
1½ **tablespoons lemon juice**
1¾ **cups sugar**
5 **eggs**
¼ **cup flour**
1 **cup heavy cream**

- Preheat oven to 450 degrees.

- Mix crumbs, sugar, butter and cinnamon. Pour into a 9-inch springform pan. Press down firmly.

- Beat cream cheese, vanilla and lemon juice together. Add sugar. Add eggs one at a time. Add flour. Stir in cream.

- Pour into crust. Bake as follows:

- 450 degrees for 15 minutes, then lower temperature to 350 degrees;

- 350 degrees for 30 minutes, then lower temperature to 300 degrees;

- 300 degrees for 45 minutes.

- When cooked, turn off oven heat. Allow cake to cool in oven. Cake will depress slightly. Refrigerate for 24 hours before serving.

Serves 12

Boston Cream Pie

A New England Tradition

2 **cups sifted cake flour**
1 **cup sugar**
2½ **teaspoons baking powder**
1 **teaspoon salt**
⅓ **cup butter**
1 **cup milk**
1 **egg**
1 **teaspoon vanilla**

- Preheat oven to 350 degrees. Grease well and flour 2 (9-inch) round cake pans.

- Sift together the flour, sugar, baking powder and salt into a large mixing bowl. Add butter and milk. Beat 2 minutes. Add egg and vanilla and beat 2 minutes.

- Pour batter into prepared pans. Bake 25 to 30 minutes. Cool in pans 10 minutes. Remove from pans and cool thoroughly on wire racks.

Vanilla Cream Filling

½ **cup sugar**
¼ **cup cornstarch**
¼ **teaspoon salt**
2 **cups milk**
4 **egg yolks, slightly beaten**
1 **teaspoon vanilla**

- In medium saucepan over medium heat, combine sugar with cornstarch and salt. Gradually add milk. Bring to boil, stirring constantly. Remove from heat.

- Add half of hot mixture to egg yolks. Mix well. Gradually stir egg yolks into remaining hot mixture in saucepan. Over medium heat, bring to a boil, stirring constantly. Remove from heat. Add vanilla. Cool completely.

Chocolate Glaze

2 **tablespoons butter**
1 **ounce unsweetened chocolate**
1 **cup sifted confectioners' sugar**
2 **tablespoons boiling water**

- Melt butter and chocolate over hot water. Let cool. In a small bowl, combine chocolate mixture with sugar and water. Beat until mixture is smooth. Let stand. Glaze will thicken.

- Spread vanilla cream between cake layers. Pour chocolate glaze over top of cake, letting it run down sides.

Serves 8 to 10

293

Italian Cream Cake

5	**eggs, separated**
½	**cup butter**
1	**cup vegetable oil**
2	**cups sugar**
2	**cups sifted flour**
1	**teaspoon baking soda**
1	**cup buttermilk or plain yogurt**
1	**teaspoon vanilla**
1	**cup pecans, chopped**
1½	**cups shredded or flaked coconut**

- Preheat oven to 350 degrees. Grease and flour 3 (8-inch) or 2 (9-inch) round cake pans.

- Beat egg whites until stiff. Set aside.

- Cream butter. Add oil and sugar. Beat well. Beat in egg yolks.

- Combine flour and baking soda. Add to mixture.

- Add buttermilk, vanilla, pecans, and coconut. Mix well. Fold in egg whites.

- Pour into prepared pans. Bake for 45 minutes, or until done. (Top will get very brown.)

Cream Cheese Frosting

½	**cup butter**
8	**ounces cream cheese, at room temperature**
1	**pound confectioners' sugar**
1	**teaspoon vanilla**

- Cream butter and cream cheese until smooth. Add sugar and vanilla. Beat until smooth.

- Spread frosting on cooled cake.

Serves 8 to 10

Cake improves after 2 or 3 days.

Mocha Cream Cake

Cake

1½ **cups sifted flour**

1½ **teaspoons baking powder**

¾ **teaspoon salt**

4 **eggs, separated**

½ **cup water**

3 **teaspoons lemon rind, grated**

¾ **teaspoon vanilla**

1½ **cups sugar**

3 **tablespoons lemon juice**

Icing

8 **ounces German chocolate**

¼ **cup brewed coffee**

2 **tablespoons cognac**

1½ **cups heavy cream**

- Preheat oven to 350 degrees. Grease sides and bottom of 2 (8-inch) round cake pans.

- Sift together the flour, baking powder and salt. Combine egg yolks, water, lemon rind and vanilla. Beat well. Add sugar and lemon juice. Blend in dry ingredients. Beat egg whites until stiff but not dry. Fold into batter. Bake in prepared pans for 20 to 25 minutes.

- In a double boiler, over but not in simmering water, melt chocolate with coffee. Stir until smooth, then add cognac. Cool.

- Whip the cream and fold in chocolate.

- When cool, split the 2 cake layers horizontally to form 4 layers. Frost with mocha cream icing. Chill overnight.

- Before serving, let stand at room temperature for 30 minutes.

Serves 8 to 10

Cranberry Cobbler

2 **cups cranberries**

1½ **cups sugar, divided**

½ **cup walnuts, coarsely chopped**

2 **eggs**

1 **cup flour**

¾ **cup butter, melted**

- Preheat oven to 325 degrees. Grease a 10-inch diameter deep pie plate.

- Line the pie plate with cranberries. Sprinkle them with ½ cup of the sugar and the nuts. Beat eggs with remaining 1 cup of sugar, the flour and melted butter. Pour over the cranberries. Bake for 45 minutes.

Serves 8 to 10

Desserts

Fresh Blueberry-Lemon Bundt Cake

3¼ cups cake flour, plus
    3 tablespoons cake flour
    for dusting blueberries
1   teaspoon baking soda
1   teaspoon salt
1   cup unsalted butter,
    softened
2   cups sugar
2   tablespoons zest of lemon,
    grated (about 2 lemons)
3   large eggs
1   teaspoon lemon extract
¼   cup buttermilk
2½ cups fresh blueberries, or
    frozen blueberries (not in
    syrup)

- Place rack in center of oven. Preheat oven to 350 degrees. Generously grease a 10-inch Bundt cake pan (12-cup capacity), then lightly dust with flour.

- Sift 3¼ cups flour, the baking soda and salt onto a sheet of waxed paper. Set aside.

- Using an electric mixer, cream butter, sugar and lemon zest until light and fluffy. Add eggs and lemon extract. Beat 3 minutes. Mixture will be thick and smooth.

- Add the sifted dry ingredients and the buttermilk. Mix well.

- Toss the blueberries with the remaining 3 tablespoons of flour to coat. Using a wooden spoon, stir blueberries into the batter. Transfer batter into prepared pan. Bang the pan on the counter to settle batter. Smooth the surface with a spatula.

- Bake 55 to 60 minutes, or until a toothpick inserted in the center comes out clean. Cool cake in its pan on a wire rack for 10 minutes, then invert it on rack.

(continued on next page)

Fresh Blueberry-Lemon Bundt Cake continued

Tart Lemon Glaze

1   **tablespoon grated zest of lemon**

1   **cup confectioners' sugar**

3   **tablespoons fresh lemon juice**

4   **tablespoons unsalted butter, melted**

Pinch of salt

- Place the lemon zest and sugar in a blender or food processor fitted with a metal blade. Process until zest is finely minced. Add the lemon juice, butter and salt and blend until smooth.

- Place aluminum foil under the cake rack. Brush cake while still warm with the glaze. Reapply glaze that drips onto foil. Cool cake completely before serving.

Serves 10 to 12

Cake may be made one day ahead and stored at room temperature in an airtight container. Do not freeze.

Golden Cointreau Cake

8   **large eggs, separated**
1½ **cups sugar**
⅓   **cup fresh orange juice**
1   **cup flour, sifted twice**
1½ **teaspoons Cointreau**
½   **teaspoon vanilla extract**
¼   **teaspoon salt**
½   **teaspoon cream of tartar**
Cointreau frosting (recipe follows)

- Preheat oven to 325 degrees.

- Beat the egg yolks with an electric mixer until they have thickened and are smooth. Beat in the sugar slowly, then continue beating until the mixture turns a lighter shade of yellow and is smooth. Add the orange juice and blend thoroughly.

- Sprinkle sifted flour over the egg yolk mixture and gently fold it in by hand with a whisk, a spatula, or an electric mixer on very low speed. Fold in the Cointreau and vanilla.

- Add the salt to the egg whites and beat until they begin to turn white and foamy. Add cream of tartar and continue beating until the egg whites hold a stiff peak but are not dry and grainy, about 4 minutes more.

- Fold a few spoonfuls of egg white into the batter to lighten it. Then add the remaining egg whites to the batter, gently folding them in.

- Spoon the batter into a 10x4½-inch ungreased angel food cake pan (a tube pan with a removable bottom). The pan should be no more than ¾ full. Place the cake pan on the middle shelf of the oven and bake until a cake tester inserted into the center of the cake comes out clean, or until the cake springs back when lightly

(continued on next page)

Golden Cointreau Cake continued

touched, about 1¼ hours. Remove cake from oven, turn upside down on the tube pan legs or a glass bottle and allow it to rest overnight before frosting.

• Loosen the cake from the pan with a thin sharp knife and unmold it. Place the cake on a plate or on a flat surface covered with wax paper or foil. Frost the cake generously in a swirl design. Allow the frosting to firm for 30 minutes before lifting the cake onto a serving platter.

Serves 12 to 14

Cointreau Frosting

8   tablespoons unsalted butter, cut into pieces

2¾ cups confectioners' sugar, sifted

⅛   teaspoon salt

1   large egg yolk

6-8 tablespoons Cointreau, or more as needed

• In a large mixing bowl, combine butter, confectioners' sugar and salt. Beat well with an electric mixer. Add the egg yolk. Slowly add 6 tablespoons of the Cointreau. Continue to beat until smooth, thick and pliable, 3 minutes. Add more Cointreau as needed to achieve desired consistency. Frosting must be thick. Allow the frosting to firm for 30 minutes before frosting cake.

Decadent Chocolate Cake

Chocolate Syrup
1   cup granulated sugar
1   cup milk
1   cup cocoa

Cake Batter
1   cup granulated sugar
1   tablespoon solid vegetable shortening
1   egg
1   teaspoon baking soda
1¾ cups flour
1   teaspoon vanilla
1   cup buttermilk, or 1 cup milk plus 1 tablespoon vinegar

- Preheat oven to 350 degrees. Grease and flour 2 (9-inch) round cake pans.

- To make the chocolate syrup, heat the sugar, milk and cocoa until smooth and sugar is dissolved. Do not boil.

- To make the batter, mix the chocolate syrup with the sugar, shortening, egg, baking soda, flour, vanilla and buttermilk. Pour into the prepared cake pans. Bake for 30 minutes or until a cake tester inserted in the middle comes out dry. Cool in pans 15 minutes, then turn out onto racks to cool 1 hour before frosting.

Mocha Rum Butter Frosting
1   ounce unsweetened chocolate
1   tablespoon strong brewed coffee
1½ tablespoons rum
4   tablespoons butter
4   tablespoons solid vegetable shortening
1   egg yolk, beaten until thick
½   cup sugar
¼   cup water

- In a small saucepan, melt the unsweetened chocolate with the coffee. Add the rum. Cool to lukewarm. Set aside.

- Cream together the butter and shortening.

- Combine the sugar and water in a small saucepan. Boil to 240 degrees, using a candy thermometer. Pour slowly over the egg yolk, beating well. Add the butter and shortening, a little at a time, beating after each addition. Add the mocha rum syrup and beat well. Cool. Frost sides and top of cooled cake layers.

Serves 8 to 10

Chocolate Marble Loaf Cake

Syrup

½   **cup cocoa**
¼   **cup sugar**
½   **cup corn syrup**
½   **cup water**
½   **teaspoon vanilla**

Cake

3¼ **cups flour**
2⅛ **teaspoons baking powder**
½   **teaspoon salt**
¼   **teaspoon baking soda**
1½ **cups butter, softened**
2   **cups sugar**
4   **eggs**
2½ **teaspoons vanilla**
1   **cup milk**
½   **cup sour cream**

- In small saucepan, combine cocoa and sugar. Add corn syrup, water and vanilla. Heat, stirring until sugar is dissolved. Set aside to cool.

- Preheat oven to 350 degrees. Butter and dust with flour 2 (9x5-inch) loaf pans.

- Stir together the flour, baking powder, salt and baking soda. Cream butter and sugar until fluffy. Add eggs, one at a time, beating well after each addition. Add vanilla on low speed. Add milk and sour cream alternately with dry ingredients.

- Remove ⅓ of the batter. Divide remaining ⅔ between the 2 loaf pans. Combine syrup mixture with the reserved batter. Mix well. Spoon dollops of the chocolate batter down center of each loaf pan, using all remaining batter, and swirl with a knife.

- Bake for 1 hour or until a cake tester inserted into the center comes out clean. Cool on a rack before slicing.

Yield: 2 (9-inch) loaves

Chocolate Pudding Cake

1   cup flour, unsifted
1⅓ cups granulated sugar, divided
6   tablespoons unsweetened cocoa, divided
2   teaspoons baking powder
¼   teaspoon ground cinnamon
½   teaspoon instant espresso coffee powder
¼   teaspoon salt
½   cup lowfat milk
¼   cup light vegetable oil (canola)
1   teaspoon vanilla extract
⅓   cup chocolate chips
1   cup water
Lowfat vanilla yogurt or heavy cream, whipped and sweetened, for garnish (optional)

- Position rack in center of oven. Preheat oven to 350 degrees. Grease an 8x8x2-inch pan.

- Blend together the flour, ⅔ cup of the sugar, 2 tablespoons of the cocoa, the baking powder, cinnamon, coffee and salt. With a wooden spoon, beat in the milk, oil, vanilla, and chocolate chips. Spoon batter evenly into prepared pan.

- In a small bowl, stir together ⅔ cup granulated sugar and 2 tablespoons cocoa. Spread evenly on top of batter.

- Boil 1 cup of water. Pour over cake batter. Do not stir. Bake 30 minutes, or until top looks crisp and a cake tester comes out clean.

- Serve warm, spooned from the pan, topped with lowfat vanilla yogurt or heavy cream, whipped.

Serves 4 to 6

A quick and easy dessert.

Texas Sheet Cake

2 **cups sugar**
2 **cups flour**
½ **cup butter**
½ **cup shortening**
4 **tablespoons unsweetened cocoa**
1 **cup water**
½ **cup buttermilk**
1 **teaspoon baking soda**
2 **eggs, beaten**
1 **teaspoon cinnamon**
1 **teaspoon vanilla**

- Preheat oven to 400 degrees.

- Mix together sugar and flour. Set aside.

- Combine butter, shortening, cocoa and water in a saucepan and bring to a boil. Pour over the sugar and flour mixture. (You may heat butter/water mixture in microwave oven if preferred.)

- Add buttermilk, baking soda, eggs, cinnamon and vanilla.

- Pour into a greased shallow 9x13-inch pan. Bake for 20 minutes.

Icing

½ **cup butter**
6 **tablespoons milk**
4 **tablespoons unsweetened cocoa**
1 **pound confectioners' sugar**
1 **teaspoon vanilla**
1 **cup pecans, chopped (optional)**

- Combine the butter, milk and cocoa in a saucepan and bring to a boil. (You may microwave until melted and bubbling if preferred.)

- Add the confectioners' sugar, vanilla and nuts. Mix well. Spread on cake while it is still hot. Cool before serving.

Serves 16 to 24

Cake is great for picnics, cookouts, meetings and socials. Stays moist and freezes well. This cake is ideal for all chocolate lovers.

Orange-Pecan Cake

¼ **pound unsalted butter**
1 **cup sugar**
1 **tablespoon orange zest, finely minced**
¼ **teaspoon vanilla extract**
1 **large egg**
1 **cup pecans, chopped and divided**
1⅓ **cups cake flour**
4 **teaspoons baking powder**
¼ **teaspoon salt**
1 **cup milk**
4 **ripe peaches, sliced**
2 **tablespoons Grand Marnier**
Whipped cream for garnish

- Adjust oven rack to middle level and preheat oven to 375 degrees. Butter and flour a 9-inch springform pan.

- Cream together butter, sugar, orange zest and vanilla extract until smooth and light in color.

- Add egg and mix until blended. Scrape down sides of bowl. Set aside.

- Place ¾ cup of pecans on a baking sheet and toast lightly in oven, about 6 minutes. Allow to cool completely.

- Place pecans in the bowl of a food processor with the flour and process until pecans are ground to powder.

- Add baking powder and salt. Pulse a few times to blend.

- Add half the flour mixture to the butter, then remaining flour mixture and milk.

- With a spatula, mix until smooth.

- Spoon batter into prepared cake pan. Sprinkle remaining chopped raw pecans on top of batter.

- Bake until center springs back, about 45 minutes. Unmold and cool on a rack.

- Combine sliced peaches and Grand Marnier. Let marinate 1 hour.

- When cool, slice and serve with marinated peaches.

- Garnish with whipped cream if desired.

Serves 8

Apple Cake

3 cups flour
1½ teaspoons cinnamon
½ teaspoon salt
½ teaspoon cloves
2 teaspoons baking soda
2 cups sugar
2 eggs
1 cup mayonnaise
⅓ cup milk
3 cups apples, peeled and chopped
1 cup raisins
½ cup walnuts, chopped

Frosting

1 pint whipping cream
1 teaspoon vanilla
2 tablespoons confectioners' sugar

- Preheat oven to 350 degrees.

- Combine flour, cinnamon, salt, cloves and baking soda. Set aside.

- Beat sugar and eggs. Add mayonnaise and milk.

- Add dry ingredients.

- Stir in apples, raisins and walnuts.

- Pour into 2 greased and floured 9-inch cake pans.

- Bake 45 minutes.

- Transfer to cooling rack.

- Beat whipping cream, vanilla and confectioners' sugar until stiff.

- Fill and frost cake with whipped cream.

Serves 10 to 12

Chocolate Toffee Cookie Crunch Bars

Cookie Base

2   **cups vanilla wafers (about 50 wafers), finely crushed**

¼   **cup firmly packed brown sugar**

⅓   **cup butter, melted**

Toffee Layer

½   **cup butter**

½   **cup firmly packed brown sugar**

1   **package (6 ounce) semi-sweet chocolate morsels**

½   **cup nuts, finely chopped**

Cookie Base

- Preheat oven to 350 degrees.

- In a large bowl, combine wafer crumbs and brown sugar. Stir in melted butter.

- Press into 13x9-inch baking pan.

- Bake 8 minutes.

Toffee Layer

- In saucepan, combine butter and brown sugar. Cook over moderate heat, stirring constantly until mixture comes to a boil.

- Boil 1 minute and immediately pour over baked base.

- Bake at 350 degrees for 10 minutes.

- Let stand 2 minutes.

- Sprinkle chips on top and let stand 2 to 3 minutes until morsels are shiny and soft. Spread evenly.

- Sprinkle with chopped nuts.

- Chill. Cut into 2x1-inch bars or break into irregular pieces.

Yield: 4½ dozen bars.

Merry Cherry Bars

1   cup butter
1   cup sugar
1   egg
½   teaspoon almond extract
2   cups flour
¼   teaspoon salt
¾   cup red candied cherries
    (8 ounces), coarsely
    chopped and divided
½-1 cup plain M&M's (red and
    green), divided
1   cup sifted confectioners'
    sugar
5   teaspoons warm water

- Preheat oven to 300 degrees.

- Beat butter and sugar until fluffy. Blend in egg and almond extract.

- Add flour and salt. Mix well.

- Stir in ½ cup cherries.

- Spread dough onto ungreased 15½ x 10½-inch cookie sheet.

- Sprinkle with remaining cherries and M&M's. Press in lightly.

- Bake 30 to 35 minutes or until edges are lightly browned. Cool thoroughly.

- Combine confectioners' sugar and water. Mix until smooth. Drizzle over top of bars.

- Cut into bars.

Yield: 24 bars

Oatmeal Caramel Bars

1   cup butter
2½ cups flour, divided
2   cups packed brown sugar
2   eggs
2   teaspoons vanilla extract
1   teaspoon baking soda
3   cups quick oats
1   cup semi-sweet chocolate
    chips
½   cup pecans, chopped
24 vanilla caramels
    (about 7 ounces)
2   tablespoons milk

• Preheat oven to 350 degrees.

• Beat butter with mixer for 30 seconds.

• Add 1 cup flour, brown sugar, eggs, vanilla and baking soda. Beat until well combined.

• Stir in remaining 1½ cups flour and oats.

• Press ⅔ of dough into an ungreased 15x10x1-inch baking pan.

• Sprinkle with chocolate chips and nuts.

• In saucepan, combine caramels and milk. Cook over low heat until melted. Drizzle over chocolate and nuts.

• Drop remaining dough by teaspoonfuls over top.

• Bake 25 minutes or until top is light golden brown.

• Cool in pan on wire rack. Cut into bars.

Yield: 30 to 36 bars

Pecan Pie Bars

2   cups unsifted flour
½   cup confectioners' sugar
1   cup butter
1   can (14 ounce) sweetened
     condensed milk
1   egg
1   teaspoon vanilla
1   package (6 ounces) almond
     brickle chips
1   cup pecans, chopped

• Preheat oven to 350 degrees (325 degrees if using glass dish).

• In a medium bowl, combine flour and sugar. Cut in butter until mixture resembles coarse meal.

• Press firmly on bottom of an ungreased 9x13-inch baking pan.

• Bake 15 minutes.

• Meanwhile, in a medium bowl, beat milk, egg and vanilla.

• Stir in chips and pecans. Spread evenly over prepared crust.

• Bake 25 minutes or until golden brown. Cool.

• Chill thoroughly. Cut into small bars. Store covered in the refrigerator.

Yield: 36 bars

Bars freeze well.

Baklava

Baklava Dough

1   **pound walnuts, chopped**
2   **teaspoons ground cinnamon**
1   **tablespoon orange rind, grated**
1   **pound unsalted butter, divided**
1   **pound phyllo dough**
Whole cloves (optional)

Syrup

2   **cups sugar**
1   **cup water**
½   **cup honey**
½   **lemon**
1   **stick cinnamon**

Baklava Dough

- Preheat oven to 350 degrees.

- Combine walnuts, ground cinnamon and orange rind.

- Melt butter, skimming foam from top of butter and avoiding solids at bottom.

- With pastry brush, coat bottom of 9x13-inch aluminum pan with a little melted butter. (Do not use glass pan. Phyllo dough will not bake properly.)

- Cut phyllo dough in half crosswise. Roll up one half, cover with damp cloth and set aside until first half is used up.

- Place a single sheet of phyllo dough in buttered pan. Brush top side of dough with melted butter. Continue layering sheets of phyllo, buttering each top side, until you have 7 to 8 layers in pan.

- Sprinkle dough evenly with ⅓ to ½ cup of walnut mixture.

- Brush another sheet of dough with butter. Place, buttered side down, in pan on top of walnut mixture.

- Quickly and gently brush top side of dough with melted butter.

- Repeat layers of walnut mixture and buttered phyllo dough until all walnut mixture is used. End with the phyllo dough layer, buttered on both sides.

Baklava continued

- Add another 7 to 8 layers of phyllo dough to the pan, brushing top side of each layer with melted butter. (This should use most of the phyllo dough.)

- With sharp knife, score top of baklava through top few layers (but not all the way through to bottom of pan), making first lengthwise lines, then diagonal lines to create a diamond pattern. Make lines about 1½ to 2 inches apart.

- If desired, press a whole clove in center of each diamond.

- Bake 30 to 35 minutes or until a rich golden brown.

- While baklava is baking, combine sugar, water, lemon and cinnamon stick in a small saucepan. (For a less lemony flavor, use only juice of lemon, not rind.)

- Bring to a boil and continue cooking for 2 to 3 minutes until sugar is melted and syrup is clear.

- Stir in honey and cool. Remove lemon rind and cinnamon stick.

- When baklava is done, remove from oven and cool 1 to 2 minutes.

- While baklava is still hot and after syrup has cooled, pour syrup over baklava dough. Cool completely.

- Slice baklava along diamond cuts to form individual bars.

Yield: 3 to 4 dozen

Triple Chocolate Brownies

2¼ cups flour

¾ teaspoon baking soda

16 tablespoons unsalted butter

2¼ cups sugar

¼ cup water

2 tablespoons instant espresso coffee powder

18 ounces semi-sweet chocolate, chopped

1 tablespoon vanilla extract

6 eggs

1½ cups white chocolate chips

1½ cups milk chocolate chips

1½ cups walnuts, chopped

- Preheat oven to 325 degrees.

- Butter a 12x18-inch or 11x15-inch baking pan. Line with parchment paper and butter the parchment.

- In a medium mixing bowl, combine flour and baking soda. Set aside.

- In a large, heavy saucepan, combine the butter, sugar, water and espresso.

- Heat just to boiling point. Remove the pan from the heat and add the semi-sweet chocolate and vanilla. Stir until the mixture is smooth and the chocolate has melted.

- Add eggs, one at a time, beating after each addition.

- Gradually add flour mixture, being careful not to overmix.

- Stir in white chocolate chips and milk chocolate chips, and then nuts.

- Spread batter into the prepared pan and bake 30 to 40 minutes for 12x18-inch pan and 50 to 60 minutes for 11x15-inch pan. Rotate the pan in oven half way through baking.

- The brownies are done when a toothpick inserted into the center comes out almost clean.

- Cut into squares.

Yield: 24 brownies

Cappuccino Thins

4 ounces sweet chocolate, cut
  into 1-inch pieces
½ cup plus 2 tablespoons
  sugar
½ cup firmly packed light
  brown sugar
1 egg yolk
1 tablespoon instant coffee
  powder
1 tablespoon unsweetened
  cocoa powder
1 tablespoon cinnamon
¾ teaspoon salt
1 cup unsalted butter, at
  room temperature, cut into
  8 pieces
1 cup cake flour
1 cup unbleached flour

- Chop chocolate in a food processor fitted with a steel blade until chocolate resembles coarse meal. Transfer to small bowl and set aside.

- Combine light brown sugar, egg yolk, instant coffee, cocoa powder, cinnamon and salt in food processor and mix for 1 minute. Add butter and process 1 minute.

- Add cake flour, flour and chocolate and pulse in food processor just until flour is incorporated in dough. Do not overprocess.

- Divide dough into four portions. Roll into logs on plastic wrap. Seal and refrigerate 1 hour. (Dough can be frozen at this point.)

- Position rack in middle of oven and pre-heat oven to 350 degrees.

- Cut dough into ¼-inch slices.

- Arrange on baking sheet spacing 1½-inches apart. Bake until set, about 8 minutes.

- Transfer to wire rack and let cool completely.

- Store in airtight container.

Yield: 5 dozen

Lemon Meringue Cookies

3 **egg whites** **½** **teaspoon cream of tartar** **1** **cup sugar** **1** **tablespoon lemon rind, finely grated** **Nonstick cooking spray**	• Preheat oven to 275 degrees. • Beat egg whites until foamy. Add cream of tartar. • Gradually beat in sugar, 2 tablespoons at a time, until stiff glossy peaks form. • Fold in lemon rind. • Drop by teaspoonfuls onto baking sheet that has been lightly sprayed with non-stick cooking spray. • Bake for 20 to 25 minutes. (Cookies will not brown on top but will be very pale brown on the bottom.) Cool on a wire rack.

Yield: 24 to 30 cookies

For the holidays, replace lemon with crushed candy cane for Peppermint Meringue Cookies.

Have egg whites at room temperature before beating to achieve maximum volume from the egg whites.

Oatmeal Chocolate Chip Cookies

1 cup butter
¾ cup brown sugar
¾ cup white sugar
2 eggs
1 teaspoon vanilla
1 teaspoon baking soda
1 teaspoon salt
2 cups quick oatmeal
1½ cups flour
11 ounces chocolate chips
1 cup raisins

- Preheat oven to 350 degrees.

- Cream butter, brown and white sugars and eggs. Add vanilla, baking soda and salt.

- Stir in oatmeal and then the flour.

- Add chocolate chips and raisins.

- Drop onto cookie sheet by well-rounded teaspoonfuls.

- Bake 10 minutes.

Yield: 2 to 3 dozen

Oatmeal Crisp Cookies

1 cup butter
2 tablespoons water
2 tablespoons maple syrup
1 cup flour
1½ cups sugar, divided
½ teaspoon baking soda
1 teaspoon baking powder
2½ cups quick cooking oats

- Heat butter and water until butter is melted. Add maple syrup.

- Sift together flour, 1 cup of the sugar, baking soda and baking powder. Add to butter mixture and mix.

- Add quick cooking oats to mixture and combine well.

- Chill dough for 15 minutes.

- Preheat oven to 350 degrees.

- Form dough into 1-inch balls and roll in ½ cup sugar.

- Place on cookie sheet and press flat with bottom of a glass.

- Bake for 12 to 15 minutes.

Yield: 4½ dozen

Molasses Cookies

⅔ **cup vegetable oil**
1 **cup sugar plus additional for dipping cookies**
1 **egg**
⅓ **cup molasses**
1 **teaspoon ground ginger**
1 **teaspoon cinnamon**
2 **cups flour**
2 **teaspoons baking soda**
½ **teaspoon salt**

- Preheat oven to 350 degrees.

- Stir together oil, 1 cup sugar, egg, molasses, ginger and cinnamon.

- Sift flour, baking soda and salt into mixture and stir well.

- Form large walnut-sized balls and dip them into a dish of granulated sugar.

- Place on greased cookie sheets and flatten with the bottom of a glass which has been greased and dipped in sugar. Space cookies 2 to 3 inches apart. (Cookies are large, 3 to 4 inches in diameter.)

- To test for doneness, bake until firm to touch. Cool approximately 12 minutes.

Yield: 2½ dozen large cookies or 3 dozen small cookies

Recipe can be doubled.

Semi-Retro Chocolate Chip Cookies

3   cups flour

1   teaspoon baking soda

1   teaspoon salt

10½-14 ounces bittersweet chocolate

3½-4   ounce high-quality white chocolate

½   cup plus 2 tablespoons butter

¼   cup solid shortening

1   cup sugar

⅓   cup brown sugar

1   teaspoon vanilla

2   eggs

1   egg yolk

¼   cup maple syrup

1   cup walnuts, coarsely chopped

- Heat oven to 350 degrees. Line baking sheets with parchment paper or butter lightly.

- Sift flour with baking soda and salt. Set aside.

- Chop the chocolates into small chunks. For butter cookies with chocolate pieces, use a colander to sift out the finer crumbs. For chocolate flavor clear through, leave chocolate crumbs.

- Cream butter with shortening, then cream in sugars. Add vanilla, then beat in eggs and yolk, one at a time. Beat in syrup.

- Stir in the flour mixture, then the chopped chocolate and nuts.

- Drop by rounded tablespoons and bake until lightly browned and dry on top, about 10 minutes. Do not overbake. Let cool on the sheets for a couple of minutes, then transfer to wire racks.

Yield: about 6 dozen

Apricot Ginger Biscotti

⅓ **cup dried apricots
    (about 2 ounces)**
2 **large eggs**
1 **teaspoon water**
1⅓ **cups flour**
½ **cup sugar**
¼ **teaspoon baking soda**
¼ **teaspoon baking powder**
¼ **teaspoon salt**
½ **teaspoon vanilla**
2 **tablespoons candied ginger
    (about 1 ounce), chopped**

- Preheat oven to 325 degrees.

- Lightly butter a baking sheet and dust with flour, knocking out excess flour.

- In a bowl, soak apricots in boiling water to cover for 5 minutes.

- Drain apricots well and pat dry with paper towels. Chop apricots fine.

- In another bowl, lightly whisk eggs and transfer 1 teaspoon egg to a small bowl.

- Whisk water into the 1 teaspoon egg and reserve egg wash.

- In a large bowl with an electric mixer, blend flour, sugar, baking soda, baking powder and salt. Add remaining egg and vanilla and beat until dough forms (dough will be sticky). Stir in apricots and ginger.

- Turn dough out onto a floured surface and knead six times.

- Working on baking sheet, with floured hands, form dough into a 6½ x 4½-inch rectangle. Brush with some of the reserved egg wash and bake in middle of oven for 30 minutes.

- Cool rectangle on baking sheet on a rack for 10 minutes.

(continued on next page)

Apricot Ginger Biscotti continued

- Loosen rectangle from baking sheet with a metal spatula and carefully transfer to a cutting board.

- Cut rectangles crosswise into ½-inch thick slices.

- Arrange biscotti slices, cut side down, on baking sheet and bake 10 minutes on each side or until pale golden.

- Transfer biscotti to rack to cool.

Yield: about 12 biscotti

Biscotti keep in an airtight container at room temperature three days or frozen one month.

Macadamia Nut Biscotti with Candied Ginger

4   ounces unsalted butter at
    room temperature
1   cup granulated sugar
2   extra large eggs at room
    temperature
2½ cups unbleached flour
4   teaspoons orange zest,
    minced
1½ teaspoons baking powder
4   tablespoons vanilla extract
½   teaspoon orange oil
2   generous pinches ground
    cinnamon
Pinch ground nutmeg
¾   cup macadamia nuts,
    chopped
¼   cup candied ginger,
    chopped
2   ounces bittersweet
    chocolate (optional),
    chopped

- Preheat oven to 375 degrees.

- Beat butter and sugar together until light and fluffy, 2 to 3 minutes.

- Beat in one egg at a time until well mixed.

- Sprinkle in flour and mix well.

- Beat in orange zest, baking powder, vanilla, orange oil, cinnamon, nutmeg and macadamia nuts.

- Add the candied ginger and chocolate, beating only until disbursed throughout the batter.

- Butter and flour baking sheets.

- On prepared baking sheets, shape batter into 2 logs, approximately 2 to 3 inches wide and 1 inch high.

- Place in center of oven and reduce heat to 325 degrees. Bake until barely golden brown, 30 to 35 minutes.

- Remove from oven and cool for a few seconds.

- Slice logs into ½-inch thick pieces and separate on the sheet so air can circulate.

- Reduce oven to 275 degrees and bake 25 to 30 minutes more or until dry and crisp.

- Remove from oven, cool and store in an air-tight container.

Yield: 3 dozen

(continued on next page)

Macadamia Nut Biscotti with Candied Ginger continued

Most macadamia nuts are salted. To remove salt, quickly rub between moistened paper towels. Do not add more salt to batter.

Chocolate can be added either chopped and mixed into dough or as a topping. To use chocolate as a topping:

• *In small saucepan over low heat, melt chocolate until smooth.*

• *Cool to about 100 degrees, stirring constantly. Pour into a thick resealable plastic bag.*

• *Line up baked, cooled biscotti, sides touching, tightly packed together.*

• *Snip off one bottom corner of the plastic bag, about ⅛-inch, and quickly drizzle the chocolate in lines over the tops of the biscotti. Cool until set.*

Layered Peppermint Crunch Bark

17 ounces good quality white chocolate, finely chopped

30 red and white striped hard peppermint candies, coarsely crushed (about 6 ounces), divided

7 ounces bittersweet or semi-sweet chocolate, chopped

6 tablespoons whipping cream

¾ teaspoon peppermint extract

• Turn large baking sheet bottom side up. Cover securely with foil. Mark a 12x9-inch rectangle on foil.

• Stir white chocolate in metal bowl set over saucepan of barely simmering water (do not allow bottom of bowl to touch water) until chocolate is melted and smooth and candy thermometer registers 110 degrees. (Chocolate will feel warm to touch.) Remove bowl from saucepan.

• Pour ⅔ cup melted white chocolate onto rectangle on foil. Using icing spatula, spread chocolate to cover rectangle. Sprinkle with ¼ cup crushed peppermints.

• Chill until set, about 15 minutes.

• Stir bittersweet chocolate, cream and peppermint extract in heavy, medium-sized saucepan over medium-low heat until just melted and smooth. Cool to barely lukewarm, about 5 minutes.

• Pour bittersweet chocolate mixture in long lines over white chocolate rectangle. Using icing spatula, spread bittersweet chocolate evenly over entire rectangle. Refrigerate until very cold and firm, about 25 minutes.

• Rewarm remaining white chocolate in bowl set over barely simmering water to 110 degrees.

(continued on next page)

Layered Peppermint Crunch Bark continued

- Working quickly, pour white chocolate over firm bittersweet chocolate layer. Spread to cover. Immediately sprinkle with remaining crushed peppermints. Chill just until firm, about 20 minutes.

- Lift foil with bark onto work surface. Cut crosswise into 2-inch wide strips.

- Using metal spatula, slide bark off foil and onto work surface.

- Cut each strip crosswise into 3 sections and each section diagonally into 2 triangles. Let stand 15 minutes at room temperature before serving.

Yield: 36 pieces

Can be stored in airtight container for two weeks.

Pecan Delights

8 ounces cream cheese
1¼ cups plus 2 tablespoons butter, divided
2½ cups flour
2 cups brown sugar
2½ teaspoons vanilla extract
2 eggs
2½ cups pecans, chopped
Confectioners' sugar for garnish

• Preheat oven to 350 degrees.

• Mix cream cheese, 1¼ cups butter and flour.

• Roll into balls and press into greased mini muffin tins.

• Mix brown sugar, 2 tablespoons butter, vanilla and eggs. Add pecans.

• Fill shells ¾ full. Bake 20 minutes.

• Sprinkle with confectioners' sugar.

Yield: 3 dozen

Toffee Grahams

12 graham crackers
1 cup butter
½ cup brown sugar
12 ounces chocolate bits
½ cup pecans, chopped
(optional)

- Preheat oven to 350 degrees.

- Line 15x10x1-inch pan with foil.

- Cover bottom with graham crackers.

- Melt butter and brown sugar. Whisk until blended. Boil 2 minutes.

- Pour mixture over graham crackers.

- Bake for 6 minutes.

- Remove from oven and sprinkle with chocolate bits.

- Return to oven for 1 to 2 minutes or until bits are soft.

- Spread bits over crackers. Sprinkle with chopped pecans.

- Place pan in freezer for 1 to 2 hours.

- Lift crackers from pan. Peel off foil and break into chunks.

Yield: 2 dozen

Substitute unsalted saltines or matzo for graham crackers.

Apple Pie

2½ **pounds apples (½ Granny Smith, ½ other), peeled, cored and sliced**

2 **cups light brown sugar, divided**

2 **tablespoons cornstarch**

2 **tablespoons dark rum**

1 **teaspoon vanilla**

1 **teaspoon lemon juice**

1 **teaspoon cinnamon**

1 **(9-inch) single pie shell**

½ **cup rolled oats**

½ **cup flour**

2 **tablespoons butter, melted**

- Preheat oven to 350 degrees. Cover cookie sheet with aluminum foil.

- Mix together apples, 1 cup brown sugar, cornstarch, rum, vanilla, lemon juice and cinnamon. Spoon into pie shell.

- In a separate bowl, combine remaining 1 cup of brown sugar, rolled oats, flour and butter to form a crumbly mixture. Sprinkle over apples.

- Set pie on prepared cookie sheet. Place in oven and bake 45 minutes, or until juices are bubbling and top is golden.

Serves 6 to 8

Bavarian Apple Tart

Dough

½   **cup butter**
⅓   **cup sugar**
¾   **teaspoon vanilla**
1   **cup flour**

Filling

8   **ounces cream cheese,
softened**
¼   **cup plus ⅓ cup sugar**
1   **egg**
½   **teaspoon vanilla**
½   **teaspoon cinnamon**
4   **cups apples, peeled and
thinly sliced**
¼   **cup almonds, sliced**

- Cream butter, sugar and vanilla. Blend in flour.

- Spread dough onto bottom and 2 inches up the sides of a 9-inch springform pan. Set aside.

- Preheat oven to 450 degrees.

- Combine cream cheese and ¼ cup sugar. Mix well. Add egg and vanilla. Mix well.

- Pour into pastry-lined pan.

- Combine ⅓ cup sugar and cinnamon. Toss with apples. Spoon apples over cream cheese layer and sprinkle with almonds.

- Bake at 450 degrees for 10 minutes. Reduce temperature to 400 degrees and bake another 25 to 35 minutes.

Serves 6 to 8

Blueberry Bottom Cobbler

2   cups fresh or frozen
    blueberries, thawed and
    drained
2   tablespoons fresh lemon
    juice
3   tablespoons shortening
1¾ cups sugar, divided
1   cup flour
1   teaspoon baking powder
½   teaspoon salt, divided
½   cup milk
1   tablespoon cornstarch
1   cup boiling water
Vanilla ice cream

- Preheat oven to 375 degrees.

- Place blueberries in bottom of a greased 9-inch square baking pan. Sprinkle with lemon juice and set aside.

- In an electric mixer, cream shortening. On medium speed, gradually add ¾ cup sugar, beating well.

- In a separate bowl, combine flour, baking powder and ¼ teaspoon salt. Stir well.

- Add to shortening and sugar, alternately with the milk, beginning and ending with flour. Mix well after each addition.

- Spread the batter over the blueberries.

- Combine 1 cup sugar, cornstarch, and ¼ teaspoon salt. Stir well. Sprinkle over batter.

- Pour the boiling water over the cobbler. Do not stir.

- Bake for 40 to 50 minutes or until golden. Serve warm with ice cream.

Serves 9

Blueberry Peach Pie

2	cups plus ⅓ cup flour
1	teaspoon salt
⅔	cup plus 2 tablespoons shortening
3-5	tablespoons cold water
¾	cup sugar
1½	teaspoons ground cinnamon
2½-3	cups fresh blueberries
2	cups fresh peaches, peeled and sliced

- Preheat oven to 425 degrees.

- Combine 2 cups flour and salt. Cut in shortening with a pastry blender or fork until mixture is crumbly. Sprinkle with cold water, 1 tablespoon at a time, stirring with a fork after each addition, until pastry can be shaped into a ball.

- On a lightly floured surface, roll half of the dough to ⅛-inch thickness. Place in a 9-inch pie plate. Set aside.

- Combine sugar, ⅓ cup flour and cinnamon in a large bowl. Add blueberries and peaches and toss gently. Spoon into pastry shell.

- Roll remaining pastry to a ⅛-inch thickness. Transfer to top of pie. Trim off excess pastry along edges. Fold edges under and crimp. Cut slits in top of pastry to allow steam to escape.

- Bake for 40 to 50 minutes, or until lightly browned.

- Let stand 10 minutes before serving. Serve warm.

Serves 6 to 8

If edges of pastry become too brown during baking, cover with strips of aluminum foil.

Desserts

Blueberry Pie

¼ **cup flour**
⅔ **cup sugar**
6 **cups blueberries**
2 **tablespoons lemon juice**
¼ **cup butter**
Pastry for a 2 crust 9-inch pie shell, unbaked

- Preheat oven to 400 degrees.
- Combine flour, sugar and berries. Add lemon juice and toss to coat.
- Pour filling into unbaked pie shell. Dot with butter. Cover with top crust. Cut 3 or 4 slits in top for steam.
- Bake for 20 minutes at 400 degrees. Reduce heat to 350 degrees and bake another 25 minutes, or until brown. Cool on rack

Serves 6 to 8

Chocolate Bourbon Pecan Pie

1 **(9-inch) single pie shell, unbaked**
3 **large eggs, lightly beaten**
⅓ **cup granulated sugar**
3 **tablespoons firmly packed light brown sugar**
1 **tablespoon flour**
¾ **cup light corn syrup**
¼ **cup butter, melted**
3 **tablespoons bourbon**
2 **cups pecan halves**
1 **cup semisweet chocolate morsels**
Whipped cream or vanilla ice cream for garnish

- Preheat oven to 350 degrees.
- Fit pie crust into a 9-inch pie plate. Prick the bottom with a fork and set aside.
- Combine the eggs, sugar, brown sugar, flour, corn syrup, melted butter and bourbon in a bowl.
- Spread pecan halves evenly over bottom of the pie crust. Top with chocolate chips. Pour the egg mixture over the pecans and chocolate.
- Bake for 50 to 55 minutes, until outer 2 inches are firm and the center looks set but quivery.
- Serve with whipped cream or vanilla ice cream.

Serves 6 to 8

Fruit Torte

1   cup sugar plus additional sugar to sweeten filling
½   cup butter
1   cup flour, sifted plus additional flour to thicken filling
1   teaspoon baking powder
Pinch of salt
2   eggs
4-6 cups of the following fruits (or a combination): blueberries, sliced apples, sliced peaches, or
12 Italian plums, halved and pitted
Lemon juice, to taste
Cinnamon, to taste

- Preheat oven to 350 degrees.
- Cream together sugar and butter.
- Add flour, baking powder, pinch of salt and eggs. Mix well.
- Place in 9-inch springform pan. Press dough to cover bottom and part way up sides.
- Cover entire surface with the fruit. If using plum halves, be sure to place skin side up. Sprinkle top with sugar, lemon juice and cinnamon. If fruit is very juicy, sprinkle with flour.
- Bake for 1 hour. Serve warm.

Serves 8

Full of Berries Pie

2   cups strawberries, hulled and quartered
2   cups fresh blueberries
2   cups fresh raspberries
1   cup plus 1 tablespoon sugar, divided
¼   cup cornstarch
¼   teaspoon cinnamon
2   teaspoons lemon zest
1   teaspoon vanilla
Pie dough for a 9-inch double crust pie

- Preheat oven to 400 degrees.
- Place strawberries, blueberries and raspberries in a bowl. Toss with 1 cup sugar, cornstarch, cinnamon, lemon zest and vanilla. Spoon berries into crust.
- Cover filling with top crust and crimp the edges. Cut slits in top and sprinkle with remaining 1 tablespoon sugar.
- Bake in lower ⅔ of the oven for 1 to 1¼ hours.

Serves 6 to 8

Cranberry Walnut Tart

Dough

1⅔ cups flour

2½ teaspoons sugar

¼ teaspoon salt

¼ teaspoon cinnamon

2 tablespoons cold unsalted butter, cut into small pieces

1 large egg yolk

¼ cup ice water

Filling

12 ounces cranberries

½ cup plus 1 tablespoon light brown sugar

½ cup plus 1 tablespoon granulated sugar

Zest of 1 orange, finely grated

Zest of 1 lemon, finely grated

½ cup fresh orange juice

⅛ teaspoon cinnamon

4 tablespoons plus 1 teaspoon unsalted butter

½ cup walnuts, coarsely chopped

Vanilla ice cream

- Preheat oven to 375 degrees.

- To make the pastry, in a food processor, combine the flour, sugar, salt and cinnamon and pulse. Add the butter and pulse until mixture resembles coarse meal. Transfer to a bowl.

- Whisk the egg yolk with the ice water and add to flour mixture. Stir until dough is evenly moistened. Transfer to a lightly floured surface and knead several times. Pat the dough into a 6-inch disk, wrap in plastic and refrigerate for at least 30 minutes.

- Meanwhile, in a medium saucepan, combine the cranberries with the brown sugar, ½ cup plus 1 tablespoon of granulated sugar, orange zest, lemon zest, orange juice and cinnamon. Bring to a boil. Lower the heat and simmer, stirring, until thickened, 8 to 10 minutes. Stir in the butter and transfer to a bowl to cool. Stir in walnuts.

- Butter a 10-inch fluted tart pan with a removable bottom. On a lightly floured surface, roll out the dough to a 12-inch round, about ⅛-inch thick. Transfer the dough to the pan and fit it into the sides. Trim off the overhang. Prick bottom of the tart shell and refrigerate until chilled.

(continued on next page)

Cranberry Walnut Tart continued

- Line the pastry with wax paper and fill with pie weights or dried beans. Bake the tart for 30 minutes, or until lightly golden around the edges. Carefully remove the paper and weights and bake the shell 5 minutes longer, or until dry on the bottom. Cool slightly.

- Spread the cranberry filling evenly in the tart shell and bake for 25 minutes, or until the edge of the pastry is golden. Let the tart cool on a rack before unmolding. Serve warm or at room temperature with vanilla ice cream.

Serves 8 to 10

The baked tart can be refrigerated overnight. Warm in a 350-degree oven for 15 minutes before serving.

Pear Cranberry Pie with Crumb Topping

Flaky Pie Dough

1¼ cups plus 2 tablespoons flour

¾ teaspoon salt

¼ teaspoon lemon zest, finely grated

¼ teaspoon cinnamon

3 tablespoons cold unsalted butter, cut into small pieces

6 tablespoons solid vegetable shortening, cut into small pieces and chilled

2-3 tablespoons ice water

1 egg

1 tablespoon milk or cream

Topping

1 cup flour

⅓ cup granulated sugar

⅓ cup packed light brown sugar

12 gingersnaps, crushed

⅛ teaspoon ground ginger

⅛ teaspoon salt

½ cup unsalted butter, melted and cooled

• In a food processor, combine the flour, salt, lemon zest and cinnamon. Add the butter and shortening and pulse until butter is the size of small peas.

• Transfer the mixture to a large bowl. Add the ice water and stir with a fork until the dough comes together in a ball.

• Pat dough into a 6-inch disk and wrap tightly in plastic. Refrigerate at least 1 hour.

• On a lightly floured surface, roll out the dough to a 12-inch round and fit into a 9-inch glass pie plate. Trim overhang to 1 inch, fold under and crimp.

• Beat egg with milk or cream to make egg wash. Brush rim with the egg wash and refrigerate until well chilled.

• In a medium bowl, combine the flour, granulated sugar, brown sugar, gingersnaps, ginger and salt.

• Stir in the melted butter until large crumbs form. Set aside.

(continued on next page)

Pear Cranberry Pie with Crumb Topping continued

Filling

2   **pounds ripe Anjou pears (about 5), peeled, halved, cored and sliced ¼-inch thick**

1½   **cups fresh cranberries**

2   **tablespoons fresh lemon juice**

1   **teaspoon lemon zest, finely grated**

½   **teaspoon pure vanilla extract**

¾   **cup sugar**

2   **tablespoons cornstarch**

- Preheat oven to 350 degrees.

- In a large bowl, toss the pears with the cranberries, lemon juice, lemon zest and vanilla.

- In a small bowl, mix the sugar with the cornstarch. Stir into the fruit.

- Pour into the chilled pie shell.

- Cover the filling completely with the gingersnap topping.

- Set the pie on a foil-lined baking sheet. Bake on the bottom rack of the oven for 1½ hours, or until crust is golden and filling is bubbling. Cover the pie loosely with foil if top browns too quickly. Let cool before slicing.

Serves 6 to 8

Festive Cranberry Torte

Dough

1½ cups graham cracker
 crumbs
½ cup pecans, chopped
¼ cup sugar
6 tablespoons butter, melted

- In a mixing bowl, combine cracker crumbs, pecans, sugar and butter. Press onto bottom and up sides of an 8-inch springform pan. Refrigerate.

Filling

1½ cups ground fresh
 cranberries, (about 2 cups
 whole berries)
1 cup sugar
2 egg whites
1 tablespoon frozen orange
 juice concentrate, thawed
1 teaspoon vanilla
⅛ teaspoon salt
1 cup whipping cream

- In a large mixing bowl, combine cranberries and sugar. Let stand 5 minutes.

- Add unbeaten egg whites, orange juice, vanilla and salt. Beat on low speed with an electric mixer until frothy. Beat at high speed for 6 to 8 minutes or until soft peaks form.

- In a small mixing bowl, whip cream to soft peaks.

- Fold cream into cranberries. Turn mixture into prepared crust. Freeze until firm.

Cranberry Glaze

½ cup sugar
1 tablespoon cornstarch
¾ cup fresh cranberries
⅔ cup water

- Stir together the sugar and cornstarch in a saucepan. Add cranberries and water. Cook and stir until bubbly. Cook, stirring occasionally, just until cranberry skins pop. Cool to room temperature. Do not chill.

- Remove torte from pan and place on serving plate. Spoon cranberry glaze in center.

Serves 8 to 10

Lime Cream Chiffon Pie

1   **envelope unflavored gelatin**

¼   **cup cold water**

4   **eggs, separated**

½   **cup lime juice (about 3 medium limes)**

1   **cup sugar, divided**

¼   **teaspoon salt**

1   **teaspoon lime rind, grated**

½   **cup heavy cream, whipped, plus whipped cream for garnish**

1   **(9-inch) baked pastry shell or vanilla wafer crust**

Lime slices for garnish

- Soften gelatin in cold water.

- In top of double boiler, beat egg yolks. Mix in lime juice, ½ cup sugar and salt. Cook over hot water until mixture thickens slightly, stirring constantly.

- Remove from heat. Add gelatin and stir until dissolved. Add lime rind.

- Beat egg whites until stiff peaks are formed. Gradually beat in remaining ½ cup sugar.

- Fold in gelatin mixture, then whipped cream.

- Turn into baked pastry shell and chill until firm.

- Serve with whipped cream. Garnish with a lime slice.

Serves 6 to 8

Rhubarb Custard Pie

3   cups rhubarb, sliced
1   (9-inch) pie shell, unbaked
2   eggs
1   cup sugar
2   tablespoons flour
1   tablespoon lemon juice
⅛   teaspoon salt

- Preheat oven to 400 degrees.

- Place rhubarb into a 9-inch crust.

- Beat eggs slightly. Add sugar, flour, lemon juice and salt. Mix well.

- Pour over the rhubarb.

- Bake for 20 minutes at 400 degrees. Reduce temperature to 350 degrees and bake an additional 30 minutes, or until a knife inserted in the center comes out clean.

Serves 6 to 8

For a deep-dish pie shell, increase all ingredients by half and add 10 to 15 minutes to baking time.

Mile High Strawberry Pie

10   ounces frozen strawberries, not in syrup, thawed
¾   cup sugar
2   egg whites
1   tablespoon lemon juice
⅛   teaspoon salt
1   (9-inch) baked pie shell
1   cup cream, whipped with 1 teaspoon vanilla plus additional whipped cream for garnish
Fresh strawberries for garnish

- Place strawberries, sugar, egg whites, lemon juice and salt in a large bowl.

- Beat with an electric mixer on high for 15 minutes until stiff.

- Fold in whipped cream.

- Pour into baked pie shell and freeze overnight.

- Serve with fresh strawberries and a dollop of whipped cream.

Serves 6 to 8

Strawberry and Blueberry Pie

Red, White and Blue Pie for the Fourth of July

The Crust

½   **cup butter, softened**
⅓   **cup confectioners' sugar**
1   **cup flour**
1   **teaspoon vanilla**
1   **tart pan with removable bottom, 10-inch diameter**

The Filling

2   **cups blueberries**
3   **tablespoons cornstarch**
¼   **cup kirsch, orange juice, or water**
2   **cups strawberries, cut in half if large**
¾   **cup sugar**
1   **teaspoon butter**
1   **teaspoon lemon juice**

The Topping

1   **cup heavy cream**
3   **tablespoons confectioners' sugar**
½   **teaspoon vanilla**
Extra blueberries and strawberries for garnish

- Preheat oven to 300 degrees.

- To make the crust, using a food processor, combine the butter, sugar, flour, and vanilla. Press the mixture into the tart pan.

- Bake for 25 minutes, or until the edges have begun to brown lightly. Remove from the oven and cool.

- Remove the ring from the pan. If the bottom comes off the tart shell easily, then remove it. Otherwise, leave it in place.

- To make the filling, fill the cooled tart shell with the blueberries, reserving a few for garnish.

- Dissolve the cornstarch in the kirsch. Place dissolved cornstarch, sugar and strawberries in a saucepan. Reserve a few strawberries for garnish. Bring to a boil. Lower heat immediately and stir until thickened. Remove from heat.

- Stir in the butter and the lemon juice. Cool thoroughly.

- Spread the strawberries over the blueberries. Refrigerate for several hours.

- Whip the cream, adding the sugar and vanilla. Spread the cream on the tart and decorate with the reserved blueberries and strawberries.

Serves 6 to 8

339

Fluffy Pumpkin Pie

Pie crust for 2 (9-inch) or 1
    (11-inch) crusts, unbaked
3½ cups cooked fresh
    pumpkin or canned
    pumpkin
1   cup light brown sugar
1   cup plus 2 tablespoons
    white sugar, divided
1   teaspoon plus pinch of salt,
    divided
3   tablespoons light molasses
3   tablespoons bourbon
    whiskey or dark rum
    (optional)
3   teaspoons cinnamon
3   teaspoons ground ginger
¼   teaspoon nutmeg
¼   teaspoon ground cloves
4   egg yolks
1   cup heavy cream
¾   cup milk, plus additional
    milk if batter is stiff
5   egg whites
Whipped cream or vanilla ice
    cream for topping

- Line the pie plate(s) with pie dough. Make a strong, fluted rim that extends about ½ inch above the rim of the dish. Do not prick.

- Preheat oven to 450 degrees.

- Blend pumpkin, brown sugar, 1 cup white sugar, 1 teaspoon salt, molasses, rum, cinnamon, ginger, nutmeg, cloves, egg yolks, cream and ¾ cup milk. If mixture is too stiff, blend in a few drops additional milk. Set aside.

- Beat egg whites until lightly foaming. Beat in a pinch of salt and continue beating to form soft peaks.

- Gradually sprinkle 2 tablespoons of sugar over the egg whites while continuing to beat until stiff shining peaks form.

- Beat ¼ of the whites into the pumpkin mixture. Delicately fold in the rest of the egg whites. Ladle the mixture into the pie shell(s) at once, filling only to the rim of the pan.

- Bake immediately on the middle shelf for 15 minutes. When the edges of the crust begin to brown, reduce heat to 375 degrees and bake 15 minutes longer. (Lower heat more if pastry browns too much.) Reduce temperature to 350 degrees and continue to bake 15 minutes more, until a pie tester or toothpick inserted 2 inches from the edge comes out clean.

(continued on next page)

Fluffy Pumpkin Pie continued

- Turn off oven, leave oven door ajar and let pie sit for 20 to 30 minutes more.

- Serve warm or cold, accompanied with whipped cream or vanilla ice cream if desired.

Serves 12 to 16

If filling cooks too fast, it will turn watery. Watch pie and reduce temperature if necessary to slow cooking.

Desserts

Strawberry or Raspberry Pie

1   **(9-inch) pie crust - pastry, graham cracker, or vanilla wafer**
6   **cups fresh strawberries or raspberries, divided**
1   **cup sugar**
¼   **cup cornstarch**
⅛   **teaspoon salt**
½   **cup water**
2   **tablespoons fresh lemon juice**
2   **tablespoons unsalted butter, cut in small pieces**
Whipped cream for garnish

• Prepare and line a 9-inch pie plate with chosen crust.

• Rinse strawberries (do not rinse raspberries). Dry and hull berries. Cut any large ones in half. Measure 4 cups of berries and set aside.

• Purée remaining 2 cups of berries in food processor or blender.

• In a medium saucepan, whisk together the sugar, cornstarch and salt. Whisk in water.

• Stir in the puréed berries along with the strained lemon juice and unsalted butter.

• Bring the mixture to a simmer over medium-high heat, stirring constantly. Cook for 1 minute.

• Pour half of the reserved berries into the crust and spoon half of the hot berry mixture over them. Gently shake the pie pan to coat the berries evenly. Cover with the remaining berries and spoon the remaining hot berry mixture over them. Gently shake pie pan to coat.

• Refrigerate the pie for at least 4 hours to set. Serve topped with whipped cream.

Serves 8

This pie is best served the day it is made.

Crème Caramel

Caramel

⅔ cup granulated sugar

⅓ cup water

Crème

5 eggs

5 tablespoons granulated sugar

3⅛ cups half-and-half

Caramel

- Dissolve sugar in water and bring liquid to a boil in an open heavy-bottom pan. Cover and boil for 1 minute. Uncover again and boil to a dark amber caramel. Do not stir.

- Pour caramel into a heated shallow metal mold or pan (approximately 7.5 inches in diameter) and swirl to coat the mold.

Crème

- Preheat oven to 325 degrees.

- Beat the eggs with the sugar.

- Heat half-and-half to boiling point and whisk into the beaten eggs.

- Pour egg mixture into the caramel-lined mold. Bake in a water bath for 40 to 45 minutes.

- Let cool in the mold and refrigerate.

- To unmold before serving, dip the mold in hot water for no more than 1 minute. Invert onto a shallow serving dish. Cut in slivers and spoon caramel on each serving.

Serves 8 to 10

Great Banana Cream Pie

5   large egg yolks
¾   cup cornstarch
5-5½   cups heavy cream, divided
1½ cups plus 4 teaspoons sugar, divided
1   vanilla bean, split and scraped
3   cups graham cracker crumbs
3-3½   pounds bananas, divided
¼   pound unsalted butter, melted
½   teaspoon vanilla extract
¾   cup caramel sauce
1   cup chocolate sauce
Shaved chocolate
Powdered sugar

- In a mixing bowl, combine egg yolks, cornstarch and 1 cup heavy cream. Whisk to blend well. Set aside.

- Combine 2 cups cream with 1½ cups sugar and the vanilla bean in a large heavy-bottomed saucepan over medium heat. Whisk to dissolve sugar and bring to a gentle boil, about 10 minutes.

- Slowly add egg yolk mixture, whisking constantly until it thickens, about 5 minutes. (Note: mixture will separate.)

- Pour mixture into a glass bowl. Press a piece of plastic wrap down over surface to prevent skin from forming. Let cool completely at room temperature.

- When cooled, remove vanilla bean and pour mixture into bowl of an electric mixer fitted with a wire whip. Beat at medium-speed to combine mixture. If mixture fails to combine, warm an additional ½ cup heavy cream and slowly add to the mixture. Whip to a thick and creamy custard.

- Preheat oven to 350 degrees.

- Mash ½ banana.

- In a mixing bowl, combine graham cracker crumbs, 2 teaspoons sugar and mashed banana. Mix thoroughly.

- Add butter. Mix well.

(continued on next page)

Great Banana Cream Pie continued

- Press mixture into a 9-inch pie pan. Bake until browned, about 25 minutes.

- Remove pan from oven and cool for 10 minutes.

- Slice remaining bananas into ½-inch slices.

- To assemble, spread ½ cup of custard on bottom of crust.

- Arrange ⅓ of banana slices over the custard, crowding them close together.

- Spread 1 cup custard over bananas. Arrange another ⅓ banana slices over custard. Top with 1 cup of custard and remaining banana slices.

- Top with remaining custard, covering bananas completely to prevent them from turning brown.

- Cover with plastic wrap and chill for at least 4 hours.

- Whip 2 cups heavy cream to stiff peaks with ½ teaspoon vanilla and 2 teaspoons sugar.

- Cut pie into wedges and serve with a drizzle of caramel and chocolate sauces.

- Top with whipped cream and shaved chocolate. Sprinkle with powdered sugar.

Serves 8 to 10

See index for chocolate sauce.

Very Rich Chocolate Mousse

1   **package (12 ounce) semi-sweet chocolate morsels, coarsely chopped in blender**
2   **eggs**
4   **tablespoons strong coffee, boiling hot**
4   **tablespoons rum**
½   **teaspoon vanilla extract**
¾   **cup boiling milk**
Whipped cream for garnish

- Place chocolate bits, eggs, coffee, rum, vanilla and milk in a blender and mix on blend setting for 2 minutes.

- Pour into custard cups or glass dessert dishes.

- Refrigerate 2 to 3 hours.

- Serve topped with whipped cream.

Serves 4 to 6

White Chocolate Mousse

8 ounces white chocolate,
   broken into small pieces
½ cup unsalted butter
6 eggs, separated, at room
   temperature
1 cup confectioners' sugar
½ cup hazelnut liqueur
2 cups whipping cream, cold
Pinch cream of tartar
Unsweetened cocoa powder for
   garnish

- Melt white chocolate and butter in small saucepan, stirring constantly. Set aside.

- Beat egg yolks, sugar and liqueur until mixture forms a slowly dissolving ribbon when beaters are lifted.

- Pour into top of a double boiler and cook, whisking constantly, over but not in simmering water until very thick, about 3 minutes. Pour into a large mixing bowl.

- Whisk in melted chocolate mixture and stir until smooth and cool.

- Beat whipping cream until stiff peaks are formed.

- Beat egg whites with cream of tartar until soft peaks are formed but not dry. Fold in whipped cream.

- Fold egg white and cream mixture into white chocolate mixture.

- Refrigerate covered until set, at least 3 hours.

- Spoon into ramekins or goblets. Sprinkle with cocoa powder.

Serves 8 to 12

White Velvet

1   **pint heavy cream**
½   **cup sugar**
1   **tablespoon unflavored
     gelatin**
2   **tablespoons light rum**
1   **pint sour cream
     (not low fat)**
Pinch of salt
Fresh fruit in season

• Oil a round mold, or use 8 individual serving bowls.

• Heat heavy cream until bubbles form. Do not let cream come to a boil.

• Add sugar.

• Soften gelatin in rum.

• Add to cream. Stir until dissolved.

• Add sour cream and mix until smooth.

• Pour into mold.

• Chill at least 2 hours.

• Serve with fresh fruit.

Serves 8

One teaspoon vanilla extract can be used in place of rum.

Bread Pudding

Bread Pudding

6-8 cups crumbled stale bread
4   cups milk
2   cups sugar
8   tablespoons butter, melted
3   eggs
3   tablespoons vanilla extract
1   cup raisins
1   cup coconut
1   cup pecans, chopped
1   teaspoon cinnamon
1   teaspoon nutmeg

Whiskey Sauce

½   **cup butter**
1½   **cups confectioners' sugar**
2   **egg yolks**
½   **cup bourbon**

Bread Pudding

- Combine bread, milk, sugar, butter, eggs, vanilla, raisins, coconut, pecans, cinnamon and nutmeg. Mixture should be moist but not soupy.

- Pour into buttered 9x13-inch or larger baking dish.

- Bake at 350 degrees for approximately 1¼ hours or until top is golden brown. (Do not preheat oven.)

Whiskey Sauce

- Cream butter and sugar over medium heat until butter is absorbed.

- Remove from heat and blend in egg yolks.

- Pour in bourbon gradually, stirring constantly. Sauce will thicken as it cools.

- Serve warm over warm bread pudding.

Serves 16 to 20

Chocolate Bread Pudding

8   ounces semi-sweet
    chocolate
4   ounces butter
5   eggs
1   cup sugar
2½ cups heavy cream
1½ teaspoons vanilla extract
Pinch cinnamon
½   pound white bread, crust
    removed and cut into
    1-inch cubes
Whipped cream or ice cream
    for garnish

• Melt chocolate and butter in double boiler.

• Mix eggs and sugar well.

• Add chocolate to egg mixture and mix well.

• Warm cream, vanilla and cinnamon in a saucepan. Add to chocolate-egg mixture.

• Place bread in buttered 13x9x2-inch baking dish.

• Pour custard over bread and let soak 1 hour at room temperature.

• Preheat oven to 350 degrees.

• Bake for 45 minutes until set.

• Serve with whipped cream or ice cream.

Serves 10 to 12

Cranberry Bread Pudding

½   **loaf (16 ounce) day-old French bread, torn into pieces**

1   **cup cranberries, coarsely chopped**

1   **cup chopped pecans or walnuts**

2   **cups milk**

2   **cups half-and-half**

3   **eggs, beaten**

1   **cup firmly packed brown sugar**

½   **cup granulated sugar**

¼   **cup dark rum**

1   **tablespoon vanilla extract**

Maple syrup or hard sauce

- Combine bread, cranberries and pecans in a large bowl. Toss gently.

- Combine milk and half-and-half. Pour over bread mixture. Cover and chill 1 hour.

- Preheat oven to 325 degrees.

- Combine eggs, brown sugar, granulated sugar, rum and vanilla. Stir well.

- Add egg mixture to chilled bread mixture, stirring gently to combine.

- Pour into a greased 13x9x2-inch baking pan. Bake uncovered for 1 hour or until set and lightly browned.

- Let cool in pan 5 minutes. Cut into squares.

- Serve warm with maple syrup or hard sauce.

Serves 10 to 12

Indian Pudding

4	**cups milk, divided**
½	**cup molasses**
¼	**cup sugar**
½	**cup cornmeal**
1	**teaspoon ground cinnamon**
½	**teaspoon ground ginger**
¼	**teaspoon ground nutmeg**
¼	**teaspoon ground allspice**
½	**teaspoon salt**
2	**tablespoons unsalted butter plus enough to grease dish**

Whipped cream or ice cream for garnish

- Preheat oven to 300 degrees.

- Place 3½ cups of milk in medium saucepan and turn heat to medium.

- Stir in molasses and sugar. When incorporated, turn heat to low.

- Slowly sprinkle cornmeal over warm milk mixture, whisking constantly and breaking up any lumps. Continue stirring until mixture thickens, about 10 minutes.

- Stir in cinnamon, ginger, nutmeg, allspice, salt and 2 tablespoons butter.

- Remove from heat.

- Grease an 8- or 9-inch square baking dish.

- Pour mixture into dish. Top with remaining ½ cup milk. Do not stir.

- Bake 2½ to 3 hours or until pudding is set.

- Serve warm, chilled, or at room temperature, accompanied with whipped cream or ice cream.

- May be wrapped and refrigerated for several days.

Serves 8

Cold Lemon Soufflé

1   package (6 ounce) lemon
    gelatin
2   cups boiling water
2   bottles (7 ounce) lemon-
    lime flavored soda
Rind of 1 lemon, grated
Juice of 1 lemon
2   cups heavy cream,
    whipped
Fresh strawberries or
    raspberries for garnish

• Pour 2 cups boiling water over gelatin, stirring until dissolved.

• Add soda, lemon juice and lemon rind.

• Chill until slightly thickened, then beat until foamy.

• Fold in whipped cream.

• Turn into a 2-quart soufflé dish. Chill until firm.

• Serve with fresh fruit.

Serves 8 to 10

Fresh Fruit Marinated in Raspberry Sauce

4-6 cups fresh fruit (bananas,
    pears, grapes, pineapple,
    strawberries, peaches,
    cantaloupe or any
    combination)
1   package (10 ounce) frozen
    red raspberries, thawed
3   tablespoons blackberry-
    flavored brandy

• Heat raspberries to boil in a small saucepan. Press through a sieve into a medium-sized bowl to remove seeds.

• Add blackberry-flavored brandy. Chill.

• Prepare fruit. Fold sauce into fruit to coat just before serving.

Serves 4 to 6

Desserts

Strawberry Deluxe

1 **quart fresh strawberries**
2 **tablespoons sugar**
¼ **cup cherry-flavored liqueur**
3 **ounces cream cheese at room temperature**
¼ **cup orange-flavored liqueur**
¼ **cup honey**
1 **cup heavy cream**
Grated or shaved chocolate for garnish

• Sprinkle berries with sugar and cherry-flavored liqueur.

• Toss and let macerate for about 1 hour.

• Beat cream cheese with liqueur and honey.

• Whip heavy cream until soft peaks are formed. Fold cream into cream cheese.

• Divide berries among 8 to 9 dessert dishes. Spoon cream mixture over berries. Refrigerate for several hours.

• To serve, sprinkle grated chocolate over top.

Serves 8 to 9

Concord Grape Granita

¾ **cup water**
½ **cup sugar**
2 **whole allspice**
1 **cinnamon stick**
½ **vanilla bean, split
   lengthwise**
4 **cups Concord grapes,
   stems removed**
1 **tablespoon lemon juice**
Fruit for garnish

- Combine water, sugar, allspice and cinnamon in a small heavy saucepan. Scrape the seeds from the vanilla bean and add seeds and pod to saucepan. Bring to a boil, stirring until the sugar dissolves.

- Reduce the heat and simmer for about 4 to 5 minutes, until the syrup has reduced to ½ cup. Strain and chill the syrup thoroughly.

- Purée the grapes in 2 batches in a food processor, including jackets and seeds.

- Press enough purée from grape mixture through a food mill into a bowl to measure 1½ cups. Blend well with chilled syrup.

- Transfer mixture to 9x5-inch glass loaf dish and place in freezer. Freeze grape mixture until flaky crystals form, about 4 hours. Rake with a fork every 30 minutes.

- Scoop into 4 glass goblets. Serve with fruit garnish.

Serves 4

Tortoni

⅓ cup macaroon crumbs
¼ cup lightly toasted coconut
¼ cup slivered almonds
1   cup heavy cream
½ cup sugar, divided
1   teaspoon vanilla extract
¼ teaspoon almond extract
1   tablespoon sherry
1   tablespoon Marsala wine
2   egg whites
10-12 Maraschino cherries

• In a small bowl, mix together macaroon crumbs, coconut and almonds. Set aside, reserving 3 tablespoons of crumb mixture separately.

• Whip heavy cream. Add ¼ cup sugar, vanilla and almond extract. Stir in sherry and Marsala wine.

• Beat egg whites until stiff, gradually adding ¼ cup sugar.

• Combine the crumb mixture, cream mixture and egg whites. Divide among 10 to 12 cupcake tins lined with paper liners.

• Sprinkle reserved crumbs on top and place a cherry in center of each.

• Freeze.

Serves 10 to 12

Odds & Ends

The Old Hill Burying Ground

The Old Hill Burying Ground

Being the highest point in Concord, the Old Hill Burying Ground has always offered a good view of the comings and goings in the surrounding countryside. By the time the defiant Liberty Pole flag fluttered in the wind from the hill's summit, the Old Hill Burying Ground had been witness to over one-hundred years of Concord history. The cemetery marker states, "On this hill the Settlers of Concord built their Meeting House near which they are buried. On the southern slope of the ridge were their Dwellings during the first winter. Below it they laid out their first Road and on the summit stood the Liberty Pole of the Revolution." The dwellings of the original 1635 Concord settlers anchored the bottom of the hill where they were partly sheltered from New England's driving rains and blinding snows. The oldest known Concord monument is on this hill in the form of Joseph Merriam's gravestone dated April, 1677. At daybreak on April 19, 1775, the older Concord men, who had remained in the militia when the more elite and agile Minutemen were formed, gathered briefly on the Old Hill Burying Ground. Over their heads, a flag fluttered from the Liberty Pole in protest to Britain's unwelcome, illegal acts. While we do not know what specific issues the flag addressed, we do know British Major Pitcairn scaled the Old Hill Burying Ground later that morning and looked out to Colonel Barrett's Farm where he could clearly see the Minutemen assembling and preparing to take a stand. Before descending to Wright Tavern headquarters below, the offensive Liberty Pole was ordered chopped down and burned. The smoke rising from the Old Hill Burying Ground could have been seen by the Minutemen waiting on another hillside at Barrett's Farm.

Odds & Ends

Hot Berry Cider

1 **quart apple cider**
1 **quart cranberry juice**
2 **tablespoons brown sugar**
2 **cinnamon sticks**
½ **teaspoon whole cloves**

- Pour cider and juice into a large sauce-pan. Add brown sugar.

- Place cinnamon sticks and cloves in pan.

- Bring mixture to a boil and reduce to simmer for 15 minutes.

- Strain and serve hot.

Yield: 2 quarts

Hot Cranberry Rum Toddy

3 **quarts cranberry juice cocktail**
¾ **cup sugar**
3 **cinnamon sticks (3½-inch each)**
4 **whole star anise, sliced**
1 **piece (3-inch) fresh ginger, peeled and thinly sliced**
2 **cups amber or dark rum**

- Bring cranberry juice, sugar, cinnamon, anise and ginger to a boil, stirring until sugar is dissolved.

- Cover and simmer 10 minutes.

- Stir in rum and serve hot.

Yield: about 14 cups

Mulled Wine

2	bottles (750ml) burgundy wine
2	cups water
1½	cups sugar
4	cinnamon sticks
4	cloves
½	teaspoon allspice

- Gradually heat the wine and water in a non-aluminum pot.

- Stir in sugar and add cinnamon sticks, cloves and allspice.

- Heat just to boiling.

- Reduce heat and simmer 10 minutes, stirring occasionally to dissolve sugar.

- Keep warm to serve.

Yield: about 2 quarts

Peach Smash

2	ripe peaches, unpeeled and cut into chunks
6	ounces frozen pineapple juice concentrate
¾	cup light rum
	Ice cubes

- Place peaches, pineapple juice concentrate and rum in blender.

- Fill blender with ice cubes.

- Blend until well mixed.

- Serve immediately.

Serves 4

Spiced Cranberry Punch

2 bottles (32 ounce) cranberry juice
1 can (46 ounce) pineapple juice
1 cup packed brown sugar
4 teaspoons whole cloves
12 inches of cinnamon sticks
1 bottle (fifth) light rum (optional)
Lemon slices (optional)

- Heat cranberry juice, pineapple juice, sugar, cloves and cinnamon sticks together in a pot on stovetop.

- Add rum before serving if desired.

- Float lemon slices on top.

Yield: 3 to 4 quarts

Spiced Holiday Punch

4 cups cranberry juice
2 cups orange juice
4 tablespoons Grand Marnier
2 tablespoons sugar
½ teaspoon cinnamon
¼ teaspoon allspice
⅛ teaspoon nutmeg

- Mix all ingredients together in a saucepan and simmer.

- Serve warm.

Yield: 6 cups

Holiday Eggnog

12 egg whites
1½ cups sugar, divided
12 egg yolks
½ teaspoon salt
4 cups heavy cream
4 cups milk
4 cups bourbon
1 cup dark rum
Nutmeg, grated, for garnish

- Beat egg whites until stiff.

- Beat ½ cup sugar into egg whites. Set aside.

- Beat egg yolks, 1 cup sugar and salt until very light.

- Blend in egg whites.

- Add cream, milk and bourbon. Beat well.

- Add rum.

- Store for 1 week in refrigerator before serving.

- Shake or stir thoroughly before serving. Sprinkle with nutmeg.

Yield: 4 quarts

Make eggnog 1 week in advance.

White Wine Punch

1   **quart rum**
½   **gallon Sauterne**
2   **bottles (2 liters each) ginger ale**
2   **bottles (2 liters each) club soda**

- Chill all beverages.

- Mix in large punch bowl.

- Garnish with decorative ice ring.

Yield: 3½ gallons

Baked Cranberries

4   **cups fresh cranberries**
1   **medium navel orange, peeled and sectioned**
1½ **cups sugar**
½   **cup fresh orange juice**
½   **teaspoon ground ginger**
½   **teaspoon ground cinnamon**
½   **teaspoon ground nutmeg**

- Preheat oven to 350 degrees.

- In a medium bowl, combine cranberries, orange, sugar, orange juice, ginger, cinnamon and nutmeg. Stir well.

- Spoon cranberry mixture into a 1½-quart casserole.

- Cover and bake for 1 hour.

- Serve warm or chilled with chicken or pork.

Yield: 2½ cups

Brandied Cranberries

4 **cups fresh cranberries**
2¼ **cups sugar, divided**
¼ **cup brandy**

- Preheat oven to 350 degrees.

- Place cranberries in a shallow baking dish.

- Sprinkle with 2 cups sugar.

- Bake 30 minutes, stirring occasionally.

- Remove from oven. Stir in brandy and ¼ cup sugar. Chill.

Yield: 2 cups

Cabernet Cranberries

1¼ **cups sugar**
1 **cup Cabernet Sauvignon**
1 **package (12 ounce) fresh cranberries**
2 **teaspoons tangerine rind, grated**
1 **cinnamon stick**

- Bring sugar and wine to a boil in a saucepan over medium-high heat.

- Add cranberries, tangerine rind and cinnamon stick.

- Return mixture to a boil, stirring constantly.

- Reduce heat and simmer, partially covered, 10 to 15 minutes or until cranberry skins pop.

- Remove cinnamon stick and discard.

- Cool slightly. Serve warm or chill 2 hours before serving.

- Serve with poultry.

Yield: about 4 cups

Sauce may be stored in refrigerator up to 2 months.

Cranberry Chutney

3   **small oranges, seeded, coarsely chopped, including peel**
4   **cups cranberries**
2   **cups sugar**
1   **cup tart apple, unpeeled, seeded and chopped**
½   **cup raisins**
½   **cup walnuts, coarsely chopped**
½   **cup orange juice or apple cider**
1   **tablespoon cider vinegar**
¾   **teaspoon ground ginger**
¾   **teaspoon ground cinnamon**
¾   **teaspoon ground cloves**
½   **cup bourbon (optional)**

- In a heavy pot, combine oranges, cranberries, sugar, apple, raisins, walnuts, orange juice, vinegar, ginger, cinnamon and cloves and simmer until cranberries are popped and mixture looks like jam, about 30 minutes.

- Stir in bourbon if desired.

Yield: 2 quarts

Chutney may be sealed in sterile jars or frozen. Keeps up to one year frozen.

Cranberry-Blueberry Chutney

¾   **cup cranberry chutney (prepared or see index for recipe)**
¾   **cup frozen or fresh blueberries**
1   **tablespoon sugar**
1   **tablespoon balsamic vinegar**
½   **teaspoon lemon peel, grated**
¼   **teaspoon ground ginger**
⅛   **teaspoon crushed red pepper flakes**

- Combine chutney, blueberries, sugar, vinegar, lemon peel, ginger and crushed red pepper in small saucepan.

- Bring to a boil over medium heat, stirring frequently.

- Reduce heat to low. Cook, stirring constantly for 15 to 20 minutes or until slightly thickened.

Yield: 1 cup

Curried Fruit Bake

⅓ cup butter
¾ cup packed brown sugar
4 teaspoons curry powder
Maraschino cherries, to taste
1 can (15 ounce) pear halves
1 can (15.25 ounce) peach halves
1 can (8.75 ounce) apricot halves
1 can (20 ounce) pineapple chunks

- Preheat oven to 325 degrees.
- Melt butter. Add sugar and curry.
- Drain and dry fruits on paper towel.
- Add to butter mixture.
- Bake 1 hour uncovered.

Serves 12

Great as accompaniment to poultry or ham.

Fresh Fruit Dip

1½ cups sour cream
3 tablespoons dark brown sugar, packed
¾ teaspoon vanilla extract

- In a small bowl, stir in sour cream, sugar and vanilla until smooth.

Yield: 1⅔ cups

Keeps up to 1 week in refrigerator. Cover.

Rosy Applesauce

3 pounds apples, cored,
   unpeeled and cut into
   chunks
1½ cups water
3 tablespoons brandy
1 tablespoon fresh lemon
   juice
½ cup packed brown sugar
1 tablespoon ground
   cinnamon
½ teaspoon grated nutmeg

• Combine apples, water, brandy and lemon juice in a large heavy soup kettle.

• Bring just to a boil over medium-high heat, then reduce to a simmer.

• Cook uncovered until apples are quite soft, about 40 minutes.

• Stir in brown sugar, cinnamon and nutmeg. Remove from heat.

• Press mixture through a food mill to purée and remove skins.

• Taste for flavor and adjust sugar and spices to taste.

• Serve at once or store covered in refrigerator until ready to use.

Yield: 2 quarts

Spiced Cranberry-Apricot Relish

1	**pound cranberries (4 cups)**
2	**cups dried apricots, chopped**
1	**cup seedless golden raisins**
1	**tablespoon grated orange rind**
¼	**teaspoon ground ginger**
2½	**cups water**
1	**cup sugar**

- Combine cranberries, apricots, raisins, orange rind, ginger and water in a large saucepan.

- Bring to a boil over high heat, then reduce heat and simmer about 10 minutes or until cranberries have popped and are tender. (While cranberries are popping, keep covered.)

- Remove from heat. Stir in sugar. Cool.

- Store, covered, in refrigerator until ready to serve.

Yield: 8 cups

Excellent with cottage cheese or as a substitute for cranberry sauce for turkey.

Spiced Pecans

1	**egg white**
2	**tablespoons water**
2	**cups pecans**
½	**cup sugar**
½	**teaspoon salt**
1	**teaspoon cinnamon**
¼	**teaspoon ground cloves**
¼	**teaspoon nutmeg**

- Preheat oven to 300 degrees.

- Beat egg white and water. Mix in pecans.

- In a separate bowl, combine sugar, salt, cinnamon, cloves and nutmeg.

- Sprinkle over the nuts and mix thoroughly.

- Spread nuts on a buttered baking sheet.

- Bake 30 minutes. Cool on wax paper.

Yield: 2½ cups

Cajun Marinade

Juice of 1 orange
Juice of 2 lemons
Juice of 2 limes
⅓   cup Dijon mustard
Generous dash Tabasco sauce
1   clove garlic, finely chopped
1   teaspoon Worcestershire
    sauce
½   teaspoon freshly ground
    black pepper
1   teaspoon cider vinegar
¼   cup olive oil
1   lemon cut into wedges

• Combine all ingredients.

• Pour over fish, pork or chicken.

• Cover and refrigerate several hours.

Yield: 2 to 3 cups marinade

Chicken Marinade

⅓   cup lemon juice
¼   cup soy sauce
¼   cup vegetable oil
2   tablespoons brown sugar
½   teaspoon ground ginger
¼   teaspoon freshly ground
    pepper
3   tablespoons ketchup
1   teaspoon garlic powder
    (or to taste)

• Combine all ingredients.

• Pour over chicken and refrigerate several
  hours.

Yield: about 1 cup

Dijonaise Marinade for Salmon or Chicken

1   **cup Dijon mustard**
1½ **cups salad oil**
2   **tablespoons fresh lemon juice**
½   **teaspoon fresh chopped dill**
⅛   **teaspoon salt**
Dash fresh chopped garlic
Dash cayenne pepper
Dash ground coriander

- Whip mustard in mixing bowl or food processor.

- Add oil slowly until all oil is incorporated.

- Add lemon juice, dill, salt, garlic, cayenne pepper and coriander. Mix thoroughly.

- Store in covered container in refrigerator until ready to use.

Yield: 2½ cups marinade

Before baking, coat salmon or chicken with marinade. Roll in bread crumbs, cracker crumbs or a mixture of both.

Marinade for Lamb

¼   **cup soy sauce**
¼   **cup lemon juice**
¼   **cup honey**
1   **teaspoon freshly ground pepper**
½   **teaspoon ground ginger**
1   **clove garlic**

- Place all ingredients in blender. Blend until smooth.

- Place lamb in a resealable plastic bag and pour in marinade.

- Refrigerate 12 hours before grilling.

Yield: ¾ cup marinade

Classic Marinade for Shish-Ka-Bob

1½ **cups salad oil**
¾ **cup soy sauce (regular or light)**
¼ **cup Worcestershire sauce**
½ **cup wine vinegar**
⅓ **cup lemon juice**
2 **tablespoons dry mustard**
1 **tablespoon freshly ground pepper**
1 **tablespoon salt**
1 **teaspoon parsley**
2 **cloves garlic**

- Blend all ingredients in a mixer or food processor.
- Marinate several hours in refrigerator.

Yield: enough marinade for 4 pounds of meat.

Good for beef, chicken or lamb.

Teriyaki Marinade

½ **cup soy sauce**
3 **tablespoons honey**
¾ **cup salad oil**
1 **chopped onion**
⅓ **cup red wine**
¾ **tablespoon ground ginger**
¾ **tablespoon garlic powder**
2 **pounds beef, chicken or seafood**

- Combine soy sauce, honey, salad oil, onion, wine, ginger and garlic powder.
- Marinate overnight.
- Remove meat from marinade about 30 minutes before grilling.
- Boil remaining marinade until slightly reduced, about 30 minutes. Use as a sauce.

Yield: 1¾ cups

Stock for Poaching Shrimp

10 cups water
2 celery stalks, cut into 2-inch lengths
1 medium onion, cut into eighths
1 small lemon, quartered
½ bunch fresh parsley
8 black peppercorns
2 bay leaves
1 tablespoon salt
½ teaspoon red pepper flakes
1 tablespoon mustard seed

• Bring all ingredients to a boil and simmer for 10 minutes. Strain and use according to recipe directions.

Stock can be used with other shellfish and seafood.

Cucumber Sauce

¾ cup sour cream
¼ cup mayonnaise
1 teaspoon finely grated onion
Small cucumber, seeded and finely diced
Salt and freshly ground pepper, to taste

• Mix sour cream, mayonnaise and grated onion.

• Press cucumber through a sieve to get out any juice or water.

• Add to sour cream mixture.

• Season to taste with salt and pepper.

• Serve with fish, potatoes or vegetables.

Yield: 1½ cups

Mint Sauce

3   **tablespoons water**
1½ **tablespoons confectioners' sugar**
⅓   **cup fresh mint leaves, finely chopped**
½   **cup strong vinegar**

- Heat water then dissolve confectioners' sugar in water. Cool.

- Add mint leaves and vinegar.

Yield: 1 cup

This sauce is best made 30 minutes prior to serving.

Joe's Stone Crab Mustard Sauce

4½ **teaspoons dry English mustard**
1   **cup mayonnaise**
2   **teaspoons Worcestershire sauce**
1   **teaspoon steak sauce**
2   **tablespoons lemon juice**
⅛   **teaspoon salt**
2   **tablespoons light cream**

- With an electric mixer on low speed, beat mustard, mayonnaise, Worcestershire sauce, steak sauce, lemon juice and salt.

- Add cream gradually, beating constantly, until mustard thickens.

Yield: 1½ cups

Make a day ahead to allow flavor to develop.

Mustard

4	ounces dry mustard	• Mix mustard and vinegar and keep over-night in the refrigerator.
1	cup apple cider vinegar	
1	cup sugar	• Add sugar and eggs.
4	eggs, beaten	

4   ounces dry mustard
1   cup apple cider vinegar
1   cup sugar
4   eggs, beaten

• Mix mustard and vinegar and keep over-night in the refrigerator.

• Add sugar and eggs.

• Cook in double boiler for 10 minutes, stirring constantly.

• Store in refrigerator.

Yield: 2 cups

Roasted Tomato Mayonnaise

3   tomatoes
1-2 drops liquid smoke
1   cup mayonnaise
½   cup sour cream
¼   cup balsamic vinegar
¼   cup tomato paste
1   shallot, minced
Salt and freshly ground
    pepper, to taste

• Smoke tomatoes in a smoker or bake in a moderate oven until tomatoes are soft.

• Peel and core tomatoes.

• Purée tomatoes in blender. Add liquid smoke if tomatoes were baked.

• Mix mayonnaise, sour cream, vinegar, tomato paste, shallot, salt and pepper.

• Add tomato purée. Mix well.

Yield: 3 cups

Sauce for Vegetables

6   tablespoons butter
6   tablespoons brown sugar
2   teaspoons Dijon mustard
2   teaspoons prepared
     horseradish
1½ teaspoons salt
Dash freshly ground pepper

- Melt butter in medium saucepan. Add brown sugar and dissolve.

- Add mustard, horseradish, salt and pepper

- Cook over low heat until warm.

- Pour over cooked green beans, peas, carrots or cauliflower.

Yield: ¾ cup

Brandy Sauce for Meat

⅓   cup brandy
1   cup beef consommé
2-3 tablespoons butter
1   tablespoon chopped
     parsley

- Heat brandy and consommé in a small saucepan until reduced to about ¾ cup.

- Remove from heat and add butter, swirling to melt. Add parsley.

- Keep warm over hot water and spoon small amount over individual slices of meat when serving.

Yield: 6 to 8 servings

Savory Lemon Sauce

2   **tablespoons butter**
Zest of 1 lemon, finely
    shredded
2   **large cloves garlic, finely**
    minced
3   **egg yolks**
1½ **cups water**
¼   **cup fresh lemon juice**
1   **tablespoon plus 1 teaspoon**
    cornstarch
3   **tablespoons dry sherry**
3   **tablespoons honey**
½   **teaspoon salt**

- Melt butter over medium heat in heavy saucepan.

- Add lemon zest and cook, stirring constantly, until lightly browned, about 1 minute.

- Stir in garlic and remove pan from heat.

- In small bowl, beat egg yolks until smooth.

- Beat in water and lemon juice.

- Whisk the yolk mixture into the saucepan and place over low heat.

- Cook, stirring, until mixture is heated and starts to thicken, about 5 minutes.

- Stir cornstarch into sherry to dissolve. Add honey. Stir into egg mixture.

- Continue cooking, stirring often as mixture thickens, until sauce coats a spoon, about 3 to 5 minutes. Do not boil.

- Stir in salt. Serve with fish or vegetables.

Yield: 6 servings

Sauces for Fish

Butter and Lemon Sauce

8   **tablespoons butter**
2   **tablespoons lemon juice**

• Combine butter and lemon juice in a food processor or blender. Refrigerate.

Yield: ½ cup

Mustard-Mayonnaise Sauce

3   **tablespoons Dijon mustard**
1   **cup mayonnaise**

• In a small bowl, combine mustard and mayonnaise. Refrigerate.

Yield: 1 cup

Horseradish-Yogurt Sauce

1   **tablespoon horseradish**
1   **cup mayonnaise**
½   **cup plain yogurt**

• In a small bowl, combine all ingredients. Refrigerate.

Yield: 1½ cups

Tartar Sauce

1   **cup mayonnaise**
2   **tablespoons minced onion**
1   **teaspoon lemon juice**
2   **tablespoons pickle relish**

• In a small bowl, combine all ingredients. Refrigerate.

Yield: 1¼ cups

Fresh Pesto Sauce

2   cups fresh basil leaves
2   cups fresh parsley
4-6 cloves garlic
2   teaspoons salt
1   cup olive oil
1   heaping cup Parmesan or
     Romano cheese, freshly
     grated
½   cup butter, softened

- Place basil, parsley, garlic, salt and oil in a food processor. Process until well blended. Add cheese and blend together. Add butter and blend together.

- Serve over pasta and garnish with additional basil leaves.

- Store in glass jars in refrigerator for up to 1 week or freeze in small plastic containers.

Freeze some in ice cube trays to add to soups. One or 2 cubes added to chicken soup adds a wonderful flavor.

Chocolate Sauce

2 **ounces unsweetened chocolate**
6 **tablespoons water**
½ **cup sugar**
3 **tablespoons butter**
½ **teaspoon vanilla**

- Melt chocolate with water.

- Add sugar. Cook until boiling.

- Add butter and vanilla and return to boiling.

- Serve warm on pound cake, angel food cake or ice cream.

Yield: about 1 cup

Crème Anglaise

5 **egg yolks**
½ **cup sugar**
2 **cups light cream**
1 **teaspoon vanilla**

- Whip egg yolks until thick and light colored.

- Bring sugar and cream to a boil. Slowly add to egg yolks, stirring constantly.

- Pour into top of a double boiler. Cook over gently boiling water, stirring constantly, until slightly thickened, 5 to 10 minutes.

- Remove from heat and place pan in a bowl of cold water to stop cooking.

- Add vanilla and stir occasionally until lukewarm.

- Serve lukewarm or chilled.

Yield: 2½ cups

Peanut Butter Fudge Sauce

1   package (6 ounce) semi-
    sweet chocolate bits
⅓   cup milk
⅓   cup peanut butter
¼   cup light corn syrup
½   teaspoon vanilla

• Combine chocolate, milk, peanut butter
  and corn syrup over low heat.

• Bring to full boil over medium heat.

• Add vanilla.

• Serve over ice cream.

Yield: about 1½ cups

Praline Sauce

1   cup light corn syrup
½   cup sugar
⅓   cup butter
1   egg, beaten
1   tablespoon vanilla
1   cup pecans

• Combine syrup, sugar, butter and egg in
  heavy saucepan.

• Bring to boil over medium heat, stirring
  constantly.

• Cook 2 minutes without stirring.

• Remove from heat. Stir in vanilla and
  pecans.

• Serve over brownies, cake or ice cream.

Yield: about 2 cups

CONTRIBUTORS

The Emerson Hospital Auxiliary would like to thank our membership, friends and families for submitting over a thousand of their favorite recipes. Due to space limitations, it was impossible to use all recipes that were received. Acknowledging your efforts is important to us. Therefore, all those who submitted recipes for consideration are listed below.

List of Contributors

Jeanne Abboud
Margaret A'Hearn
Debbie Andreson
Joan Appleton
Joanne W. Armstrong
Chris Avery
Jean Bachman
Joy Banks
Robin Beneke
Liz Berk
Doris Bieren
Genieva Billman
Sarah Bishop
Janice Black
Jean Bogart
Lorraine Bonner
Elinor Boynton
Barbara Brea-Pugliese
Bea Brown
Babs Browne
Catherine Bulger
Charlotte L. Burstad
Kathy Casaletto
Becky Casey
Lorraine Celi
Leslie Cheney
Elaine Chorich
Di Clymer
Rosaria T. Colosi
Elinor Condon
Lorraine Condow
Betty Coolidge
Jane Cronin
Mary R. Curtin

Margaret Dakesian
Elisabeth D'Arcy
Patricia DeBinder
Diane Dement
Marie Dempsey
Gert DeRuzzo
Molly Dietrich
Patsy Dietrich
Kathryn Dilworth
Gloria Donadio
Karen Donoghue
Priscilla England
Nancy Edie
Mary Elias
Cathi Esselen
Cheryl Esto
June Evans
Ginny Farwell
Odele Fidelman
Mary Fiorentino
Melissa Fire
Carol Flagg
Gerry Franklin
Annie Fredkin
Martie Fritz
Susan Furman
Isabel Gaffney
Lil Gailius
Sally Gangloff
Patricia Gerty
J. M. Gray
Jackie Graziano
Lisa Greene
Donna Grinnell

Susan Halby
Louise Hannegan
Ruth Hansen
Gloria Harpell
Lorna M. Harris
Helen F. Hartford
Claire L. Heffernan
Muffin Hester
Dorothy Higgins
Liz Hitt
Mary E. Hitt
Patti Holles
Virginia Holst
Fran Honan
Hilda Horne
Patti Howes
Carol Hughes
Carol M. Hughes
Tama Ishihara
Helen Jarvinen
Nini Jastromb
Margie Johnson
Wilma W. Johnson
Cathy Jordan
Jean P. Kelly
Mary Kemp
Jane Kennedy
Margie King
Gigi Kussin
Jayne LaForest
Lorri Langin
Caroline Larson
Joany Lawrence

(continued on next page)

List of Contributors continued

Barbara Leader
Stacey Leal
Mary Ann Lee
Jackie Leonard
Sue Luconi
Betsy Lynch
Robin MacPherson
Martha Marks
Elaine Martin
Lynn Martin
Karen McCarthy
Sharon McClellan
JoAnne McClendon
Eileen McCulley
Margie McHale
Ellen McTammany
Maria Marra
Annie Meola
Barbara Meola
Helen Millar
Lee Milliken
Laura Milton
Molly Mink
Jane Mischel
Joan C. Monger
Fran Montgomery
NeGarre H. Moore
Maryann Mullin
Ople Anne Nance
Karen Napoli
Betty Neeley
Beth Neeley-Kubacki
Jennifer Neustat

Mary S. Newman
Olivia Nields
Emily O'Hara
Nancy Ohm
Barbara O'Malley
Eleanore Payne
Betsy Peavy
Joan Perera
Jan Peterson
Steve Pickford
Joan Pollard
Lynn Porter
Sandy Porter
Priscilla Pratley
Iris Prescott
Victoria Prescott
Joan Priest
Cynthia Pugliese
Peggy Purcell
Dana Randles
Mary M. Rauscher
Jeanne Rautiola
Helen Reichenberg
Evie Reynolds
Janet Richards
Judy Richardson
Nancy Rote
Patti Sanford
Joan Schiller
Susan Seeley
Doris Segadelli
Judy Segal
Shelley Sherman

Ellen Sibley
Mary E. Silva
Marcia Slama
Carol Smith
Marsha Smith
Jackie Snelling
Judith C. Stigum Breuninger
Grace Stokes
Susan Sullivan
Dottie Swanson
Rhoda Taschioglou
Diane Tenaglia
Cathy Trainor
Paula Trebino
Sue Tunnicliffe
Susan L. Tyler
Marge VanHouten
Alicia Verhake
Carol Verhake
Rosly Walter
Susan Warner
Doris S. Webber
Shirley Webster
Helen Weinheimer
Charlotte Wetherbee
Theresa Whalen
Elinor White
Julie Wilson
Joan Wishart
Joan P. Wood
Sigrun E. Woodin
Charlotte Zurlo

Index

A

Index

Index

386

Index

387

Index

D

Index

Index

Index

Index

397

Index

Revolutionary **Recipes** *Concord à la Carte*

Emerson Hospital Auxiliary, Emerson Hospital, 133 ORNAC, Concord, MA 01742
Phone 978-287-3019

Please send me   Copies of Revolutionary Recipes @ $24.95 each _____

Postage and Handling $ 5.00 each _____

Total _____

*Prices subject to change without notice. Make checks payable to **Emerson Hospital Auxiliary**.*

Name _____

Address _____

City/State/Zip _____

Telephone _____

Fill this section out if you want books shipped to a different address.
Please print clearly and fill out completely.

Ship To: _____

_____

_____

_____

_____

Revolutionary **Recipes** *Concord à la Carte*

Emerson Hospital Auxiliary, Emerson Hospital, 133 ORNAC, Concord, MA 01742
Phone 978-287-3019

Please send me   Copies of Revolutionary Recipes @ $24.95 each _____

Postage and Handling $ 5.00 each _____

Total _____

*Prices subject to change without notice. Make checks payable to **Emerson Hospital Auxiliary**.*

Name _____

Address _____

City/State/Zip _____

Telephone _____

Fill this section out if you want books shipped to a different address.
Please print clearly and fill out completely.

Ship To: _____

_____

_____

_____

_____

Names of bookstores and gift shops in your area would be appreciated.

_____

_____

_____

_____

_____

_____

_____

_____

- -

Names of bookstores and gift shops in your area would be appreciated.

_____

_____

_____

_____

_____

_____

_____

_____